Sun Tzu in the West

It would be hard to overstate the impact of Sun Tzu's *The Art of War* on military thought. Beyond its impact in Asia, the work has been required reading in translation for US military personnel since the Cold War. Sun Tzu has been interpreted as arguing for "indirect strategy" in contrast to "direct strategy," the latter idea stemming from ancient Greece. This is a product of twentieth-century Western thinking, specifically that of Liddell Hart, who influenced Samuel B. Griffith's 1963 translation of Sun Tzu. The credibility of Griffith's translation was enhanced by his combat experience in the Pacific during World War II, and his translation of Mao Zedong's *On Guerrilla Warfare*. This reading of Sun Tzu is, however, very different from Chinese interpretations. Western strategic thinkers have used Sun Tzu as a foil or facilitator for their own thinking, inadvertently engaging the Western military tradition and propagating misleading generalizations about Chinese warfare.

Peter Lorge is Associate Professor of Pre-modern Chinese and Military History at Vanderbilt University. His previous books include *Chinese Martial Arts: From Antiquity to the Twenty-First Century* and *The Asian Military Revolution*.

T0384638

Sun Tzu in the West

The Anglo-American Art of War

Peter Lorge

Vanderbilt University

CAMBRIDGE
UNIVERSITY PRESS

CAMBRIDGE
UNIVERSITY PRESS

University Printing House, Cambridge CB2 8BS, United Kingdom

One Liberty Plaza, 20th Floor, New York, NY 10006, USA

477 Williamstown Road, Port Melbourne, VIC 3207, Australia

314–321, 3rd Floor, Plot 3, Splendor Forum, Jasola District Centre,
New Delhi – 110025, India

103 Penang Road, #05–06/07, Visioncrest Commercial, Singapore 238467

Cambridge University Press is part of the University of Cambridge.

It furthers the University's mission by disseminating knowledge in the pursuit of
education, learning, and research at the highest international levels of excellence.

www.cambridge.org
Information on this title: www.cambridge.org/9781108830652
DOI: 10.1017/9781108902687

© Peter Lorge 2023

First published 2023

A catalogue record for this publication is available from the British Library.

ISBN 978-1-108-83065-2 Hardback
ISBN 978-1-108-82246-6 Paperback

Contents

Figures

Acknowledgments

That this has been, by far, the easiest book I have ever written is due to the work of a number of archivists at several institutions in America and England. Many of those archivists did their work long before I arrived to profit from it, but I would like to mention by name as many of the people who directly helped me as I can. I am grateful to Siân Mogridge, archivist at the Royal Artillery Museum; to Dr. Jim Ginther, senior archivist at the Archives Branch, Marine Corps History Division; to Diana Manipud, archives assistant, Liddell Hart Centre for Military Archives, King's College London; to Laura Russo, Howard Gottlieb Archival Research Center, Boston University; and to the staff of the Library of Congress. This is an inadequate acknowledgment of the work of these individuals and their colleagues, which makes this sort of historical research possible.

As always, I must thank Yuh-Fen Benda, of the Vanderbilt University library, for locating and acquiring works for me as if by magic. I must also thank my very old friend Stuart Aston, for helping me on one of my visits to England. Without his assistance I might still be stuck in Larkhill. I would also like to thank Stephen Miller, for kindly answering several questions regarding his 1975 article when contacted out of the blue by an unknown researcher.

Thanks are also due to my editors at Cambridge University Press, Lucy Rhymer and Emily Plater, for (seemingly cheerfully) putting up with me. I would also like to thank the anonymous reviewers who saved me from many errors.

I dedicate this book to the memory of Dr. Jeannette L. Faurot (1943–2005), my first teacher of classical Chinese at the University of Texas, Austin. It was under Dr. Faurot that I first translated Sunzi's *Art of War*, and first conceived of some of the main ideas of this book. I hope this book goes some way to repaying her patience so many years ago.

Introduction

Speaking on the floor of the United States Senate in 2008 regarding her frustrations with the extensive, but ultimately, she feared, indecisive, discussions of the Climate Security Act, Senator Maria Cantwell remarked, "As Sun Tzu said in the 'Art of War,' 'the journey of a thousand miles begins with a single step'."[1] Senator Cantwell may well be excused for mistaking Sunzi for Laozi and *The Art of War* for the *Daodejing*, since she was apparently familiar enough with both mythical thinkers and their works to confuse them.[2] The more intriguing issue is how a United States senator came to invoke Sunzi and his *Art of War* in a discussion of a climate change bill rather than in a military context. To be fair, the Congressional Record is replete with military references to Sunzi, not only with respect to China, but more usually concerning universal strategic wisdom as well. Carl von Clausewitz (1780–1831), a key Western writer on strategy and war, is seldom mentioned, and then only concerning military strategy. When Clausewitz is discussed he is often paired with Sunzi, and even occasionally with Mao Zedong (1893–1976). To think strategically or even philosophically in contemporary American culture, then, is to speak of Sunzi.

Sunzi's *Art of War* became a popular work of strategy in America, in Great Britain, and more broadly in the West, as the direct result of Samuel Griffith's 1963 translation. His translation of Sunzi, with a preface by Basil Liddell Hart, the most famous strategist in the world at that time, inserted Sunzi into the Western imagination in ways that one earlier French and two English translations had not. Griffith, a retired Marine Corps general who had served in China and fought the Japanese in the Pacific during World War II, brought credibility and stature to the work. He was not an academic, even though he earned a doctor of philosophy at Oxford, and he had also published translations of Mao

---

[1] Congressional Record, Senate June 6, 2008, "Lieberman-Warner Climate Security Act of 2008," 110th Congress, 2nd Session, Issue: Vol. 154, No. 93. Senator Cantwell's concerns were well warranted. Republicans killed the bill that day.
[2] Laozi 老子, *Daodejing* 道德經, Chapter 64.

Zedong's *On Guerrilla Warfare*. The timing was also right, with the Chinese Communist Party in control of China after winning the civil war with the Nationalists in 1949. American power and support for the Nationalists had not been enough to defeat a seemingly less powerful opponent. China had, indeed, as Mao put it, "stood up," and became a world power, but in opposition to America and the West.

If the draw of trying to understand China as an emergent military power was not enough, there was a subtler connection of Sunzi to the Western concept of "strategy." This connection, which has only recently become clear, ties the 1772 publication of Father Amiot's (1718–1793) French translation of Sunzi, the first into a Western language, directly to Paul-Gédéon Joly de Maizeroy's transformation of the word "strategy" into its modern meaning.[3] Sunzi was, in fact, present at the creation of the modern Western concept of strategy. It is thus not surprising that Sunzi is so closely tied in the popular sense to "strategy," since "strategy" is tied in the intellectual sense to Sunzi.

This book, then, is about the place of Sunzi and strategy in Western culture, and about how these two things – an ancient Chinese text on warfare and the modern concept of strategy – became virtually synonymous in popular culture. Samuel Griffith's translation arrived just as John F. Kennedy and the United States were turning, intentionally or not, away from conventional war and massive nuclear retaliation, and toward small wars and insurgencies. While conventional and nuclear war did not disappear, and Kennedy was assassinated in the year Griffith's translation was published, America's military was already beginning its entry into counterinsurgency in Vietnam. Counterinsurgency and small wars were strongly associated with the Marine Corps, and Marine General Victor Krulak (himself a China marine) served as the military adviser on counterinsurgency in Kennedy's White House. After the great conventional wars of the twentieth century, combat was becoming unconventional, guerrilla, indirect, and non-Western. In the center of this confused and conflated mass of terms was Sunzi's *Art of War*.

Sunzi as Talisman

Sunzi's *Art of War* is a remarkable artifact of Chinese civilization. Not only has it been central to the Chinese conception of warfare and strategy for two millennia; it has also come to fulfill that same role in the non-Chinese

---

[3] Adam Parr, *The Mandate of Heaven: Strategy, Revolution, and the First European Translation of Sunzi's Art of War*, Leiden: Brill, 2019, 217–220. For Maizeroy's invention of strategy see, most recently, Alexandre David, *Joly de Maizeroy: L'inventeur de la stratégie*, Paris: L'École de guerre, 2018.

world since the middle of the twentieth century. *The Art of War* is *the* paradigmatic non-Western text on military thought. Yet it is more than that; it is *the* paradigmatic text on strategy everywhere, at least in the popular imagination. Where Clausewitz's *On War* is barely known outside academic circles, *The Art of War* is mentioned without explanation on television shows and in movies, and cited canonically by businessmen. The apotheosis of *The Art of War* says a lot about Chinese culture and the way in which Chinese culture is seen outside China. It says even more about the way war, military thought, and the non-West have been marginalized in the Euro-American realm of historical inquiry. War and the non-West have been marginalized in order to define the West itself.

The Art of War has been used to divide people since at least the late second century BCE (if we date the completion of *Records of the Grand Historian* to 109 BCE). This function is entirely external to the text itself, which is solely concerned with military thought and more generally with strategy. In the West after World War II, *The Art of War* was first connected to Liddell Hart's anti-Clausewitzian "indirect approach" strategy and the unconventional warfare strategies of Mao Zedong's communist conquest of China. Chinese clashes with the US-led United Nations force defending South Korea and the success of insurgent forces in Vietnam, among other Cold War clashes, reified the Chinese–Western military divide. Devious, underhanded Chinese strategy won or fought to a draw the most powerful modern Western militaries. Since *The Art of War* supposedly underlay Mao Zedong's strategy for anti-imperialist, anticolonial insurgent armies, the West had to contend with a non-West identified at a deep level with *The Art of War*.

Even in *The Art of War*'s first step toward canonization, Sima Qian's (145 or 135–86 BCE) biography of Sunzi in the chapter on "Militarists" in his *Records of the Grand Historian*, the text became a way to distinguish a rational way of conducting war from those rulers who waged war to satisfy their own whims and who were unconcerned with the welfare of their state and their subjects. War for Sunzi was an intellectual pursuit that, when done well, yielded no glory. In the Chinese milieu, this military intellectualism made *The Art of War* a marker of Chinese culture and Chineseness much like the other canonical Chinese texts. Sunzi divided the Chinese from the barbarians.

The Art of War subsequently became a means to divide civil and military in Chinese culture. Cao Cao (155–220 CE), a man who would become a famous (or infamous) warlord, wrote the first extant commentary on *The Art of War*. Yet he wrote the commentary before he became a military commander, and composed it as an educated civil official, not an army officer.[4] Military intellectualism was a substitute for military experience, at least in the minds of the educated. Knowledge of military texts separated the rational scholar with profound, classically sanctioned wisdom from the mere general with a narrow perspective based upon battlefield experience. Literati faith in the power of books also led to attempts in the eleventh century to improve the quality of officers by getting military men to read military books. These efforts to bridge this divide perhaps not surprisingly further clarified the separation. The private ownership of military books was prohibited for much of imperial Chinese history, and reading military books was a peculiarity noteworthy enough to be mentioned in scholars' biographies. *The Art of War* became a symbol of Chinese martial culture, feared by the government, disdained by some scholars, yet unquestionably canonical and powerful.

The Problem of "Strategy"

"Strategy" has only taken on non-military uses since World War II. Prior to that it was a term confined to questions of military planning and operations.[5] What constituted and constitutes "strategy" as opposed to "tactics," "grand tactics," or "grand strategy" is still subject to personal definition. The transfer of strategy outside the military realm has only further complicated matters. What a businessperson means when she speaks of strategy may well be very different than what a general means. While livelihoods are certainly at stake in business decisions, and managers may act ruthlessly, there remains a significant gap between what a general does and what a manager does. Even though Clausewitz used the analogy of a business transaction in one of his descriptions of war, he did not mean that war and business were the same.[6] *The Art of War* was unquestionably composed by and for men concerned with war, who would never have conceived of those lessons having any relationship to business.

Sunzi's underlying argument was that war was comprehensible, and that a thoughtful approach to its prosecution would produce more favorable outcomes. He argues in Chapter 1 that the outcome of a campaign can be predicted beforehand by calculating who has the advantages in certain areas. War is not governed by luck or spirits but by understandable

[4] Rafe De Crespigny, *Imperial Warlord: A Biography of Cao Cao 155–220 AD*, Leiden: Brill, 2010.
[5] Beatrice Heuser, *The Evolution of Strategy*, Cambridge: Cambridge University Press, 2010.
[6] Carl von Clausewitz (trans. Michael Howard and Peter Paret), *On War*, Princeton: Princeton University Press, 1976, 603 (Book 8, Chapter 6) and 182 (Book 3 Chapter 1).

factors. Someone who grasps Sunzi's method is not guaranteed of victory since those factors may not be in his favor. Part of strategy is knowing when doing what you want to do will not work. One has to know when not to fight because you will lose, and what can and cannot be done. Real strategy requires a clear understanding of real conditions.

This highlights the point that strategy is a set of actions that a person does not want to do. No one looks for a strategy if their desired actions achieve their desired results. Strategy comes into play when the desire to achieve one's goal takes precedence over the means to achieve it. *The Art of War* was a repudiation of earlier aristocratic views of war that saw it as a defining cultural practice for their class. Aristocrats achieved their personal goals to prove themselves aristocrats by going to war, hunting, and other ritual activities. Their personal goals did not, however, serve the emerging states, whose rulers used war in a very different way.[7] Sunzi's strategy served the state at the expense of the declining aristocratic class.

Sunzi's strategy did not only run counter to the interests of the aristocratic class, it also clashed with generals and rulers who sought military glory as a means to enhance their political power. Inherent in Sunzi's rationalism is an abstract *raison d'état* above that of a state's ruler. There were things so important to the state that the ruler had to set aside his personal whims and think things through (or listen to someone he employed for that purpose). War was too important to be left to emotion. It was, "a matter of life and death, the path to existence or ruin," as Sunzi points out in the first line of *The Art of War*.

The very act of writing about strategy, of making a text, seems to run contrary to most people's approach to war and conflict. It is an assertion of thought over emotion. Ultimately a book on strategy, any book on strategy, though particularly a short and pithy one like *The Art of War*, is a revelation to anyone seeking a rational approach to achieving goals (hence the attraction for people outside the military realm). But making achieving a goal into an intellectual process troubles some people. In China, the Ruist (Confucian) philosopher Xunzi (320–235 BCE) objected to the strategic practices of Sunzi and Wu Qi advanced by the Lord of Linwu, a general (which, paraphrasing Sunzi, included deception), arguing that a humane ruler would neither use deception nor be deceived.[8] (Wu Qi, also known as Wuzi, or Master Wu, was a Warring States period general, statesman, and military writer.) In the West, this is the sort of reaction people have to Machiavelli's *The Prince*. The idea of

---

[7] For the classic discussion of the transition from the Spring and Autumn period aristocracy to the state-centered Warring States period see Mark Edward Lewis, *Sanctioned Violence in Early China*, New York: SUNY Press, 1989.

[8] Xunzi 荀子, Chapter 15 (*Yibing* 議兵).

thinking strategically seems inherently underhanded because it is not genuine and straightforward. Planning a way to reach a goal is less emotionally compelling than simply trying as hard as one can without thinking too hard. Far fewer people read Machiavelli's *Art of War*, seeing it as merely a historic artifact of warfare in a particular time and place.[9] *The Prince*, in contrast, contains eternal truths about achieving power in human society.

War itself can seem to be justified as a tool of policy or politics, to echo Clausewitz, if it can be employed rationally. It seems, not without reason, immoral to calculate how much death and destruction a given policy goal is worth. War as a "crime of passion" absolves the participants of the full moral consequences of their actions because they were being spontaneous and emotional. A well-thought-out plan for fighting a war implies full awareness of the costs of those actions and acceptance of them. Worse still, if one chooses whether to go to war not because the gravamen of the dispute is just or unjust but instead based on a calculation of the chances of success, then morality is no longer fully operational. This seems true despite Vittoria and Suarez's sixteenth-century addition to the Augustinian just-war tradition that it is immoral to go to war without the likelihood of success.[10]

My point here is not to argue whether or not strategy has moral valence, but rather to highlight the culturally suspect act of thinking strategically. Using stratagems, surprise attacks, and ambushes is being clever when we do them, but a sign of underhanded, morally compromised schemers when our opponent does them. The West has constructed the success of its early modern imperialism and colonialism as an expression of its fundamental strength overcoming weak non-Western cultures and peoples.[11] When some of those non-Western peoples or cultures somehow defeated or fended off the West it was put down to underhanded, scheming behavior. Consequently, the morally compromised realm of strategy naturally seemed more at home in the weak but cunning non-Western cultures. And *The Art of War* is the earliest non-Western text on strategy.

There are three ways of approaching a text on strategy: as a key to enduring, objective wisdom on strategy; as the reflection of warfare in a place and time; and as a fundamental expression of a culture's approach

---

[9] Niccolò Machiavelli, *The Art of War* (trans. Christopher Lynch), Chicago: The University of Chicago Press, 2003.

[10] Michael Howard, "*Temperamenta Belli*: Can War be Controlled?", in Michael Howard (ed.) *Restraints on War*, Oxford: Oxford University Press, 1979, 8.

[11] See Edward Said, *Orientalism*, New York: Vintage Books, 1978, for the classic description of how Western imperialist ideology represented the Orient as weak and effeminate.

to warfare. An ancient text like Sunzi is often subjected to a fourth approach, strongly related to the first: the careful archaeological and philological effort to recover the original text. This book is none of those things; rather, it is a book about how a particular text on military thought, Sunzi's *Art of War*, has been used as a cultural talisman. *The Art of War* has much to say about strategy, but it has more often been used as a stand-in for thinking strategically without particular or even accurate reference to its actual contents. This is no less true in China today than outside it.

Very few people in fact delve deeply into the extensive intellectual traditions of strategic thought. Like any area of philosophy or abstract thinking, the systematic study and practice of a complex field are beyond the interest or needs of most people. Western strategic thought, despite a number of excellent studies of this rich tradition, remains a military specialist's field.[12] Indeed, it was only during World War II that Edward Mead Earle, recognizing how little studied strategic thought was in the United States, convened a conference and produced an edited volume, *Makers of Modern Strategy*, to address the issue.[13] World War II and its aftermath, particularly the advent of nuclear weapons and the Cold War, gave rise to the serious study of strategic thought, as well as producing new fields of research like security studies. Samuel Griffith's 1963 translation of *The Art of War* was published in that developing postwar interest in strategic studies. Not surprisingly, however, *The Art of War* was not discussed in either the first or the second editions of the Eurocentric *Makers of Modern Strategy*.

The needs of the military, military academies, and general hostility to the study of military history, at least in American universities and colleges, have still limited the study of strategy. Professional military officers, while acknowledging some value to strategic thought, tend to regard it as too time-consuming to engage in deeply and perhaps a bit too academic. Strategic thought in Western militaries (though this is generally true of all militaries) tends to be simplified down to a very few texts like Clausewitz and Sunzi. More usually, summary training manuals render a given military or service branch's doctrines into easily deliverable forms.

[12] The best overviews of the Western tradition are Azar Gat, *A History of Military Thought: From the Enlightenment to the Cold War*, Oxford: Oxford University Press, 2002; Heuser, *The Evolution of Strategy*; Edward Mead Earle (ed.), *Makers of Modern Strategy*, Princeton: Princeton University Press, 1944; and the revised version, Peter Paret (ed.), *Makers of Modern Strategy: From Machiavelli to the Nuclear Age*, Princeton: Princeton University Press, 1986.
[13] Earle, *Makers of Modern Strategy*. See also Michael P. M. Finch, "Edward Mead Earle and the Unfinished *Makers of Modern Strategy*," *Journal of Military History*, 80 (July 2016), 781–814.

Officers have too many other tasks that take precedence over deep considerations of strategy. Historically, even the highest levels of Western militaries have often been inclined to leave the setting of strategic goals to their respective governments. Civilian authorities are usually caught between encouraging the military to leave larger issues of strategy in their hands, and expecting the military to have something useful to say about strategy.

The problem of strategy is twofold: it seems to many people that states should have strategies (while still regarding the process as morally questionable), but no one is quite sure what strategy is or how one might be acquired. Moreover, the implications of a given strategy, should one be agreed upon, are often unacceptable. It is not just that a strategy may appear to be immoral, but also that it may run counter to political interests within a government or state. If a state decided that its military goals were best carried out by a strong navy, for example, then that state's army would likely find its funding cut or limited. Modern democracies purchase weapons from large companies and base troops in political constituencies who thus all have a stake in strategic planning. A strategy is a choice among possibilities that ramify throughout a military and society.

Strategy remains a morally fraught and badly misunderstood practice. It is studied and used within modern militaries, though often with as much of an eye on budgets, procurement, and resources as on ultimate goals. Outside the military, the popular discourse of strategy refers more generally to thinking of means to achieve one's goals without specific reference to military texts. The one exception to this is *The Art of War*, which, because it is ancient and Chinese, seems to excite notions of clever tricks to overcome stronger opponents or conventional obstacles. Strategy in this sense is inherently unconventional, something only a non-Western text could be. To think and plan is to "think outside the box" because most people don't usually think or plan how to achieve their goals. Invoking *The Art of War* is a declaration of thinking strategically, even if none of the resulting thinking has anything to do with the contents of *The Art of War*.

Sunzi the Myth

I have thus far spoken of "Sunzi" as if there were an individual at some time or place in the past who could lay claim to that name or title and who had some association with the text I call "*The Art of War*." I have done this and will continue to do this for rhetorical purposes, in order to make my discussion more felicitous, but it should in no way imply that there ever was such a person as Sunzi. Modern scholarship has made it abundantly clear that there was no Sunzi, and that the text of *The Art of War* was the product of a school of military thought rather than an individual. *The Art of War* is obviously the work of a number of writers or compilers, though I would argue that in its received form it has been coherently organized. The mythical nature of its putative author should in no way diminish the quality of its contents.

All that we "know" about Sunzi is contained in his biography in Sima Qian's *Records of the Grand Historian*. I will take up the question of why Sima Qian created the category of "militarist" (*bingjia*) and why he formed Sunzi's biography as he did in Chapter 1. Here I would like to explain how we know that the biography is mythical. It is important to do this at the beginning of this discussion in order to make sure the reader is clear that Sunzi is mythical. It should also make clear how much *The Art of War* has been used from quite early on as a cultural tool. *The Art of War* has always had uses beyond its mere contents. Indeed, it is likely that Sima Qian's historiography needed military texts regardless of their contents.

A brief discursus is also in order before getting to the myth of Sunzi. Most readers in the Western world know Sunzi as "Sun Tzu," "Sun-tzu," or very rarely as "Sun Zi." His text is known as *The Art of War*. "Sun Tzu" and "Sun-tzu" are romanizations of the modern Chinese pronunciation using the Wade–Giles system. That system has been superseded by the Pinyin romanization system. In the Pinyin system, the Chinese is rendered as "Sunzi" or "Sun Zi." Because the Wade–Giles system was dominant for most of the twentieth century, most Westerners are more familiar with "Sun-tzu" or "Sun Tzu." The meaning remains the same, "Master Sun" or "Our Master Sun," which in the text is frequently abbreviated at the beginning of a passage as "Zi," "The Master" or "Our Master." In English pronunciation, it would sound something like "swin dzi."[14]

The Art of War gained its Western name more from following the pattern of the names of Western books on war than any from direct translation of meaning. Father Amiot, the first translator of Sunzi into a Western language, described the work as: "a note, a compilation, or a type of translation (*espèce de traduction*) of what has been written, least badly, in this extremity of Asia, on the military profession (*art des guerriers*)."[15] This fit it into a tradition of works with titles like *Dell'arte*

---

[14] I have chosen not to use any of the phonetic alphabets (e.g. the International Phonetic Alphabet, Americanist Phonetic Notation) since they are not popularly known.

[15] Joseph Amiot to Henri Bertin, dated September 23, 1766 (Bibliothèque de l'Institut de France (BIF), MS 1515, fol. 2). Cited and translated in Adam Parr, "John Clarke's *Military Institutions of Vegetius* and Joseph Amiot's *Art Militaire des Chinois*: translating

della Guerra" (Machiavelli), *Précis de l'Art de la guerre* (Jomini), and *Art de la guerre par principes et par règles* (Puységur). Victor Mair, in his recent translation of Sunzi, managed to insert the more accurate subtitle "Military Methods," though without shifting general Western practice. Since neither the Western tradition of writing about war nor the Chinese tradition strictly defined what could or should be discussed in such a text, a more accurate rendering of the classical Chinese is hard to support against long-standing tradition. Finally, the term *bīngfǎ* 兵法 translated as *The Art of War* was often used as a general term for "the art of war," "military methods," or "strategy," rather than as a book title. Writers might discuss the work of Sun and Wu Qi, or Sun's *bīngfǎ*. In modern China, the work is usually referred to as *Sunzi bingfa*.

This returns us to the mythical nature of Sunzi himself. Our earliest recovered copy of the text attributed to him dates to the second century BCE, but we only find any information about Sunzi at the end of the second century BCE. In Sima Qian's telling, Sunzi had already composed his text before appearing at the court of King Helu of Wu (r. 524–496 BCE). The king stated that he had read Sunzi's thirteen chapters and wanted to test out Sunzi's abilities as a commander. Sunzi agreed to get 180 palace women to follow commands and stay in formation. He accomplished this by executing the two leading women when they disobeyed his commands, after which the remaining women immediately obeyed. After this iconic story, the biography goes on to attribute several military successes to Sunzi. Another biography immediately follows that of Sunzi, a descendant of his named Sun Bin, who was also an accomplished general and strategist.

Sima Qian created a sage of strategic thought to bolster the credibility of an existing military text. Curiously, neither Wu Qi, whose biography also accompanied Sunzi's, nor Sun Bin achieved a similarly elevated state. Sun Bin's text was lost within a few centuries of Sima Qian's writing and was only recovered by modern archaeology.[16] Wu Qi's work remained in circulation along with Sunzi's. Wu Qi regularly accompanied Sunzi when writers cited strategic thinkers, and he was unquestionably the second great strategist of Chinese culture. Yet he never achieved anything like Sunzi's centrality and far fewer scholars wrote commentaries of his work. Perhaps Wu Qi was burdened by having actually existed, along with several anecdotes recording quite ruthless strategic behavior on his part.

---

classical military theory in the aftermath of the Seven Years' War," PhD diss., University College London, 2016, 7. Note too that Amiot called the work "*Art Militaire.*"

[16] D. C. Lao and Roger Ames, trans., *Sun Bin: The Art of Warfare. A Translation of the Classic Chinese Work of Philosophy and Strategy*, Albany: SUNY Press, 2003; Ralph Sawyer and Mei-chün Sawyer, *Sun Pin: Military Methods*, Boulder: Westview, 1995.

One "Other Way"

China is the paradigmatic other for the West, representative of all the non-West. China holds this position partly because of its long literate tradition, which includes a classical canon of histories, philosophers, and poets, as well as a consistent imperial system, and partly because it did not fully succumb to Western imperialism. For many early modern European intellectuals China also provided the secular opposite to church-dominated European governments and society. "Confucian" literati mandarins became secular bureaucrats and intellectuals separated from Buddhism, Daoism, and folk religion. The Jesuits in China sought to portray this Confucianism as a proto-Christianity, raising the possibility of converting or at least co-operating with an influential system of ethics and morals. In this distorted European view, warped by European concerns, China was an equivalent to Europe, absent Christianity. Depending upon which European one spoke to and when, this was a good thing, an opportunity, or a disappointment.

The China-versus-the-West comparison serves just as much to define the West as to denigrate China (and the rest). Western military success in "conquering" the world in the early modern period is basic to the West's modern identity. Setting aside for the moment the question of the reality of this European conquest, its scope, depth, and effect, and acknowledging that there are a number of other equally valid approaches other than the military for discussing the early modern expansion of European involvement with the rest of the world, the global expansion of European power in the early modern period was highly dependent upon European military superiority. Improved European guns, along with advances in sailing and a desire for international trade, changed the balance of power in the world.[17] Thus superior European technology led to, or assisted, superior European military performance against the rest of the world. At least in the military and technological realms, the West was undeniably superior to the rest.

The second aspect of European military superiority was related to its military culture. Modern European armies defeated non-European armies not just because their weapons were superior, but also because their method of fighting was superior. At its simplest, European troops directly engaged their opponents in battle, confident that their unit cohesion and inherent superiority would win out over any non-Europeans. This was true often enough to be believable, which was all that mattered. Europeans defeated local rulers and established control of colonies all

---

[17] Carlo Cipolla, *Guns, Sails, and Empires: Technological Innovation and the Early Phases of European Expansion, 1400–1700*, New York: Pantheon Books, 1965.

over the world. European defeats became anomalous and the ruthless exploitation and brutalization of non-Western peoples an unfortunate aspect of imperialism.

European military culture and rationalism also explain why Europeans did so much more with gunpowder than the Chinese who invented it. Joseph Needham, who pioneered the study of Chinese science, technology, and medicine, believed that China's deeply antiwar culture prevented it from developing guns to the extent the Europeans did. Needham had been at pains to prove the Chinese origin of gunpowder, and even guns, while simultaneously arguing for China's fundamental pacifism.[18] The militarily prostrate, but historically culturally rich, China of the nineteenth century and most of the twentieth exerted an overbearing presentism on many scholars of China, both inside and outside the country. A similar modern perspective informed the assumptions of many historians outside the China field. Western dominance of the world in the nineteenth, twentieth, and even twenty-first centuries was not a recent and significant change from the past, but rather was rooted in a long-standing superiority. If that superiority was not evident for much of the time between the third and eighteenth centuries, give or take, it was a mere artifact of our limited sources, research, or imagination.

This construction of Western superiority assumes or at least implies that the success of early modern European imperialism was due to inherent and deeply rooted aspects of Western culture. The clearest expression of this has been the Western Way of War thesis, which ties the putative ancient Greek method of warfare – a direct, force-on-force clash between opposing forces without subterfuge or attempts at maneuver – to democracy and individual freedom.[19] A way of war was thus inherently tied to a way of life, a set of values, and a culture. This was consistently present in the West from the time of the ancient Greeks, and was intimately tied to politics. As F. E. Adcock said, "We can see, as Aristotle saw, that it [the art of war] is in part a cause and in part an effect, of the political development of the city-state."[20] War gains, in this reading, a critical role in Western political culture, making the direct Western approach to battle not just a superior way of fighting, in Victor Davis Hanson's view, but also a component of the West's fundamental superiority over the non-West.

There are, however, several problems with this view. As Harry Sidebottom pointed out, "War was at the core of the classical cultures.

---

[18] Joseph Needham, *Science and Civilization in China*, Volume 5, Part 7, Cambridge: Cambridge University Press, 1986.
[19] Victor Davis Hanson, *The Western Way of War*, Oxford: Oxford University Press, 1989.
[20] F. E. Adcock, *The Greek and Macedonian Art of War*, Berkeley and Los Angeles: University of California Press, 1957, 3.

Although, contrary to popular ideas, they were not always at war, and when they were they did not always seek open battles."[21] Hanson may well have overstated the case for a Western Way of War, as the most recent research indicates, but it is not a mirage.[22] Sidebottom goes on to say,

Although the links between the two are far from straightforward, it is best for us to interpret the "Western Way of War" more as an ideology than an objective reality. To do otherwise, to think of "Western War" as a continuous practice, is to homogenize history. It can lead all too easily to thinking that there has always been just one "Western Way of War" and probably by extension just one "Other Way".[23]

It is the "One Other Way" that is called into being by the Western Way of War that returns us to the importance of China in the construction of the West. China is that one other way, and must implicitly be different than the West. By definition, then, if ancient Greeks were rational, and pragmatic in war, then the Chinese were not. Hanson writes that, with respect to military strategy,

a Greek's advice succeeded or failed solely by its logic and its degree of efficacy on the battlefield. It was neither hindered nor enhanced by extraneous religious or philosophical doctrine. Compare other traditions of military scholarship. The great Chinese military strategist Sun-tzu is sometimes cryptic, often mystical, and always part of some larger religious paradigm.[24]

Hanson's statement is important on many levels; not the least of which is the perceived need to attack *The Art of War* as a means to assert the greater value of ancient Greek, and thus Western, culture. Just as important is his characterization of *The Art of War*, a text more usually seen as clear, decidedly unmystical, and generally divorced from religious considerations. Indeed, Sunzi argues explicitly for the rational comprehensibility of warfare. Classists might even argue that the ancient Greeks were quite concerned with religious issues in warfare. Hanson's assertion is

---

[21] Harry Sidebottom, *Ancient Warfare: A Very Short Introduction*, Oxford: Oxford University Press, 2004, ix. Moreover, as F. E. Adcock pointed out, "When war came it meant a great effort but a rare one, for, in early times, the evidence suggests that wars and battle were not the constant occupation or preoccupation of the Greeks. They had many other things to do than fight." Adcock, *The Greek and Macedonian Art of War*, 4.

[22] Donald Kagan and Gregory Viggiano (eds.), *Men of Bronze*, Princeton: Princeton University Press, 2013.

[23] Sidebottom, *Ancient Warfare: A Very Short Introduction*, xiii.

[24] Victor Davis Hanson, *Wars of the Ancient Greeks*, New York: Smithsonian Books (HarperCollins), 2004, 166. This was originally published in 1999 by Cassell in London as part of a series, The Smithsonian History of Warfare, edited by John Keegan.

based upon very limited Greek evidence and no Chinese evidence apart from his idiosyncratic description of Sunzi.

The other major contrast for Hanson is that Western warfare was characterized by a direct clash between armies without deception or maneuver.[25] The crux of the distinction between the West and China (represented by Sunzi) is a Western direct, open, effective approach to war versus a Chinese indirect, underhanded, ineffective approach to war. As Sidebottom and others have made clear, Hanson's construction of Western warfare is at best one ideal among others. Ancient Greeks were no less inclined toward deception, indirection, trickery, and ambushes than anyone else in Western or non-Western history. Greek histories do record strategies and stratagems, religious concerns, and the avoidance of open battle.

The construction of a Western way of warfare requires an explicit and knowing downplaying of military events other than those leading up to major battles, and the insistence on the decisiveness of those battles. Open battles were relatively rare in ancient Greece, as they were in the rest of the world for most of history. The major difference between the West and China was in the tradition of reading and commenting on military texts. Like China, ancient Greece and Rome had histories containing many battles, and even histories of campaigns and wars, as well as specialized works focusing on the conduct of warfare in the abstract. Imperial China maintained a continuous tradition of commentary on military texts, and awareness of military works as a specialized category of thought. The West's intellectual tradition of military works, like Vegetius (late fourth century CE) or Aeneas the Tactician (fourth century BCE), was considerably less robust. Machiavelli's *Art of War* functionally restarted the Western tradition of military thought, and laid the basis for its modern development.

In modern scholarship, an extensive Western tradition of military history contrasts with a weak tradition of Chinese military history. Western warfare has been extensively documented and described; Chinese warfare has not. *The Art of War* has therefore been used to stand in for the lack of a history of Chinese wars. Yet connecting military thought to actual warfare has always been extremely difficult. Whatever influence military thinkers have on war planning is indirect at best. Very few historians would be willing to argue without clear-cut evidence that a given military decision was directly caused by a commander reading a specific military text. For Western military history, it has been possible to compare military history with military thought and generally separate

---

[25] Hanson, *The Western Way of War*, xv.

the two. This has not been possible in China, for the most part,[26] but Western writers have been all too willing to substitute shallow discussions of Sunzi for actual accounts of Chinese military history.

One of the most misleading uses of Sunzi has been as a substitute for actual knowledge of Chinese military history. Sunzi is a classical text like the works of Master Kong (Confucius) or Laozi, making it part of Chinese classical culture. Chinese classical culture can be seen as parallel to Western classical culture, and part of a foundational cultural level that renders all subsequent historical development merely derivative (see Sidebottom's warning cited above). This is how the particular characterization of ancient Greek warfare has been used to generalize about a Western way of fighting, despite that characterization inaccurately describing ancient Greek warfare and later Western warfare. China's way of fighting must be the opposite of the West's because the West dominates the modern world. The only piece of evidence for this Chinese way of fighting is a misreading of Sunzi.

Conclusion

Recalling his successful campaign against the Zungar Mongol leader Galdan (1644–1697), the Kangxi Emperor opined,

For in war it's experience of action that matters. The so-called *Seven Military Classics* are full of nonsense about water and fire, lucky omens and advice on the weather, all at random and contradicting each other.[27] I told my officials once that if you follow these books, you'd never win a battle. Li Kuang-ti said that in that case, at least, you should study classical texts like the *Tso-chuan*, but I told him no, that too is high-flown but empty. All one needs is an inflexible will and careful planning.[28]

Like any imperial pronouncement, the Kangxi Emperor's position on military thought was deeply entangled with political concerns and requires some context.

The Kangxi Emperor's explicit rejection of the value of military thought was a *kenosis*, an explicit rejection of the value of written military texts as a cultural and intellectual act of independence. Kangxi's assertion of independence from the Chinese tradition of military thought was

---

[26] For an attempt to connect court debates with military decision making see Peter Lorge (ed.), *Debating War in Chinese History*, Leiden: Brill, 2013.
[27] *The Seven Military Classics* (Wujing Qishu), was a textbook created in 1083 For the military exams. It consisted of Sunzi 孫子, Wu Qi 吳起, Sima Fa 司馬法, Tang Taizong-Li Jing Wen dui 唐太宗李衛公問對, *Liu Tao* 六韜, Wei Liaozi 尉繚子, and Huang Shigong 黃石公三略.
[28] Jonathan Spence, *Emperor of China*, New York: Alfred A. Knopf, 1974, 22.

personal, anti-intellectual, and anti-Chinese. As a successful military commander, Kangxi was asserting that victory was due to his personal qualities. Of course, the emperor had to know what the *Seven Military Classics* was in order even to make that assertion. Kangxi could not claim ignorance; he could only dismiss the contents as unimportant and by doing so inadvertently reassert the cultural importance of the text. But by rejecting the value of a text on strategy he was claiming that success was based upon the commander, not upon outside, knowable, strategies.

Kangxi's dismissal of the *Seven Military Classics* was also an argument against strategy itself. Rather than directly reject strategy, he rejected the canon of military thought in the form of a particular book. War was not an intellectual process beyond a certain amount of planning. Kangxi implies that the planning he speaks of was an operational issue rather than any higher-level consideration beyond the battlefield. In fact, Kangxi, his son, and his grandson, all demonstrated a high level of strategic decision making in their decades-long war against the Zungars.[29] The *Seven Military Classics* may not have played a role in shaping their strategies, but their consistent goal and shifting strategies as time and circumstances changed showed a careful balancing of means and policies, knitting together war, politics, and diplomacy.

Kangxi was the Manchu emperor of a Manchu dynasty that ruled China. Although he spoke and read Chinese, he was unquestionably a Manchu more comfortable speaking Manchu. Some of the early Western missionaries to his court apparently communicated with him in Manchu. And when Father Amiot translated Sunzi in the eighteenth century, he used a Manchu translation of Sunzi to help him. As the non-Chinese leader of a dynasty, the Qing, that had conquered China, Kangxi had good reason to denigrate Chinese military culture. He did not need or use strategy as the Chinese did, and that was why his people had conquered the Chinese. And indeed, most of the troops who took part in defeating Galdan were Manchus or other non-Chinese. Kangxi denigrated the *Seven Military Classics* to assert Manchu superiority over the Chinese.

The cultural and political uses of Sunzi or the *Seven Military Classics* as symbols of China have little to do with the intellectual contents of those works. Yet it would be unfair and untrue to argue that it is only outsiders like modern Westerners or Manchus who use or used these texts in this way. Even within Chinese culture, military thought meant more in the broader society than its narrowly focused contents would suggest. A text about war was both a text and a discussion of war. To read Sunzi was an

---

[29] Peter Perdue, *China Marches West*, Cambridge, MA: Belknap Press, 2005.

act of differentiation by showing literacy and choosing a military text. Most people could not read it. Of those who could read it, it was not always easy to get access to a copy, one had to decide to read it, and then one had to decide openly to inform others that one had done so.

In the eleventh century, many high court officials had read military texts and the argument was over which military books military men should read. Their arguments led up to the creation of the *Seven Military Classics* in 1083.[30] Yet the canonization of Sunzi had taken place a thousand years before that for very different reasons. The commentarial tradition that commenced in the third century CE had still other cultural implications, even though that tradition was truly and deeply engaged with understanding the meaning of the text itself.

No text can be understood without interpretation and classic works are marked by their endless ability to yield new value to new interpreters in different times and places. At the same time, however, a text cannot mean absolutely anything or it would mean nothing. The modern Western reading of Sunzi is a very narrow and selective reading of the text that has broad implications for the Western understanding of China and the West. There were very specific historical reasons for this reading of Sunzi. Several factors coincided after World War II to invest *The Art of War* with its anti-Western and anti-Clausewitzian aura, and to make it a popular symbol of strategic thinking.

This history of Sunzi will try to explain how a classic Chinese text on war became the standard of unconventional thinking in the West. It will also show how strategy became Chinese. This is a strange story of how Western ignorance of Western military writing coincided with Western ignorance of Chinese military history to make a specialized Chinese work on warfare popular in the West. The story begins with the history of *The Art of War* in China.

---

[30] Song dynasty emperor Shenzong effectively established what the seven texts that made up *The Seven Military Classics* were in December of 1083, but they would not be referred to by that name until the Ming dynasty (1368–1644). Shenzong initiated the process of compilation in 1080.

1   A Brief History of Sunzi in China

In order to understand *The Art of War* and Sunzi's modern image outside China, it is important to trace their placement within their original Chinese context, and how that construction was later intentionally crafted to promote Sunzi to the wider world. The mythical author and "his" text served a specific function in Sima Qian's 司馬遷 *Records of the Grand Historian* (*Shiji* 史記) that, given the seminal nature of *Records of the Grand Historian* in creating many of the categories and interpretations of pre-imperial and very early imperial history, has persisted until the present. This is not to say that those categories and interpretations are necessarily wrong, but rather that they were and are a particular way of seeing the past. In a manner also practiced in other cultures, the value of a text was increased by association with a heroic author or designated genius. Samuel Griffith connected Sunzi to Mao Zedong, the great Chinese military genius of the twentieth century, in order to make Sunzi relevant to Western readers. He also connected Sunzi back to ancient Chinese history to establish that, if Mao was the most recent manifestation of strategic acumen, the foundation of that thought was basic to Chinese culture. Sunzi was an ancient classic that was not only an enduring piece of strategic truth, but also a description of warfare in premodern China.

Of course, the idea that Mao was a military genius was as constructed as the category of militarists in *Records of the Grand Historian*, and the inclusion of Sunzi, Wu Qi, and Sun Bin as the exemplars of that category. Mao wrote several important essays on strategy, and the Communist government and army that he led succeeded in their struggle to take control of China. Mao's writings on strategy were therefore validated by that fundamental coin of the military realm: victory. He was an important historical figure who wrote known texts with firm dates. And while it is possible that others helped write or edit his essays on war, their content and attribution are unquestionably Mao's.

The text of Sunzi, for its part, was known well before Sima Qian composed *Records of the Grand Historian*. Master Xun 荀子 (*c.* 310–*c.* 235

BCE), for example, argued against its precepts in his discussion of warfare,[1] and Master Hanfei 韓非子 (*c.* 280–233 BCE) said that everyone has a copy of the writings of Sun [zi] and Wu [Qi],[2] but the text attributed to Sunzi needed a biography for a Master Sun to validate the text. And since Master Xun knew about the Sunzi as the Sunzi, and Master Hanfei referred to Sun 孫 and Wu 吳, a notional Master Sun pre-dated Sima Qian's formulation. Later scholars did notice that none of the canonical histories covering the period of Sunzi's supposed life mentioned him at all, something that would have been almost impossible if such a prominent figure had been real. The existence or nonexistence of Sunzi the author or general had no bearing on the centrality of the written text the Sunzi to Chinese strategic thought. Whatever the merits of the text, or the justification of Sima Qian in including a mythical biography of Sunzi in his history, Sunzi was the fundamental and unquestioned primary work on war in China, even for those who disputed the value of studying it.

Sunzi and Mao Zedong stand at the chronological opposite ends of the history of Chinese military thought, and while it seems likely Sunzi will retain his place of importance, it is impossible to say whether Mao will matter much in the future. Mao's strategic orientation and concept of warfare was extremely influential in the early decades of Communist rule, but as the People's Liberation Army (PLA) changed from a relatively simple and low-tech army into a more modern, technical, and complex institution with a dramatically different set of tasks, Mao's precepts have become less relevant. The PLA is no longer a revolutionary organization, but rather a status quo organization one of whose primary missions is to preserve the power of the Communist Party in control of China. On the other hand, Mao's strategies for revolutionary and guerrilla warfare are widely applicable in other places, and his discussion of protracted war may well be a significant contribution to the broader field of military thought. The established militaries of existing nation-states and their systems of formal officer training may tend to downplay guerrilla warfare and strive to avoid protracted wars, but they recur nonetheless.

A less disputed connection to Sunzi than Mao is the relationship of Daoism to Sunzi. Although the explicit assertion of a connection between Daoism and military thought was fairly late, there were enough similarities of perspective and language to make it seem obvious. Less clear is what the value of connecting the two traditions is to enhancing understanding of either. If Daoism and military thought, especially Sunzi, share intellectual substance then the broadening of examples of concepts can

[1] Xunzi 荀子, Chapter 15 (Yibing 議兵).   [2] Hanfeizi 韓非子, Chapter 49 (Wuchong 五蟲).

help to clarify the full range of possible meanings. The juxtaposition of texts can also serve to highlight a strong strain of ruthlessness in works like the *Daodejing*. Perhaps Sunzi and military works seem more mainstream by association with Daoism, or the association is an attempt to distance Sunzi from its similarly obvious connection to Ruism/Confucianism in imperial China. There was a natural interconnectedness among what Wiebke Denecke calls the "masters discourse," a term that she uses instead of the paradigm of philosophy.[3] Sunzi was part of the Warring States period masters discourse, as was Master Lao (Laozi), and Master Kong (Confucius).

Daoism retained an association with unconventionality throughout imperial Chinese history, in both the positive and the negative sense. The Seven Sages of the Bamboo Grove (third century CE), for example, were educated men of means who rejected government service to hang around together writing poetry and literature rather than serving in a Ruist government. Much of this is legendary, and some of their interests in detachment, which was possible because of their wealth, was simply political survival. Yet they were Daoist figures because they were unconventional; they defied the accepted convention of educated men serving in government. Many subsequent Ruist officials criticized the Seven Sages for not serving in government and trying to make the world a better place. Strategy as a concept is similarly often portrayed as unconventional since it is a way to contend that involves more than a simple test of strength. The "truth" of the connection between Daoism and Sunzi cannot be resolved since it is a matter of perspective, but it must be acknowledged that it has been occasionally argued for at various times in Chinese history.

All of these issues impacted and were manipulated by Western translators of Sunzi to configure the image of the man and the text for a particular audience. Griffith chose to link Sunzi and Mao, but did not discuss Sunzi's connection to Daoism. There is no discussion in Griffith's papers of Daoism in relation to Sunzi, and it may well be that he never considered the issue. It is also the case that Griffith was trying to get Sunzi taken seriously as a strategist on par with Clausewitz and other Western strategists. He might have believed that bringing Laozi into the discussion of strategy would have tainted the seriousness of Sunzi in the eyes of military men. Griffith does mention the opposition of Ruists to Sunzi, in order to contrast the ruthless pragmatism of the strategist against the moral emphasis of the Ruists. Of course, several of the canonical

---

[3] Wiebke Denecke, *The Dynamics of Masters Literature: Early Chinese Thought from Confucius to Han Feizi*, Cambridge, MA: Harvard University Press, 2011.

commentators on Sunzi were unquestionably Ruists, and the Legalists, who were diametrically opposed to much of the Ruist program, were also opposed to Sunzi and to strategists. This chapter will consider the problem of the biography or myth of Sunzi, followed by the issue of the text itself, the relationship of Daoism to Sunzi, and finally the question of Mao Zedong's connection to Sunzi.

The Biography of Sunzi

If there was a historical Master Sun other than Sun Bin, then any real information on him has been lost. The Sunzi described in Sima Qian's *Records of the Grand Historian* is a myth. An account written during the Later Han in the *Spring and Autumn Annals of Wu and Yue* simply repeats the *Records of the Grand Historian* myth, while purporting to be an earlier text.[4] The highly stylized nature of Sunzi's biography in *Records of the Grand Historian* makes it unlikely that it is a historical account of the life of Master Sun in the modern sense. As Albert Galvany has pointed out, the use of biography in *Records of the Grand Historian* was similar in function to its use in ancient Greece, where it

> was not so much concerned with listing data relative to birth, death or other memorable events as it was used to reveal the character of the individual and to present the way that individual lived ... These biographies are not about recording all the notable events in the life of an individual. Frequently the focus is on one event alone that, because of its paradigmatic and exemplary value, is sufficient to furnish an optimal exposition of this person's moral stature.[5]

In the case of Sunzi, that event was his taking command of King Helü of Wu's (r. 514–496 BCE) palace women and training them to fight.

Samuel Griffith was well aware that there were serious questions regarding the existence of Sunzi. He was less concerned about whether a Master Sun who wrote the thirteen-chapter *Art of War* existed at some point than with dating the text itself. The Master Sun in *Records of the Grand Historian* lived too early for Griffith's dating of the text, so his interest in undermining the credibility of the Sima Qian biography was to separate firmly that Master Sun from the received book:

> One of the principal results of this scholarly endeavour has been to confirm, or more often to disprove, traditional claims relating to the authenticity of the works

---

[4] See Ralph Sawyer and Mei-chün Sawyer, *The Seven Military Classics of Ancient China*, Boulder: Westview Press, 1993, 151, for reference to the *Spring and Autumn Annals of Wu and Yue* account.
[5] Albert Galvany, "Philosophy, Biography, and Anecdote: On the Portrait of Sun Wu, " *Philosophy East and West*, October 2011, 61/4, 630.

in question. "The Art of War" has not escaped the careful attention of dozens of these learned analysts, who generally agree that "The Thirteen Chapters" could not have been composed about 500 B.C., as the Grand Historiographer Ssu-ma Ch'ien alleged, but belongs to a later age.[6]

Chinese scholars throughout the imperial period were frequently just as skeptical of historical anecdotes as modern scholars, and were far more deeply steeped in the early texts.

At least as early as the eleventh century, scholars noticed that Master Sun or Sun Wu was absent from any early histories of the period in which he was supposed to have lived and that the text attributed to him described a different period of warfare. Griffith cited Ye Shi's 葉適 (1150–1223) observation that since there was no mention of a great general named Sun Wu in the historical texts, he must have been made up.[7] Griffith goes on to cite Mei Yaochen's 梅堯臣 (1002–1060) position that the text of the Sunzi was from the Warring States period (475–221 BCE), rather than the Spring and Autumn period (771–481 BCE).[8] Mei was not only a renowned poet, but also one of the canonical ten or eleven commentators on Sunzi. His declaration effectively rejected Sima Qian's biography, or, at least, separated the received text from the figure portrayed. Subsequent writers in the Qing dynasty agreed with Ye Shi and Mei Yaochen's positions that the *Records of the Grand Historian* biography was not reliable and that the text was from the Warring States period. Despite a general desire simply to accept the Sunzi of *Records of the Grand Historian*, most modern scholars agree that Sima Qian's biography is unreliable or mythical.[9]

Even setting aside the question of how such a famous general could have escaped earlier historical mention, the warfare of the Sunzi was clearly not Spring and Autumn period warfare. It was only in the Warring States period that professional generals began to command large armies of trained commoner soldiers. The battles of the Spring and Autumn period were chariot fights carried out by small groups of aristocrats.[10] From a technical standpoint, a Spring and Autumn period general would not have composed the text of the Sunzi. The Warring

---

[6] Samuel B. Griffith (trans.), *The Art of War*, Oxford: Oxford University Press, 1963, 1.

[7] Ye Shi, *Xixue Jiyan Xumu* 習學記言序目, Beijing: Zhonghua Shuju, 1977, 46, 675–7, cited in Jens Østergård Petersen, "What's in a Name? On the Sources Concerning Sun Wu," *Asia Major*, 1992, 5/1, 8.

[8] Griffith, *The Art of War*, 1–2. Different historians give different dates for the beginning of the Warring States period, ranging from 481 to 476–5, 453, 441, or 403.

[9] Petersen, Petersen, "What's in a Name?".

[10] The classic account in English of the transition from the Spring and Autumn period to the Warring States period is Mark Edward Lewis, *Sanctioned Violence in Early China*, Albany: SUNY Press, 1990.

States feel of the text is also characteristic of its underlying ethos, that war is about *raison d'état* rather than an activity that provides the opportunity for aristocrats to prove their status by fighting in a particular manner. In that sense, the text cannot be the work of a Spring and Autumn period author.

Modern scholarship has also benefited from archaeological finds unavailable to Samuel Griffith when he was writing. The understanding of who Master Sun was, in imperial China and even well into the twentieth century, relied entirely upon a very small number of interrelated accounts of uncertain reliability. While Wu Qi was a historical figure, and likely Sun Bin as well, Master Sun's biographical details were not corroborated by any contemporaneous source. Master Sun's reputation rested on the received text of his military teachings and his persona was built on his training King Helü's palace women to act as soldiers.

In Sima Qian's biography of Sunzi, Sima relates the story of Sunzi being summoned to King Helü's palace. After telling Sunzi that he has read his "thirteen chapters" (*The Art of War*), the king asks if he can prove the effectiveness of his methods in commanding troops using palace women. Sunzi agrees to the challenge and takes charge of the 180 beautiful women, dividing them into two units, and placing one of the king's two favorites in charge of each group. He then gives them clear and simple instruction in what to do in response to each drum signal. The first time he tried to get them to respond to the drum, they laughed; he explained again, and when called upon to respond, they again laughed. Sunzi then ordered the two commanding palace ladies to be executed, rejecting the king's plea not to do so on the ground that he was now a general in the field. Not surprisingly, the women responded in good order after the executions. The king subsequently made Sunzi a general and he won important campaigns for the state of Wu.[11] It was these campaigns for which there was no mention of Sunzi that demonstrated to scholars like Ye Shi that the *Records of the Grand Historian* biography was fictitious. More recently, more information about this anecdote has emerged.

In 1972 a major archaeological find uncovered a cache of texts from two tombs, dated to 140/134 BCE and 118 BCE, at Yinqueshan. The texts were written on bamboo slips, though most of the 4,942 slips from Tomb 1, and the thirty-two slips from Tomb 2, were damaged. Thirteen fragmentary chapters from Sunzi were included in the find, as well as sixteen chapters from Sun Bin's *Art of War*. Sun Bin's *Art of War* was lost for most of imperial Chinese history. With respect to the two masters surnamed Sun, Jens Petersen points out,

---

[11] Sima Qian, *Records of the Grand Historian*, "Militarists 兵家."

The names Sun Wu and Sun Pin do not occur in the Yin-ch'üeh-shan corpus, only the expression Sun-tzu 孫子, which is used to refer to both Sun Wu and Sun Pin. Whereas the historic referent of the expression "Master Sun says" is in doubt, the context of two of the narratives about Master Sun's exploits clearly indicates that Sun Wu is the subject, and in the other four narratives it is Sun Pin.[12]

One of the fragments of historical material among the Yinqueshan texts is a slightly different version of the story of Sunzi training King Helü's palace women. In the Yinqueshan version of the story the king goes to see Sunzi, and while interested in war, says he is not knowledgeable about it. Sunzi impresses upon him that war is a serious subject. A similar experiment with training palace women takes place, only this time Sunzi's charioteers act as the officers leading the two units. After the demonstration of his ability to form military units that will respond to commands even with palace women, Sunzi then receives an official audience with the king, who announces that "'the way has been attained' 道得矣 and calls the principles illustrated by his exercise 'the way of the general' 將之道. He concludes that in warfare there is nothing more important than the general's stern assertion of his authority over his officers and soldiers."[13] The king does not, however, appoint Sunzi to command, as in the *Records of the Grand Historian* version of the story. Rather than see this as a record of a particular event, it should be seen as an event that proves that a great general is one who carries out military regulations without respect for emotion or pleas from the ruler to be merciful.

In the *Records of the Grand Historian* version, Sunzi proves to the king not only what the correct principle is, but also that he is a general capable of carrying it out. Yet this is not the only story from that period illustrating exactly the same principle. A similar story is told about Sima Rangju 司馬穰苴 (n.d.), who became a general after a discussion of military matters with the king of Qi. In order to establish his authority over his troops, who might have scorned him because he was a relatively low-status member of the Qi royal family, he executed one of the king's favorites for arriving late. The king's messenger, pleading with him not to execute the man, arrived too late to stop it, though Sima Rangju might not have listened anyway. Although the messenger had also violated military law, he was specifically protected by his status as a royal messenger, so his aides were executed instead. Another version of this sort of story is repeated in the *Shangjunshu* and the *Hanfeizi*, where Duke Wen of Jin executes his own close follower, Tian Jie, for arriving late.[14]

---

[12] Petersen, "What's in a Name?", 4.   [13] Petersen, "What's in a Name?", 7.
[14] Petersen, "What's in a Name?", 9–11.

Petersen raises strong and credible objections to the idea that the Sunzi of the anecdote acts in accord with the principles of Sunzi's *Art of War*. *The Art of War* does not advocate for motivating troops solely by the harsh administration of military law. Wu Qi was similarly careful to motivate his troops by benevolence before punishment (on one occasion, he personally sucked the pus from a common soldier's sore). Sima Qian's core biographical anecdote for Sunzi is thus inconsistent with the arguments of the text. If anything, the Sunzi who trained the palace women should be associated with the Legalists.[15] Hanfeizi, of course, was considered a Legalist, suggesting a considerable ambiguity with respect to the image of who Sunzi was supposed to be. Another story about Sun Wu in the Yinqueshan cache associates him with a basically Ruist position, positing that treating the farmers well will result in greater military power.[16]

The key point for Petersen is that the individual in anecdotes used to make certain moral points can be switched when desired without diminishing the story's impact. All that the placement of Sunzi in an account indicates is that there was a tradition of regarding Master Sun as an important enough figure that he could validate an argument by attributing it to him. This is very similar to the thousands of stories that exist outside *The Analects* in which Master Kong (Confucius) plays a role, positive or negative, to drive home an argument. The stories have literary or philosophical value, but they cannot be used as information about the life and times of an individual. And while some famous men used in these stories were historically attested, Sun Wu or Sunzi was not. To add to this literary complex, the name Sun Wu can also be read to mean "Exiled Warrior." Thus, as Petersen concludes, "The name Sun Wu is clearly an example of the literary phenomenon of personification, Sun Wu being The Exiled Warrior, and Sun Wu is thus as fictitious as his name is meaningful."[17]

The Master Sun who composed the Sunzi described in *Records of the Grand Historian* cannot have been at the court of King Helü. There is no record of a general of that name accomplishing what he is said to have done. If there was a Master Sun at King Helü's court, he could not have written the "thirteen chapters" attributed to him, since the structure of warfare was so different between the Spring and Autumn and Warring States periods. The story of the palace women is a literary device rather than a historical account, as are other stories regarding Sunzi or Sun Wu.

---

[15] Petersen, "What's in a Name?", 12.   [16] Petersen, "What's in a Name?", 12–14.
[17] Petersen "What's in a Name?", 29. Petersen sees Sun Wu as a "shadow" of general Wu Zixu. Wu Yun (style name Zixu) died in 484 BCE, and served the state of Wu as a statesman and general.

Legends grew up or were attached to the putative author of a text on war because the figure of Sunzi served to legitimize certain arguments by his presence. One of those tales, the training of the palace women, was used for Sunzi's biography in *Records of the Grand Historian* either because it had become strongly attached to him, or, more likely, because it served Sima Qian's literary purposes.

Sunzi the Text

The Sunzi as a text is mentioned, as noted above, by both Master Xun and Master Hanfei. Some version of it was well known by the third century BCE, and it seems likely that it was compiled over time beginning in the fourth century. The component parts of the received text are the work of several different authors, though I would argue that the overall arrangement of that text is coherent and orderly. Victor Mair sums up the issue of dating as follows:

modern scholarship has demonstrated conclusively that the work evolved during the second half of the fourth century and the beginning of the third century B.C. It is clear, furthermore, that the *Sun Zi* incorporates military lore that circulated broadly during the Warring States period (475–221 B.C.) and could not possibly have been exclusively the product of a single individual.[18]

In Sima Qian's Sunzi biography, King Helü says that he has already read Sunzi's "thirteen chapters." Rather confusingly, the next time the Sunzi is mentioned in the "Bibliographic Essay" (*Yiwenzhi*) of the *Hanshu*, compiled from 58 to 76 CE,[19] the Wu Sunzi's *Art of War* is listed as having eighty-two chapters. This mention, in the "Power and Planning" subsection of the "Military Books" category, raises some problematic issues that have yet to be resolved. The entry immediately afterward is for a Qi Sunzi with eighty-nine chapters, which might refer to Master Sun Bin, who had served as a general for the state of Qi. Many theories have been advanced as to why there would be an eighty-two-chapter version of Sunzi's *Art of War*, but nothing can be concluded in the absence of new information. There were thirteen chapters for Sima Qian, and there would again be thirteen chapters for Cao Cao and afterward. In the imperial library of the Han dynasty, at least, the text of the Sunzi was organized differently, or contained a lot more associated material.

---

[18] Victor Mair (trans.), *The Art of War: Sun Zi's Military Method*, New York: Columbia University Press, 2007, li. Mair was strongly influenced by the work of Bruce Brooks on this issue.

[19] Endymion Wilkinson, *Chinese History: A Manual*, Cambridge, MA: Harvard University Press, 1998, 493.

The fluidity of texts and the vicissitudes of transmission are demonstrated by the Qi Sunzi. Even if it referred to Sun Bin's military text, it would soon be lost, never to be seen again until 1972. Yet Sun Bin was one of the great "Militarists" of *Records of the Grand Historian*. The category of military book would also change over time. Not all of what would later be chosen as the *Seven Military Classics* in the Song dynasty were listed under "Military Books" in the *Hanshu*. The *Sima Fa*, for example, is in the "Rites" chapters, *Army Rituals Sima Fa*, in 155 chapters; the *Wei Liaozi* is in the "Various" section, with twenty-nine chapters. This is not the place for an extensive dissection and analysis of this critical bibliographic issue, but it is important to be aware that the category of "military books" (*bingshu*) in the Han dynasty included a wide variety of works that would later be discarded, like works on martial arts,[20] and did not include several works on strategy or military methods (*bingfa*) that would subsequently be canonical. Moreover, since the overwhelming majority of books listed are no longer extant, there is no way to match names with contents.

A major intellectual event took place toward the end of the Han dynasty. A man by the name of Cao Cao 曹操 (*c*. 155–220 CE), born into a high-status family, and extremely well educated, wrote a commentary on the Sunzi. This is the first known commentary, which makes it an important foundation for the subsequent tradition of Sunzi commentaries. One of the reasons his commentary was preserved was that Cao Cao went on to be one of the greatest warlords in Chinese history, the retroactive founder of the Cao Wei dynasty, and future villain (in some sense) of the novelized version of Three Kingdoms history. It is important to note, however, that he wrote his commentary before he became a general.[21] At least in its conception and drafting, it was an intellectual effort to explain the Sunzi by a man without military experience. He was also said to have "edited" the text, leading to an ongoing dispute as to whether he significantly changed the received version in its thirteen chapters.

The next imperial history to contain a bibliography is the *Suishu* (completed in 636), which lists seven Sunzi *Art of War* or related works.[22] The first, Sunzi's *Art of War* in two scrolls, is noted as "composed by the Wu

---

[20] For an extremely tedious discussion of works on martial arts in the bibliographic section of imperial histories see Peter Lorge, "Early Chinese Works on Martial Arts," in Paul Bowman (ed.), *The Martial Arts Studies Reader*, London: Rowman and Littlefield, 2018, 13–25.

[21] Rafe de Crespigny, *Imperial Warlord: A Biography of Cao Cao 155–220 AD*, Leiden: Brill, 2010, 319 and *passim*.

[22] The *Suishu* was composed in the middle of the seventh century, with the monographs and bibliography sections (added after 656) compiled by a different group than the annals and

General Sun Wu, with commentary by Emperor Wu of the Wei dynasty [i.e. Cao Cao]. During the Liang dynasty, there were three scrolls." The second entry is for Sunzi's *Art of War* in one scroll, "collected and explained by [Emperor] Wu of Wei, and Wang Ling 王凌." Third was Sun Wu's *Military Classic* (*Bingjing* 兵經), in two scrolls, "commentary by Zhang Zishang 張子尚." Fourth is a copy of a Sunzi's *Art of War* in one scroll,

the Wei Defender-in-Chief Jia Xu's 賈詡 copy. The Liang [dynasty] had a Sunzi's *Art of War* in two scrolls, with Master Meng's explanation and exegesis; a Sunzi's *Art of War* in two scrolls, compiled by Shen You 沈友, a private gentleman from Wu; there was also a Sunzi *Eight Formations Diagrams* in one scroll, which was lost.

The next work on the list is not a Sunzi, but rather a Wu Qi's *Art of War*, in one scroll, "with notes by Jia Xu." The final three Sunzi-related texts are somewhat different. There is a Sunzi of Wu's *Female and Male Eight Changes Formations Diagrams*, in two scrolls; a *Continued Sunzi's Art of War*, in two scrolls, "composed by Emperor Wu of the Wei dynasty"; and the Sunzi's *Mixed Observations on the Art of War*, in four scrolls. The Liang dynasty "had five scrolls of Zhuge Liang's *Art of War*, and also a Master Murong's *Art of War* in one scroll, which was lost."[23]

We begin to see what appears to be familiar ground with the bibliography of the *Old Tang History* (completed in 945), which lists a Sunzi's *Art of War* with thirteen scrolls, "composed by Sun Wu, commentary by Emperor Wu of the Wei dynasty," followed by two entries, "also two scrolls, explained by Master Meng," and "also two scrolls, commentary by Shen You."[24] Unfortunately, the assumption that the thirteen scrolls correspond to our expected thirteen chapters, since we often translate *juan* 卷, which means "scroll," as "chapters," is unprovable and likely a false similarity. Later bibliographies do not repeat the thirteen-scroll version of Sunzi in their lists, and it is not clear whether the recorded scrolls refer to the number of scrolls, or to divisions on a smaller number of scrolls. The *New Tang History* (completed in 1060) has a considerably better record of military books, beginning with an Emperor Wu of Wei commentary on Sunzi in three scrolls, also a *Continued Sunzi* in two scrolls, Master Meng's explanation of the Sunzi in two scrolls, Shen You's commentary on the Sunzi in two scrolls, and Sunzi of Wu's *Thirty-Two Ramparts Classic*, in one scroll. A few

biographies, which were completed in 636. My thanks to David Graff for this information.

[23] Wei Zheng 魏徵, *Suishu* 隋書, Beijing: Zhonghua shuju, 1973, 34.2736.

[24] Liu Xu 劉煦 and Zhang Zhaoyuan 張昭遠, *Jiu Tangshu* 舊唐書, Beijing: Zhonghua shuju, 1975, 47.2039–41.

nearby texts mention a Wu Zixu *Art of War* in one scroll, as well as a commentary on Wuzi by Fan Xu in one scroll, which the editors curiously felt necessary to note refers to Wu Qi. Further down in the list we encounter three commentaries on Sunzi, one by Du Mu 杜牧 in three scrolls, one by Chen Hao 陳暐, in one scroll, and one by Jia Lin 賈林 in one scroll.[25] Since the section does not list an individual Sunzi in any number of scrolls without commentary, it seems most likely that the first entry that is described as "composed by Sun Wu" but accompanied by Cao Cao's commentary was functionally the basic form of the text at that time: Sunzi with Cao Cao's commentary. The other commentaries or explanations were separate works.

The most popularly used versions of Sunzi in the twentieth and twenty-first centuries are most often based on Song dynasty printed editions, or Ming dynasty recensions of Song editions. Printing became widespread during the Song, allowing a much greater circulation of texts and greater survivability. There was also an enormous flowering of military texts during the Song, most notably the *Comprehensive Essentials from the Military Classics* 武經總要, the *Seven Military Classics* 武經七書, and *Sunzi with Eleven Commentaries* 十一家註孫子. Consequently, the bibliographic section for the *Songshi* contains far more military books than previous histories do. In total, it contains 347 titles, the majority of which are no longer extant.[26]

In addition to a Sun Wu *Sunzi* in three scrolls, there was also a Sunzi collated by Zhu Fu 朱服 in three scrolls. There were also Zhu Fu's collations of four of the other of the *Seven Military Classics*: *Liu Tao* 六韜 in six scrolls, *Sima Fa* 司馬法 in three scrolls, *Wuzi* 吳子 in two scrolls, and *San lüe* 三略 in three scrolls. This is not surprising, as Zhu Fu was the chief editor for the *Seven Military Classics*, though whether the work was actually done by his assistant editor, He Qufei 何去非, cannot be determined. Curiously, the *Seven Military Classics* is not listed in the bibliography, although the *Comprehensive Essentials from the Military Classics* is. There is also an Emperor Wu of Wei commentary on the Sunzi in three scrolls; a commentary by Xiao Ji 蕭吉, "or put forth by Cao [Cao?] and Xiao," on the Sunzi in one scroll; Jia Lin's commentary on the Sunzi in one scroll; Chen Hao's commentary on the Sunzi in one scroll; and Song Qi's 宋奇 *Explaining Sunzi*, together with the *Simple Essentials from the Military Classics*, in two scrolls.[27]

[25] Song Qi 宋祁 and Ouyang Xiu 歐陽修, *Xin Tangshu* 新唐書, Zhonghua Shuju, 1975, 59.1549–52.
[26] Toqto'a 脫脫, *Songshi* 宋史, Beijing: Zhonghua shuju, 1995, 247.5288.
[27] Toqto'a, *Songshi*, 247.5277.

Further along in the bibliography there is Li Quan's 李筌 commentary on the Sunzi in one scroll; *The Five Commentaries on the Sunzi* in three scrolls, "Emperor Wu of the Wei dynasty, Du Mu, Chen Hao, Jia Yinlin 賈隱林, and Master Meng; Du Mu's *Sunzi Commentary* in one scroll; and a Cao and Du commentary on the Sunzi in three scrolls, "Cao Cao and Du Mu."[28] None of these listings include "Art of War (兵法)" in the title in connection with Sunzi, though there are other works titled "Art of War." A number of commentators who would later be included in the ten or eleven canonical commentaries also do not show up in the imperial bibliography, such as Mei Yaochen. Any conclusions based on the bibliography can only be tentative at best, since the vicissitudes of collecting and history writing for books that are no longer extant is obviously fraught, but it might suggest that the *Seven Military Classics* was not canonical in the late thirteenth century when the *Songshi* was compiled, and the *Sunzi with Eleven Commentaries* similarly either was not canonical, or had not yet been compiled by then.

An abrupt shift is clear in the *Mingshi* (completed in 1739), the next imperial history to have a "Military Books" section. Only fifty-eight works are listed, none of which appeared in the *Songshi* list; works on martial arts are back; and only two texts that might contain the Sunzi, based on title, are listed, under the author Liu Yin 劉寅, *Direct Explanations of the Seven Books* 七書直解, in twenty-six scrolls, and *Collected Ancient Art of War* 集古兵法, in one scroll.[29] Although the imperial collection does not contain any identifiable works on Sunzi, this may have been because it was widely studied outside government auspices. Griffith claims that, during the Ming dynasty, "over fifty commentaries, interpretative studies, and critical essays were devoted to 'The Art of War'. Of these, the most popular was the work of Chao Pen-hsueh, which has been repeatedly reissued."[30] Certainly, by the Ming dynasty, the place of Sunzi in military thought and the text of the work were stable.

The understanding of the text of the Sunzi and the historical existence of Sun Wu in the eighteenth century is best exemplified by the preface to Sun Xingyan's 孫星衍 (1735–1818) edition of Sunzi. Griffith based his translation on Sun Xingyan's edition of Sunzi, which D. C. Lau criticized him for in reviewing the translation.[31] Sun Xingyan was an extremely distinguished scholar, official, and collector of books, notably republishing Song dynasty editions he had acquired. Griffith presented a much

[28] Toqto'a, *Songshi*, 247.5282. Jia Yinlin is a variant of Jia Lin.
[29] Zhang Tingyu 張廷玉, *Mingshi* 明史, Beijing: Zhonghua Shuju, 1995, 98.2436–38.
[30] Griffith, *The Art of War*, 19.
[31] D. C. Lau, "Some Notes on the 'Sun tzu' 孫子," *Bulletin of the School of Oriental and African Studies, University of London*, 1965, 28/2, 320 fn. 9.

more nuanced perspective on Sun in his dissertation, providing a complete and annotated translation of Sun Xingyan's preface to the Sunzi, but dropping it from the published book. The preface includes an extraordinary defense of the existence of Sun Wu as a historical figure, demonstrating the long-standing acceptance that this was not the case:

Sun Tzu was a general of Wu and with thirty thousand men destroyed a Ch'u army of two hundred thousand. He took Ying and intimidated Ch'i and Chin but as he attributed these achievements to Wu Tzu-hsu the commentaries on the Spring and Autumn Annals do not record his name. It is likely that when he achieved merit he did not accept office.

The Yüeh Chüeh Shu says: "The great tomb outside the Wu Men is that of Sun Wu, guest of the King of Wu. This is testimony to his existence."[32]

It was obviously important for Sun Xingyan to address the belief that Sun Wu did not exist, and to explain how it could be that he was not recorded as a general of Wu. He was forced to suggest the improbable idea that Sun Wu was not mentioned because he "attributed his achievements to Wu Tzu-hsu," unintentionally reinforcing the idea that, in fact, Sun Wu was a mythical shadow of Wu Zixu. Sun Xingyan then goes on to deal with the question why there were no listed editions of Sunzi with thirteen chapters, and why earlier bibliographies listed different numbers of chapters or scrolls. His arguments offer no better solutions for the various editions, or for proving or disproving whether Cao Cao or Du Mu changed the received Song text. The edition he offers is based upon a manuscript he believed was compiled in the Song by Ji Tianbao 吉天保 with ten commentators (though incomplete). Sun Xingyan said that he discovered this particular Sunzi manuscript in the Daoist Canon at a mountain temple in Huayin. This is, effectively, a secret Song dynasty manuscript that has allowed him to produce a more accurate version of the Sunzi with ten commentaries.

While Sun Xingyan, with the help of Wu Renji and the inclusion of scholarship by Wu Nianhu and Bi Tianxi, was qualified to edit the text of the Sunzi, his main goals appear to be asserting that Sun Wu existed, and rendering an accurate Song dynasty version of the work. In the final lines of the preface, Sun Xingyan claims that his family is actually descended from Sunzi. He then steps back to make the humble claim that he doesn't really understand all that his ancestor has written, and only made textual studies of it.[33] Clearly, he could not have descended from a mythical figure, which makes his special pleading against what was the scholarly

---

[32] Samuel Griffith, "Sun Tzu, First of the Military Philosophers," D.Phil. thesis, University of Oxford, 1961, 4–5.
[33] Griffith, dissertation, 6–10.

consensus at that time more understandable, though not more credible. While he produced what Griffith describes as "the first truly critical edition of the 'Thirteen Chapters,'" in over 100,000 characters[34] – that is to say, a massive work of textual scholarship consonant with the times in which he lived and his circle of connections – neither Griffith nor many other scholars of Sunzi were convinced that Sun Wu ever existed.

This exhausting, if not exhaustive, account of the mythical Sun Wu and the very real text of the Sunzi provides the basis for considering the relationship of the Sunzi to Daoism, and the relationship of Sunzi to Mao Zedong. In both cases, the problems of intellectual framework and textual connections are apparently strong, but difficult, in fact, to establish clearly.

Sunzi and Daoism

The most basic problem of connecting Sunzi with Daoism is defining what we mean by "Daoism." There are several approaches to encompassing something that might be called "Daoism," and none of them are entirely satisfactory. The inchoate, modern Western understanding seems to reduce not only a set of texts, usually the Laozi or *Daodejing*, and the Zhuangzi, but also a long, complex, and nuanced intellectual and spiritual tradition to something like "going with the flow," "be like water," or "let nature take its course." The problem is in fitting Daoism into Western categories of practice that separate religion and philosophy. Moreover, the "Dao" or "Way" is also used as a fundamental term and concept in other traditions, like Ruism/Confucianism. It is difficult to find any intellectual or spiritual tradition, native or imported, in China that does not or has not used "Dao" in its writings. Hence, just because the Sunzi uses the word *dao* in places, and even sometimes in the same sense as does Laozi or Zhuangzi, it is not possible to assert that it came from Daoism. The uncertainty and close dating of the Sunzi, *Daodejing*, and a number of other texts similarly prevent the establishment of Daoist primacy in creating or fixing the meaning of the "Dao." In particular, for the relationship between Daoism and Sunzi, current scholarship dates the text of the *Daodejing* to a period from the late third to the early second century BCE,[35] as opposed to the earlier dating for the Sunzi text. In any case, the "Dao" belongs to many traditions, and has never been exclusive to Daoism.

---

[34] Griffith, dissertation, "A Note on the Translation."
[35] William G. Boltz, "Lao tzu Tao te Ching 老子道德經," in Michael Loewe (ed.), *Early Chinese Texts: A Bibliographic Guide*, Berkeley: The Society for the Study of Early China, 1993, 269–271.

There are, nevertheless, some consistent concepts that do support a connection between Sunzi and Daoism. In addition to arguments to conform to the reality of nature, people, and circumstances, there is a strong thread of ruthless politics in the *Daodejing*. This latter aspect is frequently overlooked in popular Western concepts of Daoism. Laozi provides advice for surviving in a dangerous political environment, showing that he, like Sunzi, assumes his audience to be men of high enough standing to be navigating constant threats. Of course, where Laozi advocates withdrawal to insure survival, Sunzi is tasked with advancing military and political objectives. Laozi sees nothing to be gained by contending for power; Sunzi explains how to succeed in seeking power. Both texts recognize that the struggle for power is real, natural, and part of ordinary life. This is to say that many of their respective fundamental assumptions about the world are the same, in addition to sharing many terms and concepts.

Although some terms and concepts were common to the Sunzi and the *Daodejing*, it was not usual, initially, to associate these works together. Sunzi was clearly not associated with Daoism or with the *Daodejing* in *Records of the Grand Historian*, for example. Daoism was one of the six schools or traditions listed in *Records of the Grand Historian* (Ruism/ Confucianism, Daoism, Legalism, Moism, the School of Names, and the School of Yin–Yang), whereas Sunzi, Wu Qi, and Sun Bin were in the chapter on "Militarists." As we would expect, then, Sunzi was listed in the "Military Books" section of the *Hanshu*'s bibliographic essay, and not grouped with Daoist matters. By the Tang dynasty, some people had begun to associate Daoism and the Sunzi, most obviously in the commentary of Li Quan (fl. eighth century), who directly quoted the *Daodejing* in explicating the text. That line of interpretation has continued until today. (I was told on several occasions when I began studying Sunzi in the 1980s that I should read the *Daodejing* to complement my work.) Of course, few of these connections made explicit what they meant by Daoism. The shift in perspective on Sunzi is a further reminder that Daoism was a complex and changing thing, as was the interpretation of Sunzi. Just because the connection between Daoism and Sunzi was not originally obvious, doesn't mean either that it didn't exist, or that it was wrong to assert it later.

Another important caveat on the Sunzi–Daoism connection can be seen in the commentators on Sunzi. Only Li Quan, who became one of the eleven canonical commentators, directly quoted the *Daodejing*, making the connection one of a number of possible lines of interpretation, if not necessarily a major or predominant one. Li Quan wrote two other military works, the *Taibo Yinjing* 太白陰經 and the *Huangdi Yinfu Jingshu*

黄帝陰符經疏, in addition to his Sunzi commentary, as well as a partially extant diplomatic and military history, the *Kunwai Chunqiu* 闕外春秋, and a lost work, the *Xiangcheng Zhezhong Taizhi* 相乘著中台志. From the limited biographical information available, it appears that Li Quan was a somewhat successful official who was demoted for offending the prime minister, and then became a Daoist recluse near Mount Song.[36] Yet despite Li's clear intellectual affiliation with Daoism, his extant military works display much stronger resonance with Ruist thinking.[37] As an educated man who served in government, he would have been familiar with both Daoist and Ruist texts, and almost certainly some Buddhist works as well. Fundamentally, of course, that would simply have meant that he was a conventional member of the elite. In the eleventh century, when the *Seven Military Classics* was compiled, the Sunzi and several other military texts were seen by Ruist government officials as conventional works consistent with Ruist teaching.

Victor Mair does point out that the Sunzi was included in the Daoist canon in two versions in the middle and late Song dynasty.[38] At least at that time, then, some Daoists identified the Sunzi as a Daoist work. The timing is interesting, however, as the Sunzi and other military texts had just been the subject of a very Ruist government project to establish a military curriculum for military exams. Mair further argues that there are consistent terms between Sunzi and Laozi, and that, conversely, the Sunzi lacks many key Ruist terms. This is true from a Daoist perspective looking for similarities, but it might also be reversed to find many inconsistencies with Laozi, and many similarities in focus with Ruist thinking. For Mair, "The chief difference between the *Dao De Jing* and the *Sun Zi* is that the former focuses on how to use a *wuwei* ('nonaction') approach to rule a state, whereas the latter concentrates on applying a similar attitude toward the prosecution of war."[39] He does temper his arguments for the Daoist connection in his footnotes, however, where he notes that *wuwei* does not actually appear in the Sunzi, and that, "In pointing out the Taoistic affinities and associations of the *Sun Zi*, I by no means wish to identify it as belonging to the Taoist school of thought per se," and he goes on to quote W. Allyn Rickett that "it is difficult to associate [it] with any particular philosophical school."[40]

The word *dao* was not the only term that spread across many intellectual traditions, and has caused some confusion in translation. A much less loaded pair of terms is *zheng* 正 and *qi* 奇. These terms are extremely

[36] Christopher Rand, "Li Ch'üan and Chinese Military Thought," *Harvard Journal of Asiatic Studies*, June 1979, 39/1, 111–112.
[37] Rand, "Li Ch'üan," 118–19.   [38] Mair, *The Art of War*, 47.
[39] Mair, *The Art of War*, 49.   [40] Mair, *The Art of War*, 74.

important in the Sunzi, particularly with respect to the question whether or not Sunzi argues for indirect strategy. In the Sunzi, they first appear in Chapter 5, which Griffith renders, "That the army is certain to sustain the enemy's attack without suffering defeat is due to the operations of the extraordinary and the normal forces ... Generally, in battle, use the normal forces to engage; use the extraordinary to win."[41] One of the earliest translators, the sinologist Lionel Giles (1875–1958), renders the passage, "To ensure that your whole host may withstand the brunt of the enemy's attack and remain unshaken, use maneuvers direct and indirect. In all fighting, the direct method may be used for joining battle, but indirect methods will be needed in order to secure victory."[42] *Zheng* is translated by Griffith as normal, and *qi* as extraordinary; Giles translates them, respectively, as direct and indirect. Interestingly, this makes Griffith explicitly less close than Giles, at least in terminology, to Liddell Hart's strategy, raising the possibility that Griffith was actively avoiding both Giles's and Liddell Hart's phrasing. It also emphasizes the influence of Liddell Hart's preface on the Western interpretation of Sunzi. Benjamin Wallacker, for his part, pointed out that the terms are also used in the D*aodejing* (57): "One uses the *cheng* [*zheng*] in governing the country; one uses the *chi* [*qi*] in resorting to arms."[43]

Military methods in this Daoist sense are extraordinary or indirect, in contrast to conventional or direct governing of the state. The term to govern, *zheng* 政, is a homonym for *zheng* 正, upright, regular, or conventional. Peter Boodberg extended the homonym connection even further, by suggesting that *qi* 奇, extraordinary or indirect, became connected to cavalry *qi* 騎, through its association with cavalry as a *qi* force in concert with a *zheng* force, which was a homonym for *zheng* 征, to fix or spike in place.[44] It is very easy, and not necessarily wrong, to pull individual terms out of context and point to their similarities, but there is nothing in Sunzi that suggests the idea that war wasn't a normal, conventional activity. Indeed, a constant state of struggle or contention is a bedrock assumption in Sunzi.

Where Daoism and Sunzi conceptually coincide is in the idea of yielding, or apparently yielding, to someone else in order to attain one's goals. This is often described in female terms, relating it back to being indirect or extraordinary, in contrast to the male direct and conventional

[41] Griffith, *The Art of War*, 91.
[42] Lionel Giles, *The Art of War: Bilingual Chinese and English Text*, Burlington, VT: Tuttle, 2014., 21.
[43] Benjamin E. Wallacker, "Two Concepts in Early Chinese Military Thought," *Language*, April–June 1966, 42/2, 295.
[44] Wallacker, "Two Concepts in Early Chinese Military Thought," 298.

approach. A woman yields or is soft to conquer a direct male force, achieving her aims in the only way she can, by deception or endurance. Women don't have the option of overcoming by force, so they deceive a stronger opponent in order to survive, and then mislead him into a disadvantageous position where he can be beaten. This is a strategy of efficiency or weakness, depending upon one's perspective, aimed for Laozi at survival and for Sunzi at gaining an advantage. Sunzi would also agree that "the weaker opponent is only a prize for the stronger";[45] in other words, fighting a stronger opponent is simply foolish and will get you killed.

Generally speaking, a Daoist perspective, however that is conceived, on Sunzi may be helpful in emphasizing some aspects of Sunzi. There is no reason, however, to see a Daoist perspective as any more or less likely than a Ruist perspective to clarify some of the Sunzi's precepts. For most of Chinese history the Sunzi was not seen as a Daoist text in any categorical or intellectual way. On the other hand, there were always some scholars who saw the Sunzi in Daoist terms, or used Daoist texts to illuminate parts of the Sunzi. The particular conditions of late imperial and modern China pushed what had hitherto been a less dominant line of interpretation that posited a fundamental relationship between Daoism and Sunzi to the forefront. Those conditions were based upon a Chinese sense of weakness with respect to their Manchu rulers during the Qing dynasty, upon Chinese weakness with respect to Japan and the West, and, in the West, upon the desire, in the absence of any knowledge of China's military history, to believe that China's culture was fundamentally antiwar in contradistinction to the West. If Chinese culture was antiwar, then its most important work on war had also to be antiwar. In China, this narrative explained Chinese military weakness at the end of imperial history. In the West, Daoism's perceived unassertiveness seemed to explain a strategy of weakness in the Sunzi. The Sunzi became nonbelligerent because it was Daoist.

China began the twentieth century in a militarily weak position. The Qing dynasty had suffered several disastrous defeats before collapsing in 1912, and Republican China fared poorly against Japanese incursions and invasion. Ultimately, the Chinese Communists under Mao Zedong would defeat the Nationalist government under Chiang Kai-shek in 1949. The Communists' success made their strategy, and the relationship of that strategy to earlier Chinese culture, an important question. What was the relationship between Maoist strategy and Sunzi, and why was the issue even raised?

---

[45] Sunzi, Chapter 3.

Sunzi and Mao Zedong

One of the most important ways in which Samuel Griffith connected Sunzi with twentieth-century historical events was by asserting a direct connection between Sunzi's *Art of War* and Mao Zedong's military thought. This added immediate relevance to reading Sunzi since the Communists had taken control of China in 1949 and fought the United States and the United Nations forces to a standstill in Korea, and many revolutionaries around the world followed, or claimed to follow, Mao's precepts. Unlike Marx, Engels, Lenin, or Stalin, Mao wrote out his revolutionary military strategy.[46] There were sound intellectual reasons for making the connection between Sunzi and Mao, but, in addition to highlighting areas of similarity, Griffith supported his argument by explaining Chinese Communist strategy and tactics from the 1930s through the Korean War. The connection between Sunzi and Mao was therefore not only implied through a seeming similarity in phrasing within the translation of Sunzi; it was also explicitly laid out by Griffith in a chapter inserted before the translation. The many similarities between some passages of Sunzi and of Mao leave little doubt for many Chinese scholars of Sunzi's influence on Mao, nor was Griffith the only foreigner to make the connection.[47] Griffith had also already translated some of Mao's military writings, and was in the process of preparing a republication of those translations while he was preparing his Sunzi manuscript for publication.

Griffith came directly to the point in Chapter 6, "Sun Tzu and Mao Tse-Tung":

Mao Tse-Tung has been strongly influenced by Sun Tzu's thought. This is apparent in his works which deal with military strategy and tactics and is particularly evident in *On Guerrilla Warfare, On the Protracted War*, and *Strategic Problems of China's Revolutionary War*; it may also be traced in other essays less familiar to Western readers. Some years before Chairman Mao took his writing-brush in hand in Yan'an, Red commanders had applied Sun Tzu's precepts to their

---

[46] For a discussion of Marx and Engels's views on war, and pragmatic preparations for war, see Sigmund Neumann and Mark von Hagen, "Engels and Marx on Revolution, War, and the Army in Society," in Paret, *Makers of Modern Strategy*, 262–280. John Shy and Thomas W. Collier discuss Mao's military writings in the same edition of *Makers of Modern Strategy*.

[47] In a 1968 letter to Griffith and his wife, Robert Asprey pointed out that Robert Payne's biography of Mao referred to Sunzi, and traced Mao's slogans to Sun Wu. "Do you know anything about Payne? He is an old hand, knew or knows Mao and seems to have a splendid background in Chinese. I wonder why he didn't use your work with your researches, impressive enough, on dating Sun Tzu; also your translations which are much better and more supple than the ones he offers." Robert Asprey to Belle and Sam Griffith, May 19, 1968, BU archive.

operations in Kiangsi and Fukien, where between 1930 and 1934 they inflicted repeated defeats on Chiang Kai-shek's Nationalists whose object was to exterminate the Communists.[48]

Mao, as Griffith goes on to point out, was, in fact, much more interested in the two great classical novels of war and rebellion, *Romance of the Three Kingdoms*, and *Outlaws of the Marsh*, than in classical works of strategy. Several of the heroes of those novels were closely associated with strategy and with Sunzi, most obviously Cao Cao and Zhuge Liang (諸葛亮) (181–234 CE).[49] Mao was also interested in the Taiping Rebellion (1851–1864).

Some of Griffith's connections between Mao's reading, Sunzi, and Mao's political and military activities seem tenuous, at best. Oddly for Griffith, who was usually systematic in his citations, he does not provide direct support for most of his assertions. His explanation for the formation of Mao's military thought seems to reflect US Marine Corps General Evans Carlson's (1896–1947) view of the Communists, and why they were militarily successful:

Both Mao and Chu Teh (who took command of the army at this time) realized the need for a literate and well-indoctrinated force. This concern with morale, traceable in part at least to Sun Tzu's teachings, was to pay handsome dividends, for it was the major factor which preserved the Red Army after the disastrous reverses suffered in Hunan in August and early September 1930.[50]

Zhu De 朱德 (1886–1976), who was an experienced and educated military man, had partnered with Mao in Jinggangshan in 1928. He likely provided most of the actual military training and doctrine for his and Mao's few thousand men. An immensely humble man, he was a convert to Communism after receiving a formal military education, become a warlord, and even traveled abroad.[51] At a minimum, Mao could draw upon Zhu De's knowledge of Western strategists.

Griffith dates the "birth" of Maoist strategy and tactics to September 13, 1930, when Mao and Zhu broke with the urban-focused strategy of the Communist Party's Central Committee under Li Lisan

---

[48] Griffith, *The Art of War*, 45.

[49] Mao told Edgar Snow that he had read *Romance of the Three Kingdoms* and *Outlaws of the Marsh* when he was young and tried to model the various characters' heroic behavior. He would have picked up the general ideas of strategy and connection to Sunzi contained in those novels. Edgar Snow, *Red Star Over China*, London: Victor Gollancz, 1937, 129–130.

[50] Griffith, *The Art of War*, 47.

[51] Zhu engaged a private tutor on Western military subjects when he was attending Göttingen University in 1923 studying political science. He felt that "he had learned little that he did not already know." Agnes Smedley, *The Great Road*, New York and London: Monthly Review Press, 1972, 155.

(1899–1967). This break was caused by the total defeat of Communist forces making futile attacks on Changsha (by Peng Dehuai 彭德怀), and Nanchang (by Mao and Zhu). Mao learned in a very direct way that it was self-destructive to attack fixed positions held by superior forces. Peng Dehuai had at least captured Changsha and held it for several days before being forced to withdraw; Mao and Zhu's forces hadn't even gotten into Nanchang. Chiang Kai-shek began what would become the first of his campaigns to destroy the Communists later in 1930. Those efforts finally succeeded in driving the Communists out of Jiangxi in 1934, leading to their famous Long March to Yan'an. In 1937, Mao reflected on the lessons he had learned by writing *On Guerrilla Warfare* and, the following year, *On Protracted War*.

Griffith suggests that Mao may have had the unpleasant experience of the defeat of the Red Army in 1934 in mind when he subsequently wrote, "We must not belittle the saying in the book of Sun Wu Tzu, the great military expert of ancient China, 'Know your enemy and know yourself and you can fight a hundred battles without disaster'."[52] Griffith attributes Mao's subsequent analysis of the failures of the Red Army to "disarming honesty" rather than to the critical political struggle that Mao was waging for control over the party and the army. The Red Army's defeat in Chiang's Fifth Annihilation Campaign was due as much to better strategy and co-ordination on the part of the Nationalists as it was to failures by the Communists. Mao wanted to develop not only an effective strategy for preserving and advancing the interests of the Communist Party, but also one that would place him in charge (Mao was not the paramount leader in the Jiangxi Soviet in 1934, so he could attack those responsible for the military failures, Bo Gu 博古, Zhou Enlai 周恩來, and Otto Braun, and promote himself).

The parallels with Sunzi, Griffith goes on to point out, are clear, even if Mao did not directly cite Sunzi. Mao, like Sunzi, realized that a war could only be won by avoiding a "static attitude." While this appears to be consistent with Sunzi's thinking, there is no direct statement to that effect. Mao argued directly against "all passive and inflexible methods."[53] Griffith also goes on note the similarities between Mao's sixteen-character "jingle" formulated at Jinggangshan, and some of Sunzi's sayings: "When the enemy advances, we retreat! When the enemy halts, we harass! When the enemy seeks to avoid battle, we attack! When the enemy retreats, we pursue!" Mao's jingle was important in

---

[52] Griffith, *The Art of War*, 50, quoting Mao Zedong, *Selected Works*, Volume 1, Peking: Foreign Languages Press, 1965, 187.
[53] Griffith, *The Art of War*, 51, quoting Mao, ii, 96.

distilling strategy and tactics down to something easy to memorize by ordinary soldiers with limited literacy. A number of other passages also elaborate on concepts from Sunzi, particularly the emphasis on deception, intelligence, and mobility. The similarities of Mao's writings to Sunzi seemed obvious to Griffith, and he was therefore comfortable in asserting, "Throughout the Civil War the Communists continually threw Sun Tzu's book of war at the Generalissimo's dispirited commanders." He continued this connection into the Korean War, attributing the People's Liberation Army's initial successes against the United Nations forces to deception, intelligence, and mobility.[54]

Mao had read Sunzi, though as Xiong Huayuan 熊華源 pointed out, Mao said on three occasions that he had only done so after the Zunyi conference, which took place in 1935.[55] Yet no one has addressed the issue of why Mao did not extensively quote Sunzi's maxims, many of which would have been generally known throughout China. There is a clear split in composition between Mao's tactical "jingles" created for Red Army soldiers, and his longer essays on broader strategic, operational, and tactical issues. His longer essays were aimed at a more educated audience, many of whom would have known that Mao was rephrasing Sunzi. "Ingenious devices such as making a noise in the east while attacking in the west, appearing now in the south and now in the north, hit-and-run and night action should be constantly employed to mislead, entice and confuse the enemy," is an obvious reference to a section of Chapter 6, for example:

For if he prepares to the front his rear will be weak, and if to the rear, his front will be fragile. If he prepares to the left, his right will be vulnerable and if to the right, there will be few on his left. And when he prepares everywhere he will be weak everywhere.

It is also a direct quote from *The Thirty-Six Stratagems*, a work of uncertain date and authorship.

Most, if not all, of the educated members of the Communist leadership would have been familiar with Sunzi, and it would have been surprising if at least some of the Communist generals did not know Sunzi. Quoting Sunzi might have seemed both condescending and pretentious in a scholarly, old-fashioned way, or even backward and feudal to the Communists. Paraphrasing Sunzi, on the other hand, allowed Mao to signal that he was educated and that he expected that his audience was as well. It was then their responsibility to know the classical reference. Mao's

[54] Griffith, 55.
[55] Xiong Huayuan 熊華源, "Mao Zedong Jiujing Heshi Dude *Sunzi Bingfa* 毛澤東究竟何時讀的《孫子兵法》," *Dangde Wenxian* 黨的文獻, 2006/3.

classical education was patchy, as was, at least in his early days, his knowledge of Marxism. He had better-educated secretaries to make up for his lacunae after he had gotten to the top of the Communist power structure. Much as Mao and the Chinese Communist leadership frequently criticized traditional Chinese education, they were also often anxious to demonstrate their knowledge of it.

Liddell Hart's role, through Griffith's Sunzi translation, in connecting Sunzi and Mao was also important to Li Ling李零, the greatest living authority on Sunzi. Indeed, Professor Li thought that Liddell Hart's foreword advocating a return to Sunzi was so important that he translated it into Chinese in 1992.[56] From Professor Li's perspective, the value of drawing the connection between Sunzi and Mao was exactly the same as for Liddell Hart and Griffith: to convince people that Sunzi was relevant and valuable. He is, however, somewhat more nuanced in his dating of Mao reading Sunzi than is Xiong Huayuan. Mao was not considered a serious thinker by the Moscow-educated Communists when he and Zhu De were at Jinggangshan, regarding him as a country yokel. Mao was influenced by the *Romance of the Three Kingdoms*, and, as a man from Hunan, people like Zeng Guofan (1811–1872) and Hu Linyi (1812–1861), two military commanders of the late Qing dynasty who took part in suppressing the Taiping Rebellion.

Mao had read Zheng Guanying's (1842–1922/1923) *Shengshi Weiyan* (Words of Warning to a Prosperous Age), published in 1893, which contained the quote, "Sunzi said: 'Know the enemy and know yourself, and in a hundred battles you will have a hundred victories.'[57] Although these words are small their effect is great." Mao had also listened to Yuan Zhongqian's 袁仲謙 (1868–1932) lectures on Wei Yuan's 魏源 (1794–1856) *Sunzi Jizhu* while in Hunan, and noted down that "Master Sun Wu believed that soldiers were used when there was no alternative 孫武子以兵為不得已."[58] But it was not until Mao reached Yan'an that he had the opportunity to actually read Sunzi. Although he mentioned Sunzi on

[56] Li Ling, "Lideer Hete, 'Huidao Sunzi'," *Sunzi Xuekan*, 1992/4, 12–13.
[57] Zheng Guanying distorted Sunzi's meaning by combining two different passages with very different meanings. In Sunzi Chapter 3, it says, "Know the enemy and know yourself and in a hundred battles you will not be in danger." Earlier in Chapter 3, it says that "winning a hundred victories in a hundred battles is not the acme of skill." Zheng was a late Qing dynasty reformer, who wanted to fight Western dominance of China through economic nationalism.
[58] Li Ling, *Bing yi zhali: Wo du Sunzi* 兵以诈立 : 我读孙子, Beijing: Zhonghua Shuju, 2006, 49–50. Wei Yuan was a Qing dynasty magistrate known for his *Huangchao Jingshi Wenbian* 皇朝經世文編 (Collected Writings on Statecraft of the Reigning Dynasty). Wei's collected works, the *Guwei Tang Ji* 古微堂集, contained an essay, *Sunzi jizhu xu* 孫子集註序 (Preface to Collected Annotations on Sunzi), which appears to be what Mao's teacher Zhongqian based his lectures on. Yuan Jiliu, whose courtesy name was

several occasions, it does not appear, or at least he did not emphasize the idea, that Sunzi strongly influenced him. Professor Li concludes that Mao did not particularly venerate Sunzi, even though he allowed Sunzi to be promoted by his (Mao's) reputation.[59]

Ultimately, it is fair to say that Mao had been at least somewhat influenced by Sunzi, even if this influence was indirect. Mao later acknowledged that he had actually read Sunzi for the first time at some point after 1935, likely in 1936, but even for a modern Chinese scholar the value of associating Mao and Sunzi was to promote Sunzi in the modern day. David Graff has pointed out that Sunzi did not include, and indeed argued against, protracted war, which was a critical concept for Mao.[60] One of the most basic strategic components of guerrilla warfare is protracted war. Sunzi, by contrast, always stressed rapid warfare. From a battlefield perspective – that is, a situation in which one raises an army to fight – lengthy campaigning is always a costly problem.

It is telling that Li Ling finds the same value in attaching Sunzi to Mao that Griffith and Liddell Hart did. The Sunzi is valued by those who study it academically, but it is also popularly known. It is impossible to determine how widely Sunzi is read inside or outside the Chinese military, let alone how seriously it is studied, or how influential it is. It is likely more widely read, in modern translation, than Clausewitz, translated from the German, is in the American military (though Clausewitz, in some form, is usually required for officers of the middle and upper ranks). Sunzi has the great advantage of being extremely short, and its more obtuse sections can easily be ignored by Westerners as weird ancient Chinese mysticism. Clausewitz is long, dense, philosophical, and, as a Western work, close enough culturally that it seems it should be understandable to Westerners. But it is a rare officer in any military who has thought through Clausewitz seriously; outside the military Clausewitz is only read by a very small group of academics and enthusiasts. Sunzi, at least, has a nonmilitary and nonacademic audience. Of course, the extent of familiarity with Sunzi is impossible accurately to measure in either the various militaries or populations of the world.

The use of Mao and Mao's importance for modern Chinese history directly contributed to the profile of Sunzi in the twentieth century. This

Zhongqian, also known as "Yuan the Big Beard," was one of Mao's teachers at the Fourth Normal School in Changsha, from 1913 to 1918. Yuan taught classical Chinese literature. Mao would later write a tomb inscription for him. See Stuart Schram (ed.), *Mao's Road to Power: Revolutionary Writings, 1912–49*, Volume 1, London and New York: Routledge, 1992, 30 fn. 104 (for Wei Yuan), 9 fn. 1 (for Yuan Jiliu).
[59] Li Ling, *Bing yi zhali*, 50.
[60] David Graff, "Sun Tzu," in Daniel Coetzee and Lee W. Eysturlid (eds.), *Philosophers of War*, Volume 1, Santa Barbara, Denver, and Oxford: Praeger, 2013, 175.

was not an accident; it was a conscious decision by Samuel Griffith, strongly supported by Liddell Hart, to push Sunzi into the consciousness of people in the West. Both Griffith and Liddell Hart appear to have believed in the fundamental value of *The Art of War* as a strategic work, and felt that strategists in the West would benefit from reading it. Both men also understood that Griffith's translation of *The Art of War* would sell many more copies if a more general audience were interested in the book. From a basic marketing perspective, Griffith had every reason to tie it to Mao Zedong, the military and political genius who had led the Chinese Communists to victory in 1949, and fought the UN forces in Korea to a standstill in the Korean War. Whether fully justified or not, the connection of Mao and Sunzi vaulted *The Art of War* into a permanent place in the popular imagination in the West.

2   Journey to the West

The first Western translation of Sunzi, the *Art militaire des chinois*, was published in France in 1772. It had been rendered into French by the Jesuit Father Amiot, and was part of his correspondence with Henri Bertin. The Sunzi was one of a number of French translations of classical Chinese works to be done at that time, as part of a more general transmission of information on Chinese culture to Europe. Father Amiot's Sunzi translation did have a direct impact on European military thought, but not in the way that previous research has sought to prove. The next translation of Sunzi into a Western language was by Everard Calthrop, a British artillery officer posted to Japan. Calthrop's translation was initially undertaken as part of his training in Japanese, and published very cheaply. His death at the beginning of World War I ended a potentially fruitful career in connecting Japanese culture to the Anglo-American world, which might have raised the profile of that translation. Calthrop's translation closely preceded Lionel Giles's translation of Sunzi directly from classical Chinese, perhaps indicating that Sunzi's time was finally coming at the beginning of the twentieth century. In addition to extensively criticizing Calthrop, Giles rendered a respectable English version of Sunzi that was little noticed outside the minuscule world of Asian scholarship in the West.

The apparently limited impact of Sunzi on Western strategic thought before Griffith's translation has surprised many twentieth-century writers who found the Sunzi such an interesting book. It seemed impossible that a perceptive and pithy work on strategy was so unimportant before 1963. Samuel Griffith spent a great deal of effort in trying to track down mentions of Sunzi in other European countries, but came up empty. The audience for works of military thought was extremely small before the middle of the twentieth century, and is only marginally larger now. Partly this was due to military culture – military academies that stressed any amount of intellectual training were mostly a late eighteenth-century invention – but the overwhelming attitude of the officer corps was aristocratic and anti-intellectual until well into the twentieth century. Indeed,

44

even in the twenty-first century, a strong strain of anti-intellectualism remains prevalent in the officer corps of most countries. Edward Mead Earle (1894–1954), a professor at the Institute for Advanced Study and an important early contributor to the field of security studies, put together the first conference and edited volume on strategy, *The Makers of Modern Strategy*, during World War II because he recognized that strategy was simply not studied in America up to that time.

Strategy, strategically minded people, and strategists existed, of course, but there were very few men (and it was an exclusively male preserve) who wrote works of strategy, few who read them, and few in the military who advocated for officers to study strategy formally. Dennis Hart Mahan (1802–1871) taught military science and engineering at West Point, where his lectures on strategy and fortifications influenced many of the generals on both sides during the Civil War. Where Dennis Hart Mahan transmitted European strategic thought like that of Jomini, his son, Alfred Thayer Mahan (1840–1914) became a real strategist for naval warfare. The younger Mahan was tremendously influential around the world, but he was really the only American strategist of the nineteenth century, and it was not until John Boyd, after World War II, that there would be another. There were only a handful of important strategists in Europe before World War I, and a similar number afterward. The reason why Basil Liddell Hart and J. F. C. Fuller were so important was because few others matched their status.

Another key point with respect to impact is the conditions at the time. Father Amiot's translation had influence on French military thinking because it fit into the Enlightenment military thought of the time. Because it fit in, however, it did not cause a noticeable shift that could be attributed to Sunzi. Calthrop published his work in the wake of Japanese military success against Russia, which he tried to associate with the Japanese use of Sunzi. Yet the Japanese defeat of Russia impressed few, if anyone, strategically or tactically. It was, if anything, a negative precursor to the coming war of attrition in Europe. Moreover, as much as the Russo-Japanese War was the first example of an Asian power defeating a European power, it could be dismissed as either a victory over the only marginally European power of Russia, and a declining one at that, or due to Japan's diligent copying of the West (Japan's warrior culture, simplified as the "code" of bushido, was also a popular explanation). For Giles, even more so than for Calthrop, China hardly offered a positive military example in 1910. The nineteenth century had seen China repeatedly beaten by Western powers, defeated by tiny, poor, and backward Japan, and then the collapse of the Qing government in 1912, followed by civil war, political and military upheaval and weakness, and conquest by Japan. There was little to suggest China as an exemplar of military strategy in the nineteenth and early part of the twentieth century.

Father Amiot

Jean-Joseph-Marie Amiot (1718–1793) was born in Toulon, France, and entered the Society of Jesus in 1737. He was sent to China in 1750, where he remained until his death in Beijing in 1793. While his life in China was extraordinary, it was his translations and transmission of texts and descriptions of China back to France that made him an important conduit of sinological information in the West. In Adam Parr's description, Amiot's "first published work appeared in Paris in 1770, and for some twenty-five years he was the leading figure in the *correspondance littéraire* conducted between Paris and Beijing under the auspices of Henri Léonard Jean Baptiste Bertin (1720–1792), controller general (1759–63) and then minister of state (1763–80)."[1]

Bertin was a central figure in the representation of China in France, and it seems likely that he was responsible for Amiot translating Sunzi into French. John Finlay has argued that Bertin "truly sought to improve France based on Chinese models."[2] China served another purpose as well, since its image as an empire ruled by a benevolent emperor served by secular scholars as officials suggested a better model than the monarchies of Europe. Ironically, given the prominent place of Christian missionaries in bringing China to Europe, Enlightenment thinkers were attracted to the idea of a secular (as they had constructed Ruism to be) education system, rather than one run by the Catholic Church, supplying government officials selected by a meritocratic examination. As such, it was also "a model formulated in part to criticize elements of European monarchy and economics."[3]

Bertin had his own political reasons for conducting his long correspondence with Amiot and other informants in China, though that is beyond the scope of this discussion. Without Bertin there would not have been the same kind of movement of knowledge, images, and goods from China to France. Amiot, for his part, had a stake in maintaining the support of Bertin for the French missionaries in China, who were usually in competition with the Portuguese missionaries. In the midst of that struggle, the Jesuit order was suppressed in 1773. While the exact

---

[1] Parr, *The Mandate of Heaven*, 3.
[2] John Finlay, *Henri Bertin and the Representation of China in Eighteenth-Century France*, London: Routledge, 2020, 1.
[3] Finlay, *Henri Bertin*, 1.

motivations for each individual act of transmission are hard to pinpoint, Amiot stated that he undertook to translate Chinese military works because he was asked to do so.[4] In response to that request (presumably from Bertin), he determined, correctly, that the Sunzi was the most important military work in the classical Chinese tradition, and translated it, with help from a tutor and a Manchu translation of the text. It is important to note that the Sunzi was not the only Chinese work that he translated, and most of his work was on nonmilitary topics. Bertin and Amiot were interested in many aspects of China.

From the perspective of Sunzi's influence in the West, Bertin and Amiot's exact reasons are less important than the more general effect or impact of his Sunzi translation in France. Samuel Griffith tried to find direct indications of Sunzi's influence in France, but neither he nor the French scholar he contacted were successful in making that connection.[5] Nor, for that matter, was he successful in finding influence in Germany on Clausewitz.[6] Despite that failure, Adam Parr's recent book makes it clear that there was, indeed, influence, that there were several French reactions to Amiot's translation, and, most critically, the translation of Sunzi directly influenced the modern definition of the term "strategy." These outcomes have been somewhat obscured by the integration of the Sunzi into the intellectual milieu of late eighteenth-century France. Amiot and Bertin actively, and consciously, shaped the way that information about China was presented to support their own positions and goals.

Amiot, for example, associated Sunzi with Confucianism in part because he wanted to align it with stable government and an aversion to warfare, and in part because he, as a missionary, was loath to bring up Chinese religion. Christian missionaries described Ruism the way they did, ultimately creating in the West the concept of "Confucianism," as an entirely secular belief system, in order to emphasize the compatibility between Ruism and Christianity. Where Buddhism, Daoism, and popular religious practices were distinctly different religions or superstitions that were irreconcilable with Christianity, Ruism was effectively Christianity without Christ. The Chinese had somehow "lost" Christ (earlier Jesuits like Athanasius Kircher (1602–1680) had claimed that the original Chinese had migrated from the West, where they had been acquainted with the monotheistic "truth"), but he could easily be reinserted into Chinese culture without disrupting the dominant Ruist values.

---

[4] Parr, *The Mandate of Heaven*, 11, 58, where Amiot states in the preface to his translation of the *Sima Fa* that he wrote about war because "some persons of importance, whose wishes are my orders, want me to do so."
[5] Griffith to Paul D'emieville, MCA.   [6] Griffith to Hahlweg, July 13, 1959, LHA.

This was particularly true of the educated elites, who had been deeply inculcated with Ruist values.

Amiot's translation itself fed into the Military Enlightenment, and was interpreted in ways consistent with that intellectual tradition. This helps to explain Sunzi's later place in the eyes of men like Liddell Hart as fundamentally opposed to Clausewitz. Clausewitz was, as Azar Gat has shown, opposed to many aspects of Enlightenment military thinkers, and Liddell Hart, in his turn, made Clausewitz the straw man against which to oppose his ideas. When Liddell Hart praised Sunzi and vilified Clausewitz, establishing them as the opposing poles of strategic thought, he was simply reverting back to the Enlightenment versus the Counter-Enlightenment, or German Romantic conflict.

Recent scholarship by Christy Pichichero has expanded the consideration of the Military Enlightenment beyond intellectual history to encompass the broader engagement of French society in those debates.[7] The Enlightenment itself reflected the perspective of people in the late seventeenth to early eighteenth centuries, mostly starting in France, that the Scientific Revolution had created an intellectual break with the past among the educated. "Participants in the Military Enlightenment," Pichichero writes,

saw themselves as actors in a history of progress and they shared a conviction that the functioning of the armed forces and the conditions of warfare more generally needed to be improved. In the name of advancement in these areas, agents of the Military Enlightenment applied a critical philosophical spirit, or *esprit philosophique*, to acquire a deep understanding of war and the military, then proposed and implemented a myriad of reforms.[8]

Functionally, Enlightenment military thinkers believed they could produce a scientific approach to war, one that would reveal objective truths that transcended time and place.

Although the Military Enlightenment reached considerably beyond a narrow group of military thinkers, it was, in fact, those thinkers who directly shaped the development of the modern idea of strategy. As is often the case, battlefield results stimulated military writing. Many theorists credited Frederick the Great's victories in the Seven Years War (1756–1763) to the organization and tactics of the Prussian army. During much of the eighteenth century, French theorists debated whether infantry should be arrayed in linear formation, to maximize firepower, or in columns, to maximize shock tactics. These tactics

---

[7] Christy Pichichero, *The Military Enlightenment: War and Culture in the French Empire from Louis XIV to Napoleon*, Ithaca: Cornell University Press, 2018.
[8] Pichichero, *The Military Enlightenment*, 2.

reflected not only changing military technology, but also perceptions of national character. What was possible for Germans was not possible for Frenchmen because they were temperamentally different. These arguments over tactics, however, eventually extended to broader and higher-level theorizing. "The French Enlightenment," Azar Gat wrote,

swarmed with definitive systems intended to regulate this or that sphere of human life, and, characteristically, all the participants in the intense military controversy believed that it was to produce a system of a definitive and absolute nature. As Clausewitz wrote in his outline of the development of military theory: "tactics attempted to convert the structure of its component parts into a general system."[9]

Gat attributes the modern use of the term "strategy" to Paul Gideon Joly de Maizeroy (1719–1780). This followed on the Enlightenment use of the term "tactics," which was concerned with military organization and formations. Most theorists, Maizeroy included, focused enormous attention on tactics as the primary concern of military operations. "The conduct of operations," however, "was the second branch of the art of war. Maizeroy gave this branch a new technical term, 'strategy', whose origins in modern military theory also seem to have been lost."[10] Gat reasonably suggests that Maizeroy drew the term from the Greek word for "a general" as used in Maurice's *Strategikón*, of which he had published a French translation from the Greek. Maizeroy first used the term "strategy" in his 1777 work *Théorie de la guerre*. It was used increasingly in the following decade, though it took until the early nineteenth century to spread across the rest of Europe.[11]

Beatrice Heuser describes a slightly different history of the terms "tactics" and "strategy," seeing them present in the ancient world, if not widely used. She stresses the presence of the concepts of strategy and tactics in the works of Maurice's (539–602) *Strategikón* (c. 600) and Leo VI's (865–912) *Taktiká*. Her account, then, connects back with Gat's, though she points to Maizeroy's use of *stratégique* in the commentary to his 1771 translation of Leo VI's work.[12] The key for Heuser is the intellectual hierarchy of the terms "tactics" and "strategy," not just their meaning. The slippage in meaning when moving from ancient Greek to fine distinctions in eighteenth-century French and then to English makes the relations between terms as important in arguing for their overall meaning as direct attempts at translation.

The timing of the use of Maizeroy's new term "strategy" is suggestive. One of the most groundbreaking arguments from Adam Parr's account of

[9] Azar Gat, *A History of Military Thought*, Oxford: Oxford University Press, 2001, 41.
[10] Gat, *A History of Military Thought*, 43–44.   [11] Gat, *A History of Military Thought*, 44.
[12] Heuser, *The Evolution of Strategy*, 4–5.

the Amiot translation is his direct connection of the Sunzi translation to the formation of the Maizeroy's concept of "strategy." Amiot's translation of Sunzi was done in 1766, though it took some time to reach Bertin and then to be published in 1772. It was accompanied by three other works and subject to a number of reviews and mentions. Maizeroy had ample opportunity to encounter the work, not least because of his membership in the Académie royale des inscriptions et belles-lettres, of which Bertin and De Guignes (who edited the *Art militaire des chinois*) were also members.[13] He also used the term strategy (*stratégie*) in a 1775 essay.[14] As other scholars have noticed, Amiot's Sunzi translation appeared in the midst of this ferment of military and strategic writing. Hitherto, however, the goal of most researchers, like Griffith, was to prove whether Napoleon had read the French translation of Sunzi. Frustrated in that, no one was interested in the possibility that Sunzi had influenced the field of strategic and military thought more generally.

Parr convincingly argues for the direct influence of Sunzi on Maizeroy based upon two points: specific mention of Amiot's translation and intellectual similarity. What makes his argument particularly strong is a passage in Maizeroy that links these two. In the definition section of his *Théorie de la guerre*, under the definition of war, Maizeroy writes,

La conduit de la guerre est la science du Général, que les Grecs nommoient *stratégie* [στατηγια], science profonde, vaste, sublime, qui on renferme beaucoup d'autres, mais dont la base fondamentale est la Tactique. Les Chinois la nomment *la grande affaire*, comme le morale, la grande science. *Art Militaire de Chinois.*

[The conduct of war is the science of the general, what the Greeks called *strategy*, a deep, vast and sublime science which incorporates many others whose fundamental basis is tactics. The Chinese call it the great matter of state, just as they call ethics the great science: *Art militaire des chinois*.][15]

Of course, "la grande affaire" is a direct quote from the first line of the Sunzi, that "war is a great matter of state 兵者國之大事," or in Amiot's translation, "la grande affaire d'un État."

Maizeroy's thinking had also progressed, Parr argues, between 1771 and 1777, to see that strategy was not just the realm of the general, as the ancient Greeks understood it, but also concerned ministers of

---

[13] Parr, *The Mandate of Heaven*, 216 fn. 49.
[14] Parr, *The Mandate of Heaven*, 218 fn. 56. Alexandre David's work on the development of Maizeroy's concept of strategy is also critical in supporting his argument for the influence of Sunzi. Alexandre David, "'L'interprète des plus grands maîtres': Paul Gédéon Joly de Maizeroy l'inventeur de la stratégie," *Stratégique* 1 (2010): 63–85; and Alexandre David, *Joly de Maizeroy: L'inventeur de la stratégie*, Paris: L'École de guerre, 2018. Both of these works are cited in Parr, *The Mandate of Heaven*, 218 fn. 56.
[15] Maizeroy, *Théorie de la guerre*, 2, cited and translated in Parr, *The Mandate of Heaven*, 219–20.

government. There are many aspects of strategy that must be incorporated together, and European and Chinese classical learning are also connected to strategy. "It is highly significant that the first attempt to synthesize the European and Chinese traditions of military theory coincides with the first modern exploration, and use, of the term 'strategy'."[16] Maizeroy's shift from *stratégique* to *stratégie* in 1777 was indicative of a much more important shift in thinking, one with profound intellectual consequences for the future.

Considering the role of Amiot's translation of Sunzi in forming the modern, Western meaning of "strategy," it is much less strange that the Sunzi has become synonymous with strategy in the modern West. Clausewitz's *On War* remains a purely military text, where the Sunzi transcends mere war to provide strategic wisdom for every aspect of life. This goes beyond Maizeroy's points, perhaps, but is consistent with his new understanding of strategy. Strategy is not something outside learning; it is part of it. Amiot in that sense succeeded in incorporating Chinese learning into Western thinking. The *Art militaire des chinois* itself would be reprinted in 1782, though it would have to wait until the early twentieth century for the Sunzi to appear in English.

Lieutenant-Colonel Everard Ferguson Calthrop

Everard Ferguson Calthrop (1876–1915) published the first translation of Sunzi in English. He served as a language officer in Japan from 1904 to 1908, and then as military attaché from 1914 to 1915. Calthrop joined the Royal Artillery, and was commissioned as a second lieutenant on November 2, 1895.[17] He served, in turn, in Malta and then South Africa (for the Boer War) for three years beginning in late 1899, being promoted to captain in September 1901, and returning to England with the conclusion of the war in 1902. His desire to escape garrison life during peacetime led him to apply to go to Japan to learn Japanese, an effort by the British government to respond to its new Anglo-Japanese Alliance (1903). Calthrop began his language training in England prior to departure.

Almost immediately after he arrived in Japan he wrote to his mother on March 9, 1904 (from the Imperial Hotel Tokyo), "The day I arrived that is the day before yesterday I immediately proceeded to the legation." He quickly found that no real provisions had been made for him to undertake

---

[16] Parr, *Mandate of Heaven*, 220.
[17] Sebastian Dobson, "Lieutenant-Colonel Everard Ferguson Calthrop (1876–1915)," in Hugh Cortazzi (ed.), *Britain and Japan: Biographical Portraits*, Volume 8, Leiden: Brill, 2013, 86–87.

his language training, or to house him: "We are awful muddlers ... How different from the Japanese I have noticed already. They have the organizing powers of the Germans without their loud and impolite rigidity."[18] Calthrop rented lodgings and engaged a teacher, choosing to live as fully as he could in the Japanese manner.

Japan had declared war on Russia on February 8, 1904, though in point of fact had actually launched a naval attack on the Russian fleet based at Port Arthur three hours before its official declaration. The tsar had been stunned by the attack preceding the formal declaration. Calthrop tried to get permission to go to Korea to observe the fighting between Russia and Japan, but was turned down. This likely was for the best, as the Russians had threatened to arrest British journalists on April 15 because their reports might provide useful intelligence to the Japanese. A British officer serving with their Japanese ally would be even more suspect. On April 17, 1904, Calthrop wrote, "The Japanese are waiting for the fall of Port Arthur,"[19] though it would, in fact, take until January 2, 1905, for the Russian garrison to surrender.

In December of 1904 Calthrop told his mother that he was able to read easy pieces from the newspaper.[20] His work on learning Japanese progressed rapidly, and in January of 1905 he wrote that he had done well on his language examination. He then went on to say, "I am translating a Chinese Military Classic with the help of my teachers. It may come to nothing, but there is a chance it might be worth something."[21] He continued on February 18, 1905, "I think I told you I was translating a Chinese Classic. Although very celebrated, perhaps quite the most celebrated book on war it has turned out rather interestingly ... I am going on perhaps may publish it with a preface on Ancient Chinese and Japanese warfare."[22]

By May, he had acquired a publisher:

I told you I was translating a Chinese Classic on war with the help of my teacher ... Now it seems that one of the Tokyo publishers is willing to produce it. That is to say without my having to pay for the privilege. So I am thinking of bursting on this world as an author ... The book however will only be a paper covered affair, and books in Japan are produced so easily and cheaply that it hardly deserves the name. However to my mind it is interesting as being a very famous book and as having influenced Japanese military strategy.[23]

---

[18] Calthrop to his mother from the Imperial Hotel, Tokyo, March 9, 1904. Calthrop's letters to his mother and sister are currently held in the Royal Artillery Archive at Larkhill, Salisbury.
[19] Calthrop, April 17, 1904.   [20] Calthrop, December 4, 1904.
[21] Calthrop, January 30 [1905].   [22] Calthrop, February 18, 1905.
[23] Calthrop, May 13, 1905.

In June, he lamented that he had still not been allowed to observe the war, but, "I have got a reputation for knowing Japanese, which I do not at all deserve and which only makes the other people jealous and work harder, without boasting, however, I suppose at this moment I know Japanese better than anyone in the army."[24]

"The 'book' is done," he wrote to his mother on July 1, 1905, "and may appear daily. I will send you a copy."[25] Unfortunately, the copy of his translation he sent to his mother had somehow not reached her by November:

I am very sorry you did not get the book 'Sonshi.' I had been wondering you did not say anything about it, and was a little disappointed not to hear.

This is undoubtedly the greatest work on war in the East – interesting on that account alone (I think) but because the words bow and arrow and chariot appear it was pooh poohed, and I think now quite forgotten. Nobody, apparently, has realized the wonderful wisdom that lies hidden in the old Chinese words.[26]

Calthrop's interest in Sunzi was stimulated by its influence on Japanese military practice, as well as its value as a strategic work. He mentioned, "I was interested to hear last night that General Matsukawa maybe Japans greatest strategists [sic] considers that no European books on strategy touch Sonshi in sublimity."[27] He found that other British officers did not share his opinion, however, as "I unfortunately handed a copy to the military attaché. The beggar never looked at it, so I unceremoniously put it back into my pocket again."[28]

Calthrop was allowed to attend a year of courses at the Japanese Staff College in December of 1906.[29] His notebook from his time at the Japanese Staff College remains in the archive of the Royal Artillery at Larkhill. Calthrop left Japan in 1908 to return to England, going to Staff College in 1910. In 1911, he was assigned to Far Eastern duties in the Directorate of Military Operations, focusing on intelligence for China and Japan. He remained there until a brief stint back in garrison, before being sent as military attaché to Tokyo effective August 12, 1914. World War I had broken out while he was en route, and he wanted to return to fight in Europe. As military attaché, and a fluent Japanese speaker, he was sent as a liaison officer for the Anglo-Japanese expedition against the German concessions in Qingdao, Shandong. Most of the British soldiers would have preferred to be back in Europe fighting in more direct defense of their country. The German positions in China seemed, and were,

[24] Calthrop, June 6, 1905.   [25] Calthrop, July 1, 1905.
[26] Calthrop, November 12, 1905.   [27] Calthrop, June 25, 1905.
[28] Calthrop, November 12, 1905.
[29] Dobson, "Lieutenant-Colonel Everard Ferguson Calthrop," 93

extremely peripheral to the British. They were important to the Japanese, however, for whom the expedition marked a further expansion of their influence on the Asian continent after the Russo-Japanese War. Consequently, there was very little co-operation between the Japanese and the British, and Calthrop was left with very little to do.

After the German surrender of Qingdao, Calthrop sought to return to Europe to fight. His language skills were valuable for the British embassy, but he did not see his duties as important, especially given the fighting in France. A different man would have been content to serve in Japan during the war. He got transferred back to England, arriving in June of 1915, and rushed to the front, arriving in Ypres on September 24. Assigned to an artillery brigade in the Ypres salient, he was struck by a shell fragment on December 19, 1915, and died several hours later.

Calthrop had published a revised and expanded version of his Sunzi translation in 1908, which added Wu Qi's text, this time with a British publisher.[30] An anonymous reviewer of his *The Book of War: The Military Classic of the Far East*, in the *United Services Magazine*, wrote,

The sayings of Sun and Wu make one "furiously to think". Strike out Bell, Drum, obsolete weapons, and Forest of Banners, we find that twenty-five hundred years ago is as to-day. Thanks to a very competent translator we have been furnished with a treatise equivalent to a précis of Clausewitz – and infinitely more interesting.[31]

That reviewer, at least, saw Sunzi as consistent with Clausewitz, if shorter and more engagingly composed. Of course, whoever the reviewer was, he was one of a minority of more intellectually inclined officers who had read Clausewitz, or at least thought it worthwhile to suggest that he had. Clausewitz's was not a widely read work even (some might suggest "especially") among British officers in the early twentieth century. Apart from the many areas of similarity, Clausewitz and Sunzi were similar simply by being works of strategy.

One of the main problems with Calthrop's Sunzi translation was that it was actually a translation of a Japanese translation of Sunzi, rather than a rendering directly from classical Chinese. Calthrop had no pretensions of being a sinologist or reading classical Chinese, even in the manner that traditional Japanese scholars of Chinese texts did. His goal was to make an important text available in much the same way it was to Japanese

---

[30] C. E. Calthrop, *The Book of War: The Military Classic of the Far East*, London: John Murray, 1908.

[31] Anonymous, *The Book of War: The Military Classic of the Far East*, in *United Services Magazine*, 38, 1908–1909, 333, cited in Dobson, "Lieutenant-Colonel Everard Ferguson Calthrop," 92.

officers. As a purely military work, Calthrop sought to transmit its strategic lessons to British officers. This foundered for the most part not on his sinological failings, but on the general contempt for study of most British officers at that time, and their particular contempt for foreign strategic thinking. Apart from a very few exceptions, like the anonymous reviewer in the *United Services Magazine*, British officers did not believe they had anything to learn from the Japanese, Chinese, or any nonwhite culture. Interest outside the military in strategy was virtually nonexistent, with the exception of sinologists.

Calthrop's translation appears to have deeply bothered Lionel Giles. It bothered him so much that when he undertook his own translation of Sunzi, he included a relentless discussion of Calthrop's failings. It was, however, Calthrop's translation that was, at least in Liddell Hart's telling, first brought to Liddell Hart's attention in 1927.[32] Interestingly, Griffith's translation would suffer a similar fate by another sinologist, D. C. Lau, though in a pointed review. The aim of both Calthrop and Griffith was to bring Sunzi into military discussions of strategy, rather than to engage the scholarly community of Asianists. Calthrop's translation arrived fifty years too soon to find a general audience. The time was not right.

Lionel Giles

Lionel Giles (1875–1958) began working at the British Museum in 1900, and became keeper of the Department of Oriental Manuscripts and Printed Books at the British Museum from 1936 until his retirement in 1940. He was the son of Herbert Giles (1845–1935), a British diplomat serving in China from 1867 to 1892, and subsequently professor of Chinese at Cambridge University from 1897 until his retirement in 1932. Lionel Giles was an accomplished sinologist and translator of classical Chinese works, like his father. Lionel was by all accounts a pleasant, studious man, quite unlike his difficult father. Herbert Giles is today mostly remembered for his modification of Thomas Wade's romanization system for Chinese, the now outdated Wade–Giles system that produced the romanization "Sun Tzu" for the characters 孫子. Lionel Giles is best known today for his translation of Sunzi.

One of the oddest aspects of Giles's Sunzi translation is the still inexplicable bile this mild-mannered scholar unleashed on Everard Ferguson Calthrop's translation of Sunzi. Although he could be blunt in his

---

[32] John Duncan to Liddell Hart, May 7, 1927, Liddell Hart Archives. Duncan wrote to Liddell Hart from Shanghai, but the edition of Calthrop was the 1908 revised edition published in England by John Murray.

published reviews of the work of other sinologists, Calthrop's translation aroused a unique fury in him. As John Minford remarked in his foreword to a new edition of the Giles translation,

Giles occasionally made errors of judgement. For example, he misjudged the early French translation of Amiot, which he deemed "little better than an imposture". In fact, Amiot was working (as did many Jesuits) from a Manchu paraphrase of the eighteenth century, which makes his "free" and discursive version all the more interesting. Giles's recurring and often ill-tempered broadsides against the unfortunate Captain Calthrop and his flawed 1908 translation (he almost seems to have been emulating his notoriously irascible and often petulant father) are the only feature that mars and dates an otherwise splendid book. This defect is not to be found in his other writings.[33]

Minford does not mention that Calthrop, like Amiot with Manchu, was using a Japanese translation of Sunzi.

As Giles set the context for his work,

Throughout the nineteenth century, which saw a wonderful development in the study of Chinese literature, no translator ventured to tackle Sun Tzu, although his work was known to be highly valued in China as by far the oldest and best compendium of military science. It was not until the year 1905 that the first English translation, by Capt. E. F. Calthrop. R.F.A., appeared at Tokyo under the title "Sonshi" (the Japanese form of Sun Tzu). Unfortunately, it was evident that the translator's knowledge of Chinese was far too scanty to fit him to grapple with the manifold difficulties of Sun Tzu. He himself plainly acknowledges that without the aid of two Japanese gentlemen "the accompanying translation would have been impossible." We can only wonder, then, that with their help it should have been so excessively bad. It is not merely a question of downright blunders, from which none can hope to be wholly exempt. Omissions were frequent; hard passages were willfully distorted or slurred over. Such offences are less pardonable. They would not be tolerated in any edition of a Greek or Latin classic, and a similar standard of honesty ought to be insisted upon in translations from Chinese.[34]

It is possible that Giles was particularly annoyed by Calthrop's publication of a new edition of his translation in 1908 with a London publisher. He mentions in his preface that the 1908 edition appeared while three of Giles's chapters had already been completed with the printer (Giles's translation was published in 1910), and admits that the revised and expanded translation had fixed some of its earlier problems. Giles's uncharacteristic venom, and the extensive research he displayed in the preface to his translation, also suggest that he might have begun his work

---

[33] John Minford, "Foreword," in Lionel Giles, *Sunzi: The Art of War*, Burlington, VT: Tuttle, 2008, vii–xxv.
[34] Giles, *Sunzi*, "Preface."

on Sunzi before Calthrop's 1905 edition came out. Perhaps while Giles was meticulously working through the background materials on the Sunzi, and figuring out how to set the Chinese text with the translation and notes (keeping in mind the cumbersome typesetting technology of the time), Calthrop's cheaply produced, Japanese-printed basic version of just the translation of the Sunzi arrived to take precedence as the first English translation. The revised and expanded 1908 translation by a London publisher only exacerbated his disappointment.

Giles's scholarly apparatus was, indeed, extremely impressive, and he, like Griffith after him, relied upon Sun Xingyan's edition of the Sunzi. After reviewing all of the evidence for Sun Wu's life, he concludes,

It is obvious that any attempt to reconstruct even the outline of Sun Tzu's life must be based almost wholly on conjecture. With this necessary proviso, I should say that he probably entered the service of Wu about the time of Ho Lu's accession, and gathered experience, though only in the capacity of a subordinate officer, during the intense military activity which marked the first half of the prince's reign. If he rose to be a general at all, he certainly was never on an equal footing with the three above mentioned. He was doubtless present at the investment and occupation of Ying, and witnessed Wu's sudden collapse in the following year. Yueh's attack at this critical juncture, when her rival was embarrassed on every side, seems to have convinced him that this upstart kingdom was the great enemy against whom every effort would henceforth have to be directed. Sun Wu was thus a well-seasoned warrior when he sat down to write his famous book, which according to my reckoning must have appeared towards the end, rather than the beginning, of Ho Lu's reign. The story of the women may possibly have grown out of some real incident occurring about the same time. As we hear no more of Sun Wu after this from any source, he is hardly likely to have survived his patron or to have taken part in the death-struggle with Yueh, which began with the disaster at Tsui-li.[35]

Giles, then, sided with men like Sun Xingyan, who assumed that there was a Master Sun, author of a text on war, that was transmitted in some form from the fifth century BCE, or shortly thereafter. He was skeptical of many of the claims about Sunzi's biography (like training the palace women), and sought to resolve them through a judicious review of the available literature. Giles expended a great deal of scholarly effort and produced sophisticated arguments to bridge the obvious problems with Sunzi's biography and text. For some reason, he seemed resolved to overcome the well-founded skepticism and criticisms of many imperial-period scholars. Giles did not see the text as a compilation of writings or oral traditions from many authors, or accept the arguments of the Song dynasty and later scholars who believed Master Sun to be a myth and the

---

[35] Giles, *Sunzi*, "Preface."

Sunzi text to be a Warring States-period work. While much of his scholarship on both the text and Master Sun remains valuable, his dating of the work, strained and untenable efforts to support the existence of the Master Sun of *Records of the Grand Historian*, and belief that the text is the work of a single author have aged poorly.

Giles's preface was aimed at a narrow scholarly audience. Although he dedicated the work to his younger brother, who was in the army, "To my brother, Captain Valentine Giles, R.E. in the hope that a work 2400 years old may yet contain lessons worth consideration by the soldier of today this translation is affectionately dedicated," it is worth noting that Valentine, like Lionel and his two older brothers, Bertram and Lancelot, and sisters Edith and Mable, had been born in and grew up in China. Bertram and Lancelot went into British diplomatic service in China, and all of them were well educated and must have spoken and been literate in Chinese. In any case, Giles's translation of Sunzi was appreciated within the sinological and Asian (what would have then been called "Oriental") studies field, but had as little impact on the British military as Calthrop's translation.

Léonard Eugène Aurousseau (1888–1929), who would later serve as the director of the École française d'Extrême-Orient, reviewed Giles's translation in *Bulletin de l'École française d'Extrême-Orient*, in late 1910, almost immediately after it was published.[36] Aurosseau noted Giles's criticisms of both Father Amiot and Calthrop, finding those of Calthrop more justified. He also points out in a footnote that Giles ignored the bibliographic detail that Amiot's translation was published for the first time in 1772, and that its publication in the Memoirs was not a reprint. Overall, however, Aurosseau believes that it was fortunate that Giles found the other two translations unusable because it induced him to produce his excellent one.

J. Dyer Ball (1847–1919) reviewed Giles's translation for the *Journal of the Royal Asiatic Society of Great Britain and Ireland* in its July 1910 issue.[37] Ball emphasizes the importance of Sunzi to Chinese; however, "Writers on military affairs have occupied rather an inconspicuous position in Chinese literature." After asserting that Sunzi must have been a knowledgeable student of war who also practiced it, and emphasizing

---

[36] Léonard Aurousseau, Review of *Sun Tzŭ on the Art of War*. 孫子兵法, *the oldest military treatise in the world* by Lionel Giles, *Bulletin de l'École française d'Extrême-Orient*, October–December 1910, 10/4, 709–710.

[37] J. Dyer Ball, review of "*Sun Tzu on the Art of War* by Lionel Giles," *Journal of the Royal Asiatic Society of Great Britain and Ireland*, July 1910, 961–966.
James Dyer Ball was born in Guangdong to missionary parents, and was educated in Great Britain and Guangdong. He spent most of his adult life as a translator in Hong Kong, and was known at the time as the best European speaker of Cantonese.

the mostly conjectural biography of Sunzi, he turns to Giles's attacks on the Amiot and Calthrop translations. Having not seen the Amiot translation himself, he must take Giles's word for it that it wasn't very good. Calthrop, for his part, while a military officer, was unfortunately not a "Sinologue." Ball's characterization of Giles's treatment of Calthrop is understated: "Our present translator is most scathing in his denunciation of the omissions and mistakes and blunders which he detects. One hundred and seventeen or eighteen times in the course of 175 pages reference is made to the former translation, and nearly always to animadvert strongly on it." This would appear to be a criticism of Giles's unnecessarily extensive comments against Calthrop, though it is presented merely as an observation.

The remainder of Ball's review both lauds Giles's skills as a translator and emphasizes the value of Sunzi for the present. Ball is especially pleased that Giles illustrated some concepts with battles from Western history, and ancient Greece. He further suggests that it would be useful, "To any fearing the Yellow Peril," to read Sunzi, since it is so central to Chinese ideas of warfare. Sunzi, for Ball, is an illustration of the unchanging attitudes of China to war, to wit, that Chinese people are opposed to "militarism." Giles also argued that Chinese thinkers from Laozi through Confucius were all pacifistic and opposed to "militarism."

Most of the scholarly work that Giles did on his translation, his preface, the pairing of Chinese text with English translation, and notes, was discarded in subsequent editions. His translation of the Sunzi text alone has been repeatedly reproduced for every imaginable application of strategy. A Taiwanese reprinting of the bilingual edition was available in Taiwan by at least 1985,[38] and in 2008 the entire bilingual text was reprinted with a foreword by the distinguished scholar and translator John Minford. Professor Minford began by asserting that

Napoleon is reputed to have possessed a copy of the earliest (1782) French translation by the Jesuit, Père Jean-Joseph-Marie Amiot (1718–1793). It has also exerted a huge influence in the modern Chinese world. Both Chiang Kai-shek and Mao Zedong are known to have studied the book carefully, and Chiang was an avid collector of *Art of War* editions. As for Mao, he learned many lessons from Master Sun . . .[39]

Minford goes on to say that B. H. Liddell Hart's principles of strategy (particularly the indirect approach) stemmed from his reading of Sunzi.

---

[38] From Dunhuang (Caves) Shuju, a press that frequently copied Western books without necessarily, at that time, obtaining copyright permission. I am grateful to David Graff for bringing this edition to my attention.

[39] Minford, "Foreword," vii.

As we shall see in later chapters, this is uncertain. Liddell Hart's indirect approach may have preceded rather than followed his reading of Sunzi, or it may have come from his reading of the Giles translation.

Minford's foreword reproduced Samuel Griffith's suggestions regarding the place of Sunzi in the twentieth century. The famous novelist James Clavell followed a similar argument in his foreword to a 1983 edition of Giles's translation, saying, "it is also, almost word for word, the source of all Mao Tse-tung's Little Red Book of strategic and tactical doctrine."[40] Even though the edition of Sunzi issued under Clavell's imprimatur used Giles's translation, Giles is only mentioned toward the end of his foreword, and not on the cover. The only part of Giles's impressive preface left is the story of Sunzi training the palace women, and a few lines of background history. More subtly, both Giles and Griffith's perspectives on Sunzi were incorporated into Clavell's and Minford's prefaces, Clavell reproducing Griffith's emphasis on strategy to succeed in conflict, and Minford and Giles's insistence on Chinese culture being antiwar and Sunzi following Daoist thought. Many other reproductions of Giles's translation offer the same unattributed and unchallenged transmissions of Giles and Griffith.

Giles's translation has lasted into the twenty-first century because it is excellent and because it has long been in the public domain. Calthrop's translation, by contrast, has effectively disappeared even though it is also in the public domain. In order to make Sunzi more accessible to a broad audience, most of Giles's meticulous scholarship has been stripped away. This was the case in Major Thomas Phillips's 1943 anthology of military texts, *Roots of Strategy*, in which he chose what he believed were the five most important pre-nineteenth century military classics:

all are an indispensable part of an officer's military education, and the foundation of a military library. *The Art of War*, by Sun Tzu, is not only the oldest military work in existence but is unquestionably the greatest military classic in any language. It has had little influence in the Western world, but has guided Chinese and Japanese military thought for 2,400 years.[41]

A well-read and broad-minded officer placed the Giles translation of Sunzi front and center, hoping that it would not remain as neglected as it had been in the three decades since its publication.[42]

---

[40] James Clavell, "Foreword," in Lionel Giles (trans.), *The Art of War by Sun Tzu*, New York: Dell Publishing, 1983, 2.

[41] Major Thomas R. Phillips (ed.), *Roots of Strategy*, London: John Lane and the Bodley Head, 1943, "Foreword."

[42] I located only two reviews of Phillips's book, one by Clive Garsia, *International Affairs Review Supplement*, September 1943, 19/13, 676–677, who disparaged it, and one by an anonymous reviewer, *Military Engineer*, July–August 1940, 32/184, 312, who praised it.

Not Entirely Dead on Arrival

Amiot, Calthrop, and Giles agreed on several important points. All of them believed that the Chinese were fundamentally opposed to war, and argued for that interpretation in their prefaces or notes. Their reasons for arguing for Chinese antimilitarism varied, however, because the circumstances and audiences for their translations were very different. Nevertheless, they used the authority of Sunzi as the exemplar of Chinese military thought, and their own positions as translators of Sunzi, to make blanket generalizations about all of Chinese culture for all of its history. This characterization would carry unopposed through Griffith's translation and into almost all of the scholarship on Chinese culture until the end of the twentieth century. It is strange that it has made sense to many people in the West to persist in the idea that a history laden with just as many wars and just as much violence as anywhere else was notably antiwar, particularly when stated in the context of an unbroken tradition of military texts that far exceeded the similar Western tradition.[43]

The idea of an antimilitary China, however, was promoted by experts on Chinese military thought and on China, and continues to be perpetuated by Western experts on China. Many twenty-first-century Chinese scholars and politicians also insist on this idea, though it has begun to wear more thin as China's current military expands.[44] There has long been a political value inside and outside China for insisting upon Chinese opposition to war. The nonmilitary Chinese claim also connects Sunzi with Daoism, on the presumption that since Daoism is fundamentally peaceful, then Sunzi, and all Chinese strategy, must also be peaceful. When China appears to be militarily weak, it is simply a Daoist-based strategy, expressed in Sunzi, of using weakness to overcome strength. Even so, none of the early translators (including Griffith) connected Sunzi and Daoism.

All of these early translators also agreed on the fundamental value of Sunzi as a work of strategy. They did not present Sunzi as an oriental curiosity, or an example of a historically limited description of warfare. Sunzi presented universal strategic wisdom applicable beyond premodern China. This connects back to the Enlightenment search for universals and the belief that a scientific or rational approach to war would reveal objective truths about strategy. Obviously, a text with universal value was

---

[43] Peter Lorge, "Discovering War in Chinese History, " *Extrême-Orient Extrême-Occident*, 2014, 38, 21–46.

[44] See, for example, Andrew Scobell, *China's Use of Military Force: Beyond the Great Wall and the Long March*, Cambridge and New York: Cambridge University Press, 2003.

much more worth translating and being read than an idiosyncratic cultural artifact, so there was an inherent justification for the translator in making such a claim. Unlike philosophical works that express culturally specific values, Sunzi provides objective strategic teachings.

Finally, they all believed that Sunzi had contemporary value. It was not just that the Sunzi was a sound strategic work, but also that, if taken seriously, it could improve the current circumstances of France in the late eighteenth century or Europe in the early twentieth. The Sunzi provided good strategy, and was relevant to ongoing or recent conflicts. Japanese success against the Russians was, for Calthrop, partly due to the Japanese use of Sunzi in strategy. The Sunzi was not mysterious oriental wisdom, but concrete and practical advice for war. It was also not just an academic work for scholarly study. Statesmen and officers should study Sunzi to gain strategic judgment.

The point here is not to argue whether these areas of agreement between the early translators were right or wrong. They wrote what they wrote motivated by many different factors, and their work was received in the time and the place in which it was published. Their opinions matter because they were absorbed into the Western view of Sunzi, and of China. Even in the twenty-first century, generalists and comparatists usually read Sunzi as a substitute for learning about Chinese military history and military culture, and absorb the consistent Western translators' view that the Chinese were fundamentally antimilitary; that the Sunzi is a human, not just Chinese, classic of strategy; and that the Sunzi remains relevant. This shortcut extends to Western military education, where familiarity with Sunzi is substituted for the study of Chinese military history and the current Chinese military. Similar views of Chinese military history and military thought still permeate the field of Chinese studies. We are thus still unconsciously living with the views of the early translators of Sunzi and of China's military past.

3 The Armchair Captain

> In art and in life he made and unmade Great Captains. It is not too simplistic to believe that he longed to be one. He wanted desperately to be great, and he almost succeeded.[1]

Basil Liddell Hart popularized the idea of an "indirect approach to strategy," though it is unclear if he created it entirely on his own, or drew it, consciously or not, from Lionel Giles's translation of Sunzi.[2] He first mentioned it in 1927, and it then appeared in its fully developed form in his 1929 book *The Decisive Wars of History*. He would repeat it in several of his subsequent works. Indeed, *The Decisive Wars of History* would eventually, after several iterations, be republished as *Strategy: The Indirect Approach* in 1967. Liddell Hart's views on warfare made him a controversial figure in the 1920s and 1930s, and his legacy after his death in 1970 remains unclear. For a time in the 1930s he was considered one of the greatest writers on war, if not *the* greatest, at least in the Anglo-American world. This hyperbolic, and unprovable, claim, amplified and spread by Liddell Hart himself, exposed him to public criticism and resentment even before his reputation crashed at the beginning of World War II. His reputation recovered after the war so that by the late 1950s, when he met Samuel B. Griffith, he was once again, at least in Griffith's eyes, the most important strategist in the world. Indeed, even one of his harshest critics, John Mearsheimer, believed Liddell Hart to be the greatest strategist in the world when he died in 1970.[3] Today he is entirely unknown outside a very narrow academic community.

His contributions to strategic thinking in the 1920s and 1930s were distorted by two factors: his commitment to preventing Britain from

---

[1] Alex Danchev, *Alchemist of War: The Life of Basil Liddell Hart*, London: Phoenix Gant, 1998, 6.
[2] Giles used the terms "direct" and "indirect" in his 1910 translation, and while it is hard to imagine that Liddell Hart did not read either the Giles or the Calthrop translations before 1927, there is no evidence that he did. Calthrop did not use "direct" or "indirect" in his translation.
[3] John J. Mearsheimer, *Liddell Hart and the Weight of History*, Ithaca: Cornell University Press, 1988, 1.

Figure 3.1 B. H. Liddell Hart. © Hulton-Deutsch Collection/CORBIS/
Corbis via Getty Images

repeating its performance in World War I, and his need to earn a living as
a writer. The former issue drove his thinking about changes in warfare and
the need for a different overall approach to strategy, but also warped his
judgment about the Nazi threat. The latter issue forced him to write
quickly, simply, and forcefully in order to maximize his audience.
A number of his books were compilations of previously published articles.
Consequently, Liddell Hart was a consummate popularizer and self-
promoter. His strengths as a writer enlivened military history for a wide
audience, and he was a positive influence for military reform. But he also
took intellectual shortcuts, found the answers in history that he wanted to
find regardless of the evidence, and argued for negotiating with Hitler
during World War II. German aggression and subsequent military successes proved him publicly wrong, a failure made all the more damaging
because he was *The Times*'s military correspondent and a close military
adviser to the government.

Liddell Hart played an important role, along with his friend
J. F. C. Fuller (and Giffard Le Quesne Martel), in promoting mobile,
mechanized warfare, particularly tanks. His articles and books were the

means to promote both change within the British military and his own career. Between the world wars Fuller and Liddell Hart fought a partially unsuccessful war against the conservatism of the British military establishment, which was reluctant quickly to adapt to the new technologies of tanks, planes, and mechanization. To be fair, the army had very few resources between the wars with which to pursue new technology. Liddell Hart himself actively and influentially argued against building a large army designed to intervene on the Continent. His advice to government officials and his newspaper columns directly contributed in some small measure to the unpreparedness of the British Army at the beginning of World War II.

To Liddell Hart's great frustration, his concepts of mobile warfare were much less influential in the British Army than in the German army (though there was great resistance in the German army as well). As he sought to rebuild his reputation after the war, he claimed credit for the success of the German army at the beginning of World War II. He had legitimate claims to forming some of the earliest concepts of what would later be called blitzkrieg, but so did others. He was generous to and supportive of many people working to establish their careers, though this sometimes appeared to be in service to creating and maintaining his status as a leading military thinker. Many of the people he helped were inclined to accept his postwar rewriting of his prewar history. In his *Memoirs* (1965), Liddell Hart presented himself as prescient, correct, and ignored, except by the Germans. This view was largely accepted.[4]

In retrospect, Liddell Hart had many failings as a historian and military thinker. But it must be understood that his central concern before World War II was to prevent Great Britain from repeating the slaughter of World War I. He was fundamentally a polemicist bent on keeping Great Britain out of a land war in Europe. This noble goal, however, was essentially impossible in the face of Nazi Germany's rise. Idealistically driven, he found in history what he wanted to find and ignored what contradicted that. Much the same could be said for his strategic writing, which was only partly based on his reading of history. He began writing in a period of dramatic technological change following a traumatic war, placing him in the middle of a wave of new thinking and new doctrines.

Liddell Hart was able to rebuild his reputation after World War II in part by riding his prewar reputation. The opportunity to interview captured German generals was certainly fortuitous as well, allowing them to praise him while he pushed the idea that they were simply professional military men and not Nazis. His time of creative thinking was long past by

---

[4] Mearsheimer, *Liddell Hart*, 7–9.

the 1950s, however, and he spent his energies on recycling older work, helping up-and-coming people (like Samuel Griffith), and offering opinions as an *éminence grise* to further enhance his reputation. It is important to note that there were many important people who sought out his advice and valued his opinions. No reputation alone, whether true or false, could have made him a valued adviser absent useful advice. His personal generosity was at the root of his many, many friendships, despite some of his less attractive personality traits.

World War I

Basil Liddell Hart was born in Paris on October 31, 1895, to H. Bramley Hart, a Methodist minister, and Clara Liddell. The family returned to England in 1901. Liddell Hart eventually went to Cambridge in 1913, where his education, like that of so many other young Englishmen, was interrupted by the outbreak of World War I in 1914. He took a temporary commission as an officer to avoid the three months of training a regular commission would have required, and with his parents' reluctant consent joined the King's Own Yorkshire Light Infantry as a second lieutenant on December 7, 1914. He was an entirely conventional young man of his time who imagined war could have a generally positive effect Europe, "If the war ends by Easter [1915] it will be a great thing for the virility and manhood of Europe. If it continues until Xmas 1915 it will be a disaster."[5] Also like so many men of his generation, World War I would be the greatest influence on his life.

He was sent to Morlancourt north of the Somme in late September of 1915, where he generally enjoyed himself until a high fever sent him back to England. He had seen no fighting in his three weeks at the front. It took him two weeks to get back to France, this time to the Ypres salient. After an anxious day commanding some fifty men on the front line, he and his unit were rotated out. A shell that hit near his dugout apparently concussed him, however, resulting in nosebleeds, grogginess, and vomiting. He was sent back to England to convalesce.

February of 1916 found him overseeing troops in Hull guarding the coast road. It was uneventful except for witnessing a Zeppelin raid on the city. As with his experience of being shelled, he found it terrifying to be attacked from above by indiscriminate bombing. He made it back to France shortly afterward, and in June was second in command of a company just before the Battle of the Somme. Liddell Hart was in the immediate reserve when his unit took part in the assault on July 1. After

---

[5] "Credo" (November 28, 1914), 7/1914/10, cited in Danchev, *Alchemist of War*, 44.

the slaughter of British forces that morning, he was called up along with the other reserve officers to gather the remaining troops and reform them into units. In the end, it would take them until nearly midnight to locate what was left of their battalion. He and his fellow officers then spent two days with their men enduring artillery barrages before being pulled back on July 3. Liddell Hart had been under fire, but was fortunate enough to have escaped serious injury. Ignorant at that time of the colossal slaughter he had missed, he was full of praise for both a military career and the organizational skills of the British Army.

Liddell Hart may not have known the enormity of the casualties suffered during the Battle of the Somme, but he was clear about the devastating losses among the King's Own Yorkshire Light Infantry battalions, including many of his friends. He saw more of the terrible consequences of war when his battalion moved up a week later, passing the decaying bodies of British and German soldiers. Liddell Hart sustained a minor wound to his hand while leading his men into Mametz Wood on July 16. Their position was shelled around midnight of the 17th to the 18th, this time with phosgene gas. He led his men out of the area, and, while receiving medical attention for his hand wound, began to feel the effects of the gassing. In short order, he found himself back in England, disabled enough by the gas to be fit only for office duty.

His extremely limited war experience, lack of distinction in combat, and sometimes questionable "disability" left him defensive about his military service. There was no official mention of his personal actions to prove his courage under fire, nor any eyewitnesses to attest to his bravery. While he appeared to recover from the gassing quickly, he remained subject to "breathlessness and palpitations." Was this physiological or neurotic? Both were possible, and the psychological trauma of war, even brief periods of it, was widespread among men of his generation. Nevertheless, it was not taken as a positive sign of character to have been invalided out of combat without a visibly disabling injury. The war had not gone well for Liddell Hart, at least in the way he had hoped, despite his concerted efforts to take part in combat. On the other hand, apart from the obvious value of surviving mostly intact, his forced restriction to noncombat service back in England pushed him in the direction that would become the focus of the rest of his life.

Liddell Hart's military writing began in September of 1916, soon after the end of his battlefield experience, with a short book called *Impressions of the Great British Offensive on the Somme*. The War Office would not give permission to publish it, despite its fawning praise for the British General Staff and the commanding officer, Sir Douglas Haig. It did circulate among a small circle of admirers, and helped him begin to establish a network of patrons. He also circulated some booklets that he had written on drill and training while adjutant to volunteer units in Stroud and Cambridge in the last years of World War I. These too gained him valuable connections inside and outside the military.[6]

Despite the support of several influential men, however, Liddell Hart was generally frustrated in his efforts to advance within the military after the war. The strength of his pen could not overcome the limitations of his body. He was not completely healthy, and looked physically frail. In any event, the British peacetime army was far smaller than it had been, and competition for the remaining places was fierce. He was finally released from service in 1924 and placed on half-pay.

Liddell Hart began to establish himself as a writer on military affairs even before leaving the military. He published an article on his "man-in-the-dark" theory of tactics in a military journal, and then republished it in the June and July 1920 issues of the *National Review*, bringing his ideas to the general public. Around the same time, he also began to revise his earlier praise for the British High Command. Partly fueled by greater knowledge of what had actually transpired during World War I, and partly by his own difficulties in gaining a position in the army, Liddell Hart became extremely critical of his former heroes.

Infantry and the "Man in the Dark"

Liddell Hart's initial foray into military theory developed out of his work training units in infantry tactics beginning in 1916. In April of 1920 he published an article in the *United Service Magazine* setting out his "man-in-the-dark" theory of tactics. It was an effort to theorize from tactical training up to a larger strategic vision. Liddell Hart of necessity had to think and write creatively in order to make up for his lack of combat experience and his extremely limited education. This set a pattern for all of his publications. He was a fast and fluent writer, able to synthesize pre-existing ideas into a simplified and understandable form. This skill complicated the identification of his unique contributions to discussions of military affairs, particularly when they overlapped with those of other thinkers, like his friend and frequent interlocutor J. F. C. Fuller. Liddell Hart could not ever, of course, obtain the combat experience he lacked, and so was inclined to downplay physical courage in evaluating the quality of commanders. He was only partly successful in addressing his patchy education, reading broadly but not very deeply, and discounting the value of footnotes (despite

---

[6] Brian Bond, *Liddell Hart: A Study of His Military Thought*, New Brunswick: Rutgers, 1976, 19.

Fuller's admonition to use them). Just as significantly, as a man who would make his living on selling his writing, he had to write for the general audience.

The man-in-the-dark theory proceeded from the analogy of an unarmed man fighting another unarmed man in the dark. Like any two hostile forces, the man must first grope for his enemy. Upon discovering him, he then reconnoiters his way to his opponent's throat, fixes him in place by grasping his collar or throat, and launches a decisive attack to knock him out. He then exploits his advantage to attack again in order completely to defeat him. A similar formulation of this theory would later be produced by another autodidact, John Boyd, whose OODA loop (observe, orient, decide, act) was also based on individual combat. In Boyd's case, this stemmed from his experiences as a fighter pilot. What the man-in-the-dark theory meant in tactical terms was that when a unit advanced and came into contact with an enemy force, it would use part of the unit to fix the enemy in place while the rest of the unit went around its flank to destroy it – a sound idea, and one that had been used by many armies in history.

Of much greater importance was Liddell Hart's emphasis on firepower over numbers of men. Maneuver was critical, but the force that was to be brought to bear to achieve success needed to be measured in firepower:

While manoeuvre is the key to victory, it is manoeuvre of the units of fire power and not of masses of cannon fodder. We must learn to depend for success, not on the physical weight of the infantry attack, but on the skilful offensive use in combination of all available weapons, based on the principle of manoeuvre.[7]

Liddell Hart's proposed innovations in infantry training grew out of German infiltration tactics developed in 1918. His tactics required highly motivated, independent soldiers whose individual initiative would allow them to penetrate an enemy line in dispersed, small units. The goal was to regain mobility and thus avoid the static trench warfare of World War I. To that end, he was open to integrating tanks into his infantry-centric thinking.

While he was by no means the first person to emphasize firepower or even maneuver, his interest in the use of tracked vehicles, machine guns, tanks, and airplanes (for ground attack) showed that he was alert to the possibilities of these new technologies. In retrospect, the importance of these technologies may seem obvious, but there was still considerable resistance in many parts of the British military establishment to their

---

[7] "The Essential Principles of War and Their Application to the Offensive Infantry Tactics of Today," *United Service Magazine*, April 1920, 30–44, cited in Bond, *Liddell Hart*, 24.

adoption. Liddell Hart was not alone in arguing for their value in future conflicts, but he was part of a vanguard of theorists who played an important role in the 1920s and 1930s in laying the intellectual foundations for modern mobile warfare. He was also, along with Fuller, one of the first significant British strategic theorists, after, of course, Julian Corbett (1854–1922).[8]

During the summer of 1920 Liddell Hart was asked to write the British Army's *Infantry Training Manual*. He set out his ideas based upon the man-in-the-dark theory and German infiltration tactics, christening them in the offensive mode as the "expanding torrent," and in the defensive mode as the "contracting funnel." His writing over subsequent years would vary between asserting the greater power of the offensive with new technologies and tactics, and admitting that mobile defensive tactics were at least the equal of offensive tactics. The possibility of a war bogging down into a static war of attrition like World War I always loomed over his theorizing. If defense was nearly as strong as offense, let alone equal to it or stronger, then even a weaker defender could, and logically would, delay, wear down, and draw out a conflict.

Liddell Hart's infantry phase came to an end soon after writing the *Infantry Training Manual*. In 1920, he read J. F. C. Fuller's essay in the *Journal of the Royal United Services Institution* that argued that tanks would be the main force on the future battlefield. Liddell Hart wrote to Fuller, initiating an exchange of ideas and a lifelong friendship. Fuller was far more established than Liddell Hart, and much further along in thinking through the implications of new military technology. It took him nearly two years of effort, but by 1922 Liddell Hart had admitted that he had come to see that tanks, not infantry, were the future of the battlefield.

J. F. C. Fuller and Tanks

John Frederick Charles "Boney" Fuller was born on September 1, 1878. After an indifferent education and lacking any direction, he began his military career by attending the Royal Military College, Sandhurst, in 1897. He served in South Africa from 1899 to 1902, and then in India in 1904. Illness sent him back to England in 1905, where he remained in various capacities until attending the Staff College in 1913. His military education was entirely conventional, stressing the centrality of infantry and the

---

[8] Julian Corbett was a naval historian and strategist, who distinguished between land and naval strategy. His most important work of strategy, *Some Principles of Maritime Strategy* (1911), argued for the importance of sea lines of communication, in contradistinction to Mahan's emphasis on decisive battle. Corbett was influential in British naval circles, though his differences with Mahan's ideas conflicted with inclinations of many officers.

overriding importance of offense. Even so, he began to rebel against the strictures of British Army doctrine during his time in the Staff College, through either a dawning awareness of the need for new thinking, instinctive rebelliousness, or both. At a minimum, Fuller was a thinker in an institution that frowned upon that, at a time when most officers were proudly amateurish.

Fuller's progress in strategic thought was very similar to Liddell Hart's except that he began about twenty years before him. His first forays into strategy and tactics were concerned with the infantry. He published *Hints on Training Territorial Infantry* in 1913. His openness to reform, and that of the British Army at that time, was due to an interest in professionalizing, or, at least, making more professional, the army after the Boer War. Fuller's thinking was also influenced by the reading he'd done while in South Africa, particularly Napoleon's *Correspondence.*[9] He would retain a lifelong interest in Napoleon, hence his nickname "Boney," and also a strong attachment to Clausewitz.

It would take him many years to shake off the military education which had insisted upon the power of highly motivated infantry to close with their enemy and defeat them at bayonet point. Strategy was confined to trying to envelop the enemy's flanks. Where he first began to diverge from orthodoxy, then defined by the teachings of Ferdinand Foch, was in seeing the importance of firepower. Even before the widespread introduction of machine guns and rapid-firing artillery, the general distribution of rifled muskets had increased the lethality of ordinary soldiers on the battlefield. There were obvious precursors to the coming "desolation of the battlefield," where troops needed to disperse and go to ground to avoid being picked off, as early as the American Civil War. Force of habit, and a belief that the ability to motivate troops to face murderous fire was a test of moral value, downplayed the growing futility of such assaults. Many European officers drew precisely the wrong lesson from the Japanese victory over Russia in the Russo-Japanese War. Japanese willingness to take immense casualties from artillery and machine guns eventually overwhelmed Russian forces fighting from fortified positions, thus, in the minds of some, proving that courage could defeat firepower. There was, and had been, more than enough evidence that modern weapons had vastly enhanced the defensive power of entrenched troops long before World War I.

By the time he reached the Staff College in 1913, Fuller had begun to think through the implications of the power of modern field guns. His

[9] Brian Holden Reid, *J.F.C. Fuller: Military Thinker*, New York: St. Martin's Press, 1987, 22.

appreciation for artillery increased when he observed modern artillery exercises and read a British account of the Russo-Japanese War. Artillery now appeared to be more powerful than infantry, though he expected them to work in concert. When Fuller proposed in an early essay at the Staff College the possibility of concentrating men and artillery to penetrate, rather than envelop, an enemy's line, he was called into the commandant's office and told to read *Field Service Regulations* more carefully.[10] Undiscouraged, Fuller continued to think creatively and to read widely. Although he made enough concessions to form to remain in the army, he was abrasive and never really fit in with the culture. He also finished writing his second book at that time, *Training Soldiers for War*.

Training Soldiers for War was still a transitional work, as might be expected from someone who was beginning to see the implications of new technologies that had been neither fully tested nor deployed in large numbers. He did argue that the objective was "the line of least resistance," where an army could be decisively defeated, and concentration of forces was critical. He also saw, echoing in many respects Clausewitz, that breaking down an enemy to the point where he could not resist was the way to impose one's will upon him. All of this would also come up in Liddell Hart's work, and could be found in Sunzi. In other respects, Fuller remained committed to the conventional views of infantry warfare that would soon prove so costly.[11]

It was Fuller's experiences in World War I that pushed his thinking away from infantry and toward tanks. In 1916 he was assigned to what became the Tank Corps. This put him at the cutting edge of new technology and forced him to take part in formulating doctrine for the new weapon. He was deeply involved in planning the Battle of Cambrai, which took place on November 20, 1917, and used, among a number of other recent innovations, a significant mass of tanks (437) in what was initially a successful attack. Although by no means the first massed tank assault, it was extremely instructive in both the strengths and the limitations of the tanks which were then available. The effect of massed tanks was overwhelming, but in 1917 not enough tanks were available and those that were available were unreliable.[12]

Fuller himself learned an even more important lesson when he observed the collapse of British troops during the German spring offensive in March 1918. What struck Fuller from his position on Mount St. Quentin was that the rout of some British units was not due to direct attack, but rather to the moral collapse precipitated by the British Corps and Army headquarters pulling back. The psychological dislocation

[10] Reid, *J.F.C. Fuller*, 27.   [11] Reid, *J.F.C. Fuller*, 28.   [12] Reid, *J.F.C. Fuller*, 48.

caused by a failure of the "brains" of an army resulted in disproportionate effects in its "body." Slowly, through reading, thinking, and experience, Fuller was assembling his own collection of strategic principles and operational doctrines. They were not unique or original individually, but coupled with the new technology they placed Fuller in a position to lay some of the foundation stones for mechanized warfare. The key enabling technology, of course, was the tank.

Fuller was transferred to the Tank Corps in December of 1916, and produced his first essay on tank tactics in February of 1917.[13] His thinking continued to evolve as he and others worked to exploit the new technology. This culminated in 1918, after the German spring offensive, in what would later be called "Plan 1919." Fuller's plan was, in fact, preceded by two very similar works, John Capper's (1861–1955) report to the Supreme War Council, and on March 19 Hugh Elles's (1880–1945) report to the War Office, "The Future of Tank Operations and Production Requirements." A further, shorter, and more general report was also submitted to the Supreme War Council on May 14 by Lieutenant Colonel C. N. Buzzard, "Tanks and Mechanical Warfare."[14] There were several different plans for the use of tanks and combined-arms operations being proposed in 1918, including under the auspices of General Haig. As David Childs pointed out,

> The myth surrounding the originality and viability of Fuller's "Plan 1919" owes much to the prevailing anti-Haig/GHQ propaganda of the inter-war years and beyond. Fuller's undoubted gift for writing, the friendship and support of Captain Sir Basil Liddell Hart ... combined with a need for a national scapegoat for the losses incurred on the western front, have assisted the perpetuation of this myth.[15]

Setting aside the many problems of all of the proposals for using tanks, most prominently the technological and logistical limitations of the available weapons, what emerged was an idea of combining tanks with airplanes to effect rapid penetrations of the enemy's defenses. Fuller stressed striking at the command and control centers of the opposing forces. The speed of the attack on the brain of the opposing force would disable the body quickly and with a minimum of casualties. The end of the war rendered Fuller's, and everyone else's, plans for tanks and combined-arms operations temporarily moot. It was nevertheless a blueprint for future development.

Fuller finished the war fully converted to the need for highly mobile, combined-arms forces that exploited the power of tanks, planes, and

---

[13] Reid, *J.F.C. Fuller*, 40–41.
[14] David J. Childs, *A Peripheral Weapon? The Production and Employment of British Tanks in the First World War*, Westport, CT: Greenwood Press, 1999, 155.
[15] Childs, *A Peripheral Weapon?*, 156.

well-trained professional soldiers. He would go on to write several dozen books on military history and military theory. Contrary to the later myth that he was marginalized and ignored, Fuller was given significant positions from which to promote his ideas of mechanization, notably chief instructor at the Camberley Staff College in 1923, and military assistant to the head of the Imperial General Staff in 1926. Despite his interest in promoting mechanized warfare, he turned down command of the Experimental Mechanized Force in 1927, and retired in 1933 at the rank of major general. His retirement allowed him more time to write. Unfortunately, he also joined the British Union of Fascists, attended Nazi German military maneuvers in 1935, and began praising Hitler. He was even a guest at Hitler's fiftieth birthday parade. Consequently, when World War II broke out, Fuller was not brought back into military service.

Fuller's long friendship with Liddell Hart began by converting Liddell Hart from a focus on infantry to a focus on mobile, combined-arms warfare. Liddell Hart might have made the shift on his own, of course, given that interest in the topic was widespread in the interwar period. The significance of their friendship and extensive discussions of this kind of warfare (as well as the strategic thinking behind it) goes far beyond the development of their thinking. Because of their personal connection, Liddell Hart, as David Childs alluded to, folded Fuller into his narrative of the origins of blitzkrieg. Liddell Hart would also, in later years, include Martel among the important early advocates for the tank. The distinguishing characteristic of those who received credit in Liddell Hart's schema of tank theorizing appears to have been writing a book on the subject. Martel, like Fuller and Liddell Hart, but unlike so many others who had written similar sorts of essays on the tank for the military or the government, published several books on tanks beginning in 1922.

The British Way of War and Limited Liability

At the height of his fame and influence before World War II, Liddell Hart grew increasingly alarmed at the prospect of Great Britain again raising a vast army in order to fight on the Continent. He struggled to formulate a specifically British strategy for which he claimed historical precedent. His principle of not waging a land war in Europe could perhaps be seen as similar to Field Marshal Montgomery's later second rule of war: "Do not go fighting with your land armies in China," which he subsequently revised to: "don't go fighting with your land army on the mainland in Asia."[16]

---

[16] *Pace* Vizzini in *The Princess Bride* (1987), Montgomery first set out his two rules of war in the House of Lords on May 30, 1962, and his revised version in an interview with the

Liddell Hart proceeded from arguing for certain operational strategies, "lightning war," to the indirect approach to strategy, and then to a British strategy of mostly offshore power balancing on the Continent. His influence continued to rise throughout the interwar period when, contrary to his later rewriting of events, he was very much listened to by the government and parts of the military. In no way was he an ignored prophet, rejected by his own people and embraced only by the Germans.

Liddell Hart's intellectual journey in the interwar years was complex and inconsistent. It is important to recognize that his occasional mentions of "lightning war" were never combined with the indirect approach to strategy. He never formulated a grand synthesis of his theories that ranged from the tactical to the strategic. He was certainly not a systematic thinker, but it is also true that many of his theories conflicted with each other. His central aim was always to prevent large British conscript armies fighting on the Continent as they had done in World War I. The external factors that mitigated against his efforts make him seem foolish in retrospect. Technology had moved on, and with it tactics, a process he was part of, so that while there would be conscript armies, they would not be locked in trench warfare. On the strategic level, Britain could not balance out the Continent with naval blockades, money, and small expeditionary forces because Germany had grown so much more powerful than its neighbors. Nor could Great Britain expect to remain free if Germany conquered Western Europe.

Hitler's rise to power in 1933 was the pivot point for Liddell Hart's shift from his earlier theories of lightning war and indirect approach, to the "British way of war" and "limited liability." In some sense, Hitler's aggressive rebuilding of German power diminished the significance of Liddell Hart's earlier work for Britain. It is also possible that he had already worked out the broad outlines of his tactical and operational theories by that time, leaving little more to say on the matters. Those theories were fully expressed and supported in his well-received series of biographies, including a biography of William Tecumseh Sherman, that he published between 1926 and 1934. Those biographies were more imagination than history, and they enabled Liddell Hart to put a historical sheen on his theories. But with respect to lightning war and the indirect approach to strategy, in later years he mostly recycled his early work.

The shift in Liddell Hart's thinking also coincided with increasing hostility to the senior leadership in the British army. He had already

New York Times on July 3, 1968, and may have been motivated by the war in Vietnam. Montgomery's first rule of war was "Don't march on Moscow," rather than "Never go in against a Sicilian when death is on the line."

been moving away from his youthful praise for the generals of World War I before his own forced departure from the army. He then overreacted in the opposite direction as more information about the high command during the war came out and the mood in England turned against the war. To compound matters further, his status as a journalist and writer outside the military created some resentment and resistance to his ideas. Liddell Hart, in turn, regarded that hostility as a further indictment of the conservatism of the high command. The fact that they resisted or rejected his ideas demonstrated that they were bad generals.

Perhaps counterintuitively, Liddell Hart's hostility to the generals grew as his own influence with the government over military affairs grew. Not only were there many officers receptive to his ideas, even if some opposed them, but also he became a close adviser of Leslie Hore-Belisha when Chamberlain appointed Hore-Belisha Secretary of State for War upon becoming prime minister in 1937. For a time, Liddell Hart really could make and break officers, though his power was not total. This allowed him directly to influence critical strategic decisions, including the rejection of a continental commitment. He was therefore partly responsible for delaying British Army development in a critical period before the war.

His influence with the general population had also grown, as his books in the 1930s were extremely well received. He had moved as military correspondent from the *Daily Telegraph* to *The Times* in 1935.[17] From his position at *The Times* and in his books, he dramatically shifted his views on the effects of new military technology, arguing that they actually enhanced the defense rather than the offense, as he had previously argued. Where the tank and lightning warfare had originally opened up the possibility of highly mobile warfare that would result in short wars with small armies and limited destruction, Liddell Hart now argued that defense was still so fundamentally strong that a lightning offensive would not work. This was an effort on his part to deter the obviously rising German power from thinking that a mechanized, combined-arms force making a deep penetration raid could rapidly overwhelm an opponent.

Even as Germany was rearming and moving aggressively against her neighbors, Liddell Hart was pushing the notion that England had traditionally relied upon naval blockades, on funding her allies on the Continent, and on small expeditionary forces to maintain a balance of power. This British way of war had served well in the past, and it would certainly serve better than a disastrous Continental intervention like World War I. This ignored the facts that British blockades and balancing had more often failed horribly, that Germany was a Continental power

---

[17] Mearsheimer, *Liddell Hart*, 102.

less susceptible to naval blockade, that submarines were a greater threat to England, and that German power required more than just tipping a balance.

Liddell Hart also tried to restrict Britain's commitment to France and the Continent through "limited liability." The idea was to lend some support without fully committing to sending large numbers of troops to help the French against Germany. He was deeply concerned that England could be pulled into a war again if it made a larger commitment to aiding France. Of course, the calculus was essentially the same as in World War I, but France was in a weaker position than in 1914. Anything short of a full commitment backed up by a large army ready to cross the Channel would neither deter Germany nor reassure France. Liddell Hart opposed building a large army because to do so would allow the sort of Continental intervention he feared. His position undercut British preparedness even as it was becoming clear that Hitler could not be appeased.

Fall and Rise

Liddell Hart was never as influential as he wanted to be, nor as much of a rebel as he would later suggest. His views, particularly in the 1930s, were essentially in keeping with *The Times*, where he was the military correspondent, and later with Chamberlain's government. As a journalist and prominent writer, his opinions were very public. As with any writer, it is difficult to quantify how influential his opinions were. Those who agreed with him, and wrote to him to tell him so, were grateful for his public expression of their views, but, of course, they already believed what he was saying. Some in the military disagreed with his views, particularly those who felt his advocacy of air defenses for England and a limited commitment to Continental intervention meant less funding for the army and for tanks. Still, it was Chamberlain's government that made the decisions regarding budget and allocation of resources, and the military leadership that deployed those resources.

It is clear that Liddell Hart had, indeed, fallen from grace at the beginning of World War II. The most prominent military writer in England during the 1930s was mostly invisible during the war. His *Memoirs*, published in 1965, which were so instrumental in reviving his reputation and creating a series of myths about his role in strategic thought before World War II, end in 1940. Indeed, Liddell Hart concentrated in his *Memoirs* on his writings from the 1920s, when he discussed tank warfare and the indirect approach to strategy, rather than the 1930s, when he had argued for the British way of war, limited liability, and the greater strength of defense. Liddell Hart's greatest campaign would ultimately be waged after World War II to recover his reputation. In the course of that successful campaign, he helped numerous writers and historians to advance their careers, including Samuel Griffith.

Liddell Hart's reputation collapsed for two very good reasons: first, he publicly made predictions and supported a series of military and diplomatic policies that proved to be spectacularly wrong; and second, he held on to some of those policies long after most people, including Chamberlain and his government, had abandoned them. His absolute opposition to sending a large army to the Continent forced him to insist until the fall of France that defense would defeat offense, and that Hitler could be appeased. Even after the German attack on May 10, 1940, which he had thought unlikely in the first place, Liddell Hart was confident that Belgium and France would be able to defend themselves. He published articles to that effect as late as the 19th, and it was only on the 20th that he finally realized how wrong he had been.[18] He had certainly not been alone in his mistaken judgments, but he had been very public in those mistakes and in posing as a great strategic mind.

The contrast between Liddell Hart's positions in 1939 and in 1940 was remarkable. He had published a well-received collection of his articles, *The Defense of Britain*, in July 1939 that insisted upon the growing power of defense over offense. By September of 1939 he had stopped writing for *The Times*, though he published articles in other newspapers and magazines through the early part of 1940 ridiculing the idea that Germany would attack France. He had moved gradually to a position of appeasement during the late 1930s, and continued to imagine that Hitler was a rational politician seeking reasonable concessions while reluctant to go to war. He was so worried that events were pushing England to war on the Continent that he criticized *The Times*'s coverage of the successful fascist offensives in the Spanish Civil War; if modern offensive power really could overcome defensive power, then there could be no deterrence without England creating a large army. Liddell Hart ultimately left *The Times* and stopped supporting the Chamberlain government because both shifted from appeasement to seeing the need to threaten military action against Hitler. He maintained his support for appeasement, or at least a negotiated settlement with Hitler, well into World War II.

In the wake of his reputational failing, Liddell Hart began a long process of reworking his own intellectual history, as well as his position with respect to the militaries of Britain and Germany, and the British government. He became in his own telling a perceptive military sage who foresaw everything but was ignored by the British military and

---

[18] Mearsheimer, *Liddell Hart*, 125–26.

government. This required him to emphasize his work from the 1920s and mostly to skip over his work from the 1930s. Mearsheimer broke down Liddell Hart's efforts into four lines: arguing that he was unable to speak openly of what he knew; rewriting the historical record to his own advantage; manipulating the record of his relationships with British, German and Israeli military leaders; and challenging the influence of Fuller and de Gaulle.[19]

Mearsheimer explains the course of Liddell Hart's self-rehabilitation convincingly and at length. For my purposes, the critical points concern how and why this rehabilitation was important for Samuel Griffith and Sunzi. Liddell Hart's preface to the Sunzi was written in exactly the period in which he published *The German Generals Talk*, an account of World War II as told to him by captured German generals; wrote the preface for Guderian's memoir; edited Rommel's papers; and republished his book on strategy. The Sunzi preface came out in 1963, and Liddell Hart's *Memoir* in 1965. Liddell Hart patronized many people, including Michael Howard, Kenneth Macksey, Brian Bond, Robert O'Neill, Jay Luvaas, Samuel Griffith, and Robert Asprey, which Mearsheimer saw as part of his campaign of rehabilitation. While this may have been true to some extent, it may also have been true without contradicting the fact that Liddell Hart also truly wanted to help people.[20]

Liddell Hart refocused his reputation primarily on taking credit for the development of blitzkrieg, and secondarily on the indirect approach to strategy. The question then became, was he responsible for blitzkrieg? The answer to that could never be more than "partially." This drove him constantly to try and discount Fuller and de Gaulle's respective contributions to the idea, as well as those of a number of other lesser figures like Martel. Credit for blitzkrieg was a much more fundamental issue of influence and legacy, and much more difficult to argue, than brushing away the mistakes of the 1930s and 1940s. The idea that he had been forced to be circumspect about what he really knew before World War II was as ridiculous as his assertions that he was an ignored outsider who had predicted accurately the course of the German invasion of France.

Liddell Hart's focus on taking credit for blitzkrieg led him to distasteful acts of playing down the roles of others, including his friend Fuller, but,

[19] Mearsheimer, *Liddell Hart*, 178–208.
[20] Jay Luvaas, "Liddell Hart and the Mearsheimer Critique: A Pupil's Retrospective," *Parameters*, March 1990, 9–19; and Robert O'Neill, "Liddell Hart Unveiled, " *Twentieth-Century British History*, 1990, 1/1, 101–113. Neither Luvaas nor O'Neill reject the idea that Liddell Hart had certain personality flaws, or that he had manipulated the record, but they do emphasize that he had legitimate claims to theorizing about blitzkrieg and that he also had many very positive personal qualities as well.

even worse, to dishonest acts of manipulating the accounts given by captured German generals. Liddell Hart invested considerable time and effort in cultivating the group of captured senior German generals held in England (Field Marshals Brauchitsch, Rundstedt, and Manstein), or on the Continent (Guderian), and later corresponding with the family of Rommel. He sent care packages to the generals while also working to improve the conditions of their captivity. He later interviewed many of them in order to write his book *The German Generals Talk*. His questions were designed to elicit statements praising his work and attributing blitz-krieg to him. The generals could see that they, in turn, had received and would receive not only better treatment but, more significantly, help in de-Nazification. In Liddell Hart's telling, the generals were just military professionals who fought for their country and were only incidentally Nazis. It was Hitler's interference in military matters than had diminished their effectiveness. This construction of the German senior commanders became an important strand of interpretation in England and America.

His praise of the German generals was the flip side of his criticisms of the British generals and British government who had not listened to him. As he mentioned, "Most of them, I found, were old students of my military writings, so that they were all the more ready to talk and exchange views."[21] This was self-serving and mostly inaccurate, or at least know-ingly deceptive. As Mearsheimer points out,

He needed evidence that showed his prewar writings had influenced the German plan to defeat the Allies in the West, but in *The German Generals Talk* Liddell Hart does not point to a single instance of a German general claiming such an influ-ence. Liddell Hart had to manufacture the evidence.[22]

Thus began Liddell Hart's distinctly dishonest efforts, concentrated on Manstein, Guderian, and Rommel's family, to get critical German mili-tary heroes to insert credit for his theories into their accounts of the development or use of blitzkrieg. He did not try to pull in British generals, although he did emphasize some connection to Patton. Those efforts were not entirely successful, and scholars like Kenneth Macksey and Brian Bond, not to mention Mearsheimer, began to notice flaws in the manufactured record.[23] Manstein, despite great efforts on Liddell Hart's part to help the former field marshal in his postwar trials, flatly refused to

---

[21] B. H. Liddell Hart, *The German Generals Talk*, New York: Morrow, 1948, 113.

[22] Mearsheimer, *Liddell Hart*, 187.

[23] Mearsheimer also noted that the two letters from Liddell Hart to Guderian requesting additions in his favor in April of 1968 were mysteriously, and extremely uncharacteris-tically, missing from Liddell Hart's archives. Liddell Hart obsessively kept copies of every letter he sent or received, except for those. They were recovered from Guderian's papers by Kenneth Macksey, who knew they were missing, and copies reinserted into the Liddell

insert into his writings language saying that he got the idea of attacking
France through the Ardennes from Liddell Hart's work.[24]

The crux of Liddell Hart's manipulation is one of two paragraphs in
Guderian's *Panzer Leader*. The first paragraph appeared in both the
German and English versions:

It was principally the books and articles of the Englishmen, Fuller, Liddell Hart
and [Gen. Giffard] Martel [a British tank expert], that excited my interest and
gave me food for thought. These far-sighted soldiers were even then trying to
make of the tank something more than just an infantry support weapon. They
envisaged it in relationship to the growing motorization of our age, and thus they
became the pioneers of a new type of warfare on the largest scale.[25]

It was the paragraph that immediately followed, which did not appear
in the German version, that provided a key piece of evidence supporting
Liddell Hart's arguments that he was the true father of blitzkrieg:

I learned from them the concentration of armour, as employed in the battle of
Cambrai. Further, it was Liddell Hart who emphasized the use of armoured forces
for long-range strokes, operations against the opposing army's communications,
and also proposed a type of armoured division combining panzer and panzer–
infantry units. Deeply impressed by these ideas I tried to develop them in a sense
practicable for our own army. So I owe many suggestions of our further developments to Captain Liddell Hart.[26]

The finer points of Guderian attributing "long-range strokes," attacking
communications, and combined armor–mechanized infantry forces are
critical. It was these points, which Liddell Hart claimed as his own, that
distinguished his ideas from those of Fuller, Martel, and others. The
struggle over the precise origins of blitzkrieg is fought over very specific
nuances of how a mobile force should be constituted, and how it was
supposed to operate.

Mearsheimer traced the origin of the second paragraph to a letter that
Liddell Hart wrote to Guderian while Liddell Hart was editing the
English translation:

I appreciate very much what you said in the [first] paragraph . . . So, I am sure, will
Fuller and Martel. It is a most generous acknowledgement. But because of our
special association, and the wish that I should write the foreword to your book,
people may wonder why there is no separate reference to what my writings taught.

Hart archive. This strongly suggests that Liddell Hart knew how dishonest the request
was, and attempted to conceal it. See Mearsheimer, *Liddell Hart*, 191.
[24] Mearsheimer, *Liddell Hart*, 164.
[25] Heinz Guderian (trans. Constantine Fitzgibbon), *Panzer Leader*, London: Joseph, 1952,
20, cited in Mearsheimer, *Liddell Hart*, 164.
[26] Guderian, *Panzer Leader*, 20, cited in Mearsheimer, *Liddell Hart*, 164.

You might care to insert a remark that I emphasized the use of armoured forces for long-range operations against the opposing army's communications, and also proposed a type of armoured division combining panzer and panzer–infantry units – and that these points particularly impressed you.[27]

As is obvious from the quoted paragraph that was included in the English version, Guderian accepted and simply inserted Liddell Hart's language where suggested.

Kenneth Macksey, who was a friend of Liddell Hart's, demonstrated in his biography of Guderian that Guderian's ideas of tank warfare had been mostly influenced by Fuller, not Liddell Hart. He also noticed that Liddell Hart's influence had been inserted into the English version of Guderian's memoir, *Panzer Leader*, although it did not exist in the German version. Speaking of the sources Guderian looked to for tank armies, Macksey wrote, "The brain behind these ideas was Fuller's, whose talents for analysis, organization and penetrating expression had marked him out as a staff officer and a reforming military genius of the very first water." While also mentioning a 1919 book by the brothers Williams-Ellis,[28] he goes to say, "at that time Captain Basil Liddell Hart was beginning to make a name for himself by his early lectures and writings on infantry tactical systems which were very similar to those already in use in the German Army."[29]

Macksey attributed Liddell Hart's understanding of the importance of tanks to Fuller, who was also Guderian's early inspiration. This directly undermined any claim that Liddell Hart had to originating the ideas of blitzkrieg, at a minimum handing Fuller most of the credit. But Macksey went further, providing three pieces of evidence not only that Liddell Hart was not the intellectual inspiration for Guderian's construction of blitzkrieg, but also that Liddell Hart had dishonestly inserted himself into the history of blitzkrieg in the English translation of Guderian's memoir. Mearsheimer emphasized Macksey's discussion, since it both spoke directly to Liddell Hart's rewriting of the past and came from a friendly source.

First, the critical paragraph giving so much credit to Liddell Hart only appears in the English version, *Panzer Leader*, but not in *Erinnerungen*

---

[27] Liddell Hart to Guderian, April 6, 1951, quoted in Mearsheimer, *Liddell Hart*, 165.

[28] Major Clough Williams-Ellis (1883–1978) and Amabel Williams-Ellis (1894–1984), *The Tank Corps*, New York: George H. Doran Company, 1919. Macksey was mistaken that the book was written by the "brothers Williams Ellis." The "A. Williams-Ellis" was Mrs. Amabel Williams-Ellis (*née* Strachey), Major Clough Williams-Ellis's wife. She also wrote a book in 1929, *The Exquisite Tragedy: An Intimate Life of John Ruskin*. Clough Williams-Ellis was a well-known architect beginning in the interwar period.

[29] Kenneth Macksey, *Guderian: Creator of the Blitzkrieg*, New York: Stein and Day, 1976, 62.

eines Soldaten, the German version. Second, although Fuller, Martel, de Gaulle, and Liddell Hart are mentioned in the text of *Achtung! Panzer!*, Guderian's 1937 book, which was the summation of his articles and lectures from the previous ten years published to gain public support for the *Panzertruppe*, neither Liddell Hart's books nor articles were in the bibliography, though Fuller's, Martel's, and de Gaulle's were. (The book was an unexpected best seller, enabling Guderian to buy his first car).[30] Third, and finally, Guderian's eldest son made it clear that it was Fuller, not Liddell Hart, who was important to Guderian, and implied that mention of Liddell Hart was a postwar change:

> As far as I know it was Fuller who made the most suggestions. Once before the war my father visited him. Fuller was almost certainly more competent as an active officer than Captain B. H. Liddell Hart ... At any rate my father often spoke of him [Fuller] while I cannot remember other names being mentioned at that time [before 1939] ... The greater emphasis upon Liddell Hart seems to have developed through contacts after the war.[31]

From Guderian's son's point of view, Liddell Hart was at best secondary to Fuller.

Liddell Hart's other attempt to bolster his legitimacy came in 1949 after he was asked to edit the English translation of Rommel's letters. His first reaction was to ask whether the family (Rommel, of course, having committed suicide in 1944) really wanted him as editor, and if they believed he had influenced Rommel. After being assured that Rommel had been interested in his works, he wrote Frau Rommel directly to ask for specific evidence for that interest. Her son, Manfred, replied in general terms that his father had read one or more of his books and some of his articles during the war, but that neither he nor his mother knew precisely what. Manfred did include two sections from Rommel's papers that referred to "British military critics" and that an officer who had served under Rommel, General Fritz Bayerlein, explained that this referred to Liddell Hart and Fuller. Liddell Hart asked Manfred to rewrite what he had told him in German, so he could get it translated, and told him that Guderian had referred to himself as a disciple of Liddell Hart when it came to the tank.

In a remarkable repeat of what had happened with Guderian, Liddell Hart managed to extract a statement from Bayerlein that Rommel could be regarded as a pupil of Liddell Hart. He further got him to write that Fuller and Liddell Hart were taken more seriously by the German officers than by the British. This was then incorporated in the English translation

[30] Macksey, *Guderian*, 92.   [31] Macksey, *Guderian*, 62.

of Rommel's papers, in a footnote (written by Liddell Hart) explaining the reference "British military critics":

Note by General Bayerlein – Rommel was here referring to Captain Liddell Hart and General Fuller. In his opinion the British could have avoided most of their defeats if only they had paid more heed to the modern theories expounded by those two writers before the war. During the war, in many conferences and personal talks with Field-Marshal Rommel, we discussed Liddell Hart's military works, which won our admiration. Of all military writers, it was Liddell Hart who made the deepest impression on the Field-Marshal – and greatly influenced his tactical and strategical thinking. He, like Guderian, could in many respects be termed Liddell Hart's "pupil".

And, again, Bayerlein did not include any of this statement in the German version of the papers, *Krieg ohne Hass*, which came out in 1950.

The original manuscript of the English version only had the narrower footnote explaining that "British military critics" meant Fuller and Liddell Hart, and not the longer footnote drafted by Liddell Hart and sent to Bayerlein. Liddell Hart successfully insisted on including the longer version.[32] To the English-speaking world, Rommel's papers, which came out in 1953, firmly linked Liddell Hart to Rommel and disparaged the British generals who had ignored him. Careful readers noted these links, and Liddell Hart himself tried to publicize them.

By the early 1950s at the latest, Liddell Hart had maneuvered himself back into a prominent position as a military writer. The German generals had seen the advantage of associating with Liddell Hart, and he, in turn, had exploited their military fame to enhance his own legitimacy and take credit for blitzkrieg. The Germans only went along with this in the English-speaking world, however, where the lie was of less importance to them. Liddell Hart was useful to many people, not least himself, as a famous strategist, the "Clausewitz of the 20th century," and the "captain who taught generals." No one opposed this myth-making because the only people who might have done so were Fuller, who didn't care, and Martel, who also seems to have raised no serious objections. Liddell Hart could thus be lauded by the Israelis on a visit in 1960, to his delight, and for their own political use. He endorsed them when they needed endorsing by a prominent British personage. His actual influence on them in tank warfare or the indirect method appears to have been nil, but they were happy to claim his imprimatur and tell him whatever he wanted to hear.[33]

---

[32] Mearsheimer, *Liddell Hart*, 192–197.   [33] Mearsheimer, *Liddell Hart*, 201–204,

Conclusion

In 1988, John Mearsheimer wrote, "When he died in 1970, Sir Basil H. Liddell Hart was the most famous and widely admired military historian and theorist in the world, and he probably remains so today."[34] This is a remarkable statement for the beginning of a book that constitutes an extremely harsh critique of Liddell Hart. It is even more remarkable because, without an important caveat, it is entirely wrong. Liddell Hart was not well known outside the West during the twentieth century or after. Several of his books were popular with general readers of military history in Britain and America, but his reputation as a strategist or military theorist was mostly confined to the security studies audience in academia, government, and the military. But, again, the critical caveat for these claims is "in the West." Outside the West, he was hardly known while he was alive, and that limited recognition faded very quickly after his death. Even in the West today, he is only known to an older generation or in very narrow fields of study. Measured purely in numbers of readers, for example, Mao Zedong's military writings were far more famous, and likely far more widely read, in the twentieth century.

Liddell Hart's influence exceeds his current recognition, though for a time in the second half of the twentieth century his recognition exceeded his influence. His biography of William Tecumseh Sherman does retain some influence for nonacademic historians of the Civil War, and even for nonmilitary historians.[35] His biographies, books, and articles, however, are only of historiographical interest, or useful for those studying Liddell Hart and twentieth-century military thought. His histories, excepting perhaps his 1959 book *The Tanks: A History of the Royal Tank Regiment and Its Predecessors*, were never scholarly. I will leave aside comment on his writings on tennis or women's fashion as beyond the scope of this study and my own competence. But a number of his strategic concepts continue to be important even though they are no longer associated with his name.

Liddell Hart made important contributions to early thinking about mechanized warfare, along with J. F. C. Fuller and Martel. They were not the only people writing about these issues, but Liddell Hart and Fuller in particular were extremely prominent in the 1920s and 1930s. They were read and their ideas taken up by many others, notably men like Heinz Guderian in Germany, who then further advanced their thinking and brought to fruition many of their proposals. The success of Nazi German armies at the beginning of World War II ignited a struggle for

[34] Mearsheimer, *Liddell Hart*, 1.
[35] Albert Castel, "Liddell Hart's 'Sherman': Propaganda as History," *Journal of Military History*, April 2003, 67/2, 405–426.

credit. The greatest proof of value for a strategist, or a military thinker, is to have one's predictions turn out to be true in a real war. Liddell Hart was profoundly wrong on several major points of strategy in World War II, but generally correct on some operational and tactical issues. And, of course, his own thinking changed during the 1920s and 1930s.

Ironically, one of Liddell Hart's central concepts, "the indirect approach to strategy," shortened to "indirect strategy," has achieved a lasting place in strategic thinking, but become attached to Sunzi. It was never a well-defined concept, and has become even less so with time. As an ambiguous term with a vague origin, indirect strategy has become all things to all people. This has also made it popular in ways that more clearly defined and thought-out strategies are not. Despite the complex origins and variations of meaning that Liddell Hart argued for indirect strategy, at root it meant: not World War I trench warfare. Anything which was not a static, grinding contest of strength was not only strategic, but indirect. And because Liddell Hart attributed the slaughter of that war to Clausewitzian thinking, indirect strategy was by definition not Clausewitzian. Furthermore, by this chain of reasoning, Clausewitz must have argued for direct strategy.

Liddell Hart succeeded for a time in making himself important, though the historical significance of the Liddell Hart Archive far outweighs the long-term importance of his strategic contributions. He was a strategic thinker entirely in keeping with Western traditions of strategic thought. His thinking with respect to tanks, planes, and mechanized warfare was similar to that of many others around him, most prominently his friend J. F. C. Fuller and Giffard Martel. It is telling in this context that Fuller was very much a Clausewitzian thinker, and that others pointed out that Liddell Hart was as well. If there was a real opposition between Clausewitz and Liddell Hart, it was that Clausewitz was a profound and careful thinker who is very difficult to understand, and Liddell Hart was a shallow and facile thinker who is very easy to understand. Moreover, Clausewitz had a lifetime of military experience, including direct combat, behind his very well-read education. Liddell Hart was not even an armchair general; he was an armchair captain.

4   Stilwell, Chiang Kai-shek, and World War II

Samuel Griffith's experience in China was rare, but not unique. Many Americans had lived in China in the first half of the twentieth century, and several American military units, as well as individual officers, served in China. From 1935 to 1938 Griffith was stationed in Beijing, where he learned Chinese, witnessed the dramatic expansion of Japanese power into China in 1937, and translated Mao Zedong's *On Guerrilla Warfare* for the *Marine Corps Gazette*. In order to understand why Griffith's background was critical for establishing the importance of Sunzi after World War II, it is useful to see him in relation to other renowned American officers who also served in China. This context will make it clear both why the particular American understanding of what happened in China turned out as it did, and also why particular men, but not others, emerged to represent that understanding. In the simplest terms, the individuals and groups who succeeded gave their associated, if not actual, strategic frameworks a positive reputation, and the individuals and groups who failed tainted their associated strategic frameworks.

The reality is, unsurprisingly, more complicated than portraying the Communists, Mao Zedong, Samuel Griffith, Evans Carlson, Merritt Edson, and Sunzi as winners, and the Nationalists, Chiang Kai-shek, Joseph Stilwell, and Clausewitz as losers. At a minimum, at least for the Americans in this group, it is vital to explain who Samuel Griffith, Evans Carlson, Merritt Edson, and Joseph Stilwell were, and why they mattered to America and its relationship to China. But it is also vital to understand the contingent events that interacted with these individuals to produce winners and losers, and the way in which those people and events were presented to the wider world. During World War II and immediately afterward, Evans Carlson and Joseph Stilwell were well-known and widely admired military leaders. Merritt Edson was less famous, but had won the Medal of Honor, America's highest military award, for his leadership on Guadalcanal. Griffith was connected to all three of these men in one way or another, but only became widely known as a result of his postwar publications. He served under Edson on Guadalcanal, knew

Carlson, and, in an interesting historiographical turn, supported Barbara Tuchman in the research that resulted in her 1971 book *Stilwell and the American Experience in China, 1911–45*.[1]

Barbara Tuchman (1912–1989) was a best-selling author of histories, winning the Pulitzer Prize twice, the first time for her book on World War I, *The Guns of August*, and the second time, in 1972, for her biography of Joseph Stilwell. As a prominent writer of popular history, Tuchman's views of Stilwell, Chiang Kai-shek, and China were extremely influential in the decades after World War II. She reflected, amplified, and disseminated a particular American understanding in the 1960s that Chiang Kai-shek had been defeated both by the Japanese and by the Chinese Communists because he and his Nationalists were corrupt and inept, and that, in the face of such corruption, there had been only so much that Stilwell (and America) could accomplish. Through heroic effort, and in the face of Chiang's active resistance, Stilwell managed to eke out some victories before Chiang got him recalled. Recent scholarship has significantly modified the wholly negative appraisal of Chiang, and positive view of Stilwell. At a minimum, Chiang faced almost impossible military, political, and economic problems, and Stilwell's abrasive personality and simplistic focus on military matters exacerbated Chiang's problems. Up to 1971, and certainly for some time afterward, however, Stilwell exemplified the idealistic American defeated by Asian corruption, and was part of the narrative of how America "lost" China.

If America, Chiang, and Stilwell had lost China, the Chinese Communists and their methods of warfare had won it. Quite fortuitously for Griffith, his Sunzi translation arrived at a perfect time to be taken seriously in ways that neither Calthrop nor Giles had been. By the time Tuchman was researching and writing her biography of Stilwell, following the Korean War and in the midst of the ongoing Vietnam War, Sunzi seemed extremely relevant. Tuchman, whether because of her personal connection to Griffith or not, mentioned and quoted Sunzi twice, using Griffith's translation, in her biography of Stilwell. From her perspective in 1971 at least, Sunzi explained something about recent Asian history. It was also true that she thought Stilwell was a pivotal figure in America's twentieth-century history with China. Given how well her book sold, and the Pulitzer Prize she received for it, that view was widely shared.

There were further connections among these men, particularly Stilwell, Carlson, and Griffith, who all learned Chinese in China, and lived among the Chinese people rather than being ensconced in an American military

---

[1] Barbara Tuchman, *Stilwell and the American Experience in China, 1911–45*, New York: The Macmillan Company, 1971, xiv.

unit, as Edson was when he was in China. Griffith, Carlson, and Edson were all marines, and all three were key leaders of the Marine Raiders during that unit's brief existence in World War II. Stilwell knew Carlson from Hankou and regarded him as

"a good scout, not overeducated ... but a solid citizen and a soldier" and, though he wore all the wrong clothes at dinner, "a gentleman anyway." Privately he called him "Captain Courageous" and was not impressed by Carlson's glowing reports of the 8th Route Army's military training methods which Stilwell told him he had seen in practice under Feng Yu-hsiang 15 years before.[2]

Despite Stilwell's skepticism of Communist aims, he found Zhou Enlai and his entourage "uniformly frank, courteous, friendly and direct. In contrast to the fur-collared, spurred KMT new-style Napoleon – all pose and bumptiousness."[3]

Carlson would no doubt have agreed with Stilwell's view of both the Communists and the Nationalists–Guomindang (GMD/KMT). The contrast between these respective political groups, the straightforward and ultimately victorious Communists versus the corrupt, untrustworthy, and ultimately defeated Nationalists, was a virtually unquestioned truth (outside Taiwanese GMD circles) until fairly recently. Tuchman's biography of Stilwell reflected that position, and promoted it to the general public. Less clear is whether she amplified or downplayed the opinions of Stilwell and the other Americans in China. Regardless, this was the general sense of the main players in America during and after World War II. America had ended up supporting a distasteful and dishonorable government led by an incompetent military man. Despite Stilwell's best efforts, the Guomindang lost. Carlson, by contrast, had advocated for the Communists, who won.

Stilwell had in fact advocated for or at least considered channeling some US military aid to the Communists during World War II because they appeared to be competent and willing to fight the Japanese. This was, not surprisingly, completely unacceptable to Chiang Kai-shek and the GMD, who understood that the Communists were an existential threat to their power in the short and long term. Stilwell's interest grew out of frustration with Chiang Kai-shek's reluctance to commit his ground forces to fighting the Japanese and the long-standing, if likely forlorn, American hope for a political resolution of the GMD–Communist split. In any case, Stilwell did not perceive the Communists as having a distinctive strategy or fighting style. Like Carlson, the Communist forces distinguished themselves in political indoctrination. This political

---

[2] Tuchman, *Stilwell and the American Experience in China*, 184.
[3] Tuchman, *Stilwell and the American Experience in China*, 184.

indoctrination, which Carlson would bring to the 2nd Marine Raider Battalion, and Griffith would later spread to the 1st Marine Raider Battalion, relied, in part, on explaining to the troops why they were fighting in order to enhance their fighting spirit. This would become known in the Raiders as "gung ho," from the Chinese Communist admonition to "work together" or "work harmoniously."[4] Its association with the elite Marine Raiders and subsequent spread into the Marine Corps as a whole changed its meaning into its current, American definition of being "extremely enthusiastic."

Carlson's new training methods clashed with Merritt Edson's, who stressed the core, conventional fighting skills of the marines. Both Raider Battalions would perform admirably in battle, so there was no clear advantage to either method. Samuel Griffith, who served under Edson as his executive officer, and later took over the unit after Edson's promotion, had consulted with Carlson earlier and saw enough value in gung ho as a doctrine to institute it when he was in command. Despite the centrality of political indoctrination, what would mark Carlson and the Raiders was their association with special operations and unconventional warfare, an association that would connect them to Chinese Communist guerrilla warfare, Mao Zedong, and, ultimately, Sunzi. By contrast, Merritt Edson and Stilwell, who were higher-ranking and extremely distinguished commanders, were entirely conventional leaders in terms of training and tactics.

The strong, and not unreasonable, association of Mao Zedong and the Communists with guerrilla warfare set up a false clash in the American perception between guerrilla warfare and conventional, American warfare during the Chinese Civil War of 1945–1949. After all, Griffith himself had made Mao's book, *On Guerrilla Warfare*, available in English. The failure of Chiang Kai-shek's American-trained troops against the Chinese Communists became part of the "loss" of China to Communism in the early stages of the Cold War. What was not apparent to many in the American military or public was that the Communists' guerrilla warfare of the first stages of the Chinese Civil War (1927–1937) and World War II (1937–1945) in China gave way to mobile warfare after the defeat of Japan. This process began at least as early as the Shangdang campaign of 1945, during which Liu Bocheng (1892–1986), an advocate and practitioner of conventional warfare, successfully defeated a Nationalist force in north China at the beginning of the second phase

---

[4] The phrase has also been attributed to Rewi Alley (1897–1987), a New Zealander who was a member of the Chinese Communist Party, and lived in China from the 1930s until his death.

of the Chinese Civil War.[5] Not only was the Chinese Red Army in the late 1940s no longer a guerrilla army, but Mao was not the central military "genius" that CCP propaganda made him out to be. Mao did have a written corpus of military thought to support his image as a great strategist, but credit for the skilled generalship that defeated Chiang's admittedly inept plans belongs mostly to Lin Biao, not Mao.[6] Mao's military writings did influence doctrine in the People's Liberation Army (PLA), but it was a conventional army by the time of Communist victory in the civil war.

Sunzi, through Mao and guerrilla warfare, "won" World War II in China in the popular sense, though it would take a series of insurgencies and wars afterward to retrospectively make that clear. Chiang's loss in China could be dismissed as either Chiang's failure as a leader or the lesser quality of the American-trained Nationalist troops. Many of those units had been trained by Stilwell and equipped with American arms. In the Korean War, however, American troops, as well as other UN forces, directly clashed with the Chinese army. Despite superior equipment, the UN forces were not able to defeat the Chinese army, and suffered early reverses. The Chinese forces stressed night marches and close combat to negate UN air power, just as they had used similar tactics to negate superior Nationalist artillery. This was not a case of guerrilla, unconventional, or indirect tactics, but rather an intelligent response to an obvious operational weakness. As the initial shock of the Chinese entry into the war wore off and UN troops adapted to Chinese tactics, Chinese casualties increased dramatically. Logistical limitations took a further toll on Chinese troops and they paid an enormous price in lives as they held the line against superior firepower. Indeed, a tenuous argument could be made that it was political indoctrination that allowed the Chinese "volunteers" in Korea to fight the materially superior UN forces to a standstill. Given that many of the Chinese troops were politically unreliable surrendered Nationalist units, many of whom refused to return to China after being captured, it is, however, difficult to attribute their tenacity to a commitment to the cause.

---

[5] The Communist forces perceived the Nationalists as being good at positional warfare. They emphasized night attacks and close combat to minimize the effects of Nationalist artillery. See Harold Tanner, "The Shangdang Campaign," paper presented at the 2020 Chinese Military History Society.

[6] Harold Tanner, *The Battle for Manchuria and the Fate of China: Siping, 1946*, Bloomington: Indiana University Press, 2013; Harold Tanner, *Where Chiang Kai-shek Lost China: The Liao-Shen Campaign, 1948*, Bloomington: Indiana University Press, 2015; Christopher Lew, *The Third Chinese Revolutionary Civil War, 1945–49: An Analysis of Communist Strategy and Leadership*, London: Routledge, 2009.

During World War II, the US military fought against Japan and, to some extent, on the side of China. It was only in Korea after World War II was over that America directly opposed Chinese troops in any capacity. Stilwell invested considerable effort in proving that Chinese troops, when well trained, well equipped, and well led, could defeat the Japanese. Near the end of his tenure as commander in Burma, Chinese troops under Stilwell's command did, in fact, defeat the Japanese. This was vindication for Stilwell, yet it seems to have done very little to convince either the American military or the American government that Chinese troops could make up effective armies. The most that could be said was that, perhaps, Chinese soldiers under American leadership could defeat Japanese troops, but only second- or third-rate Japanese troops at that.

Stilwell's success was a further indictment of Chiang Kai-shek and the GMD leadership. This implicit criticism was one of several reasons why Chiang demanded Stilwell's removal. If the same Chinese troops under GMD command, and even the direct command of Chiang, suffered an almost unbroken string of defeats against the Communists and the Japanese, then why were they suddenly able to fight successfully under Stilwell? Again, as with all of these American perspectives, the facts and personalities were simplified to the point of fantasy. Chiang was portrayed in glowing and heroic terms for many years by both the American govern-ment and press, if often privately condemned. Chiang's public image in the United States was that of a Westernized, Christian convert, whose wife spoke fluent English, and who wanted to lead a new, modern Chinese state with American values. That this was nonsense was far less important than the fact that he did not fight the Japanese successfully, and then lost to the Chinese Communists.

While China connected all four of these American officers, Guadalcanal occupies a prominent place in the lives of the three marines, all of whom served and distinguished themselves in battle there. Samuel Griffith went on to write a historical account of the Battle for Guadalcanal (rather than a personal memoir of his time there), which he also published in its original edition in 1963.[7] The Makin Island raid, carried out by the 2nd Marine Raider Battalion under Evans Carlson on August 17–18, 1942, and often described as the first American use of special operations, and the struggle for Guadalcanal amplified the influence of Chinese training and tactics on the United States Marine Corps. While the term "China marines" refers most narrowly to the 4th Marine Regiment, stationed in China between 1927 and 1941, I will use it more generally

---

[7] Samuel B. Griffith, *The Battle for Guadalcanal*, New York: Bantam Books, 1963. It was originally published by J. B. Lippincott in 1963.

here to refer to any of the marines who served in China in the first half of the twentieth century.

Joseph Stilwell

Army Chief of Staff George Marshall was forced to appoint Joseph Stilwell (1883–1946) to command American forces in the China–Burma–India theater in 1942. Marshall and Stilwell both knew that it was a nearly impossible position to succeed in given the poor logistics, complicated politics, and unclear military objectives inherent in it. Marshall's first choice, General Hugh A. Drum (1879–1951), had lost out to Marshall for the position of army chief of staff. One of the main reasons for wanting to send Drum to China was that Marshall believed it would kill two birds with one stone; it would rid him of the pompous and ineffective Drum, and it would satisfy Chiang Kai-shek with a sufficiently high-ranking, but ignorant, American representative in China (Drum had been promoted to lieutenant general at about the time he lost out to Marshall for the position of chief of staff). Chiang had even encouraged assigning an officer who knew nothing of China, suggesting that someone

Figure 4.1 Joseph Stilwell. US National Archives

with previous experience would be biased by earlier conditions that no longer obtained. Drum, however limited as a military commander (he had actually been captured when in command of the First Army during the 1941 Carolina maneuvers), was politically astute enough to see that the China assignment, despite its grandiose titles and scope, was a military dead end, and turned it down. Stilwell, then considered to be the best corps commander in the US Army, was the obvious choice to fill the position because he spoke Chinese and had extensive experience of the country. It was a decision that pleased no one (except, perhaps, Drum).

Absent all of the obvious military and political problems, Stilwell was ideally suited for the job. After a somewhat rebellious youth, he went to West Point, which he graduated from in 1904. He was an accomplished athlete and linguist, performing particularly well in French, which proved a useful skill when he served in France during World War I. Stilwell went to the Philippines immediately after graduating West Point, which was the only place where the army was actively fighting. He spent time involved in suppressing the local rebellions against American rule, and in the ordinary exploits of garrison life. He exercised his language skills in French and Spanish there by translating documents for the War Department. In early 1906, he was ordered back to West Point, where he would teach English, French, and Spanish for the next three years, before being also assigned to teach tactics, and then moved over to history.

Stilwell went to China in November of 1911, arriving in the midst of the revolution that was in the process of overthrowing the Qing dynasty, the last imperial regime. He spent a little over two weeks there, in Shanghai, Hong Kong, Canton, and Wuzhou. Stilwell returned to Manila on December 9, missing the formal abdication of the emperor and official end of the Qing on February 12, 1912. Early 1912 found him back in the United States, where he would remain until joining the American Expeditionary Force (AEF) in France on January 21, 1918. Stilwell saw the destruction of the World War I battlefield while accompanying patrols along the front lines, returning to America in July of 1919.

The prospects for advancement or interesting service were poor in the postwar army, and Stilwell sought a foreign posting. His timing was fortunate, coinciding with a new initiative to send intelligence officers with good language skills abroad. Since the Japanese slots were already full, Stilwell was sent to China. He first undertook a year of Chinese language training at Berkeley, before being shipped with his family to Beijing in the fall of 1920. Stilwell began intensive Chinese language study at the North China Union Language School, five hours a day of class, along with lectures on other aspects of Chinese history and culture.

He was almost immediately in love with China, though his interest in getting out of Beijing to see the rest of the country put his language training temporarily on hold. Within six months he had got himself assigned to a road-building project for the Red Cross. After successfully completing the project from April to July, he and his family were back in Beijing. He would make a subsequent trip to consult on road building, during which he met Feng Yuxiang (Feng Yu-hsiang), the "Christian General," who invested time in politically indoctrinating his soldiers to make them more effective fighters.[8]

Stilwell traveled extensively in China, and by the time he and his family had left China in July of 1923, he had firsthand knowledge of large parts of China. Back in the United States, Stilwell caught up on the courses of study required for higher command. He went through the infantry course at Fort Benning, followed by the Command and General Staff School at Fort Leavenworth. Fate once again stepped in, diverting him from an assignment at the École de guerre, and back to China, this time as a battalion commander for the 15th Infantry Regiment stationed in Tianjin. Tianjin was not Beijing, and the situation in 1926 was far less foreigner-friendly than when the Stilwells had been in China only a few years before. The 15th Infantry Regiment's executive officer was George C. Marshall, whom Stilwell had last seen in France during World War I. Their deep mutual respect, developed over the next eight months, would be an important factor in Stilwell's posting to China in 1942. Marshall knew firsthand how well acquainted Stilwell was with China, as well as his qualities as an officer and leader of men.

Stilwell left China in 1929 to head the Tactical Section of the Infantry School at Fort Benning. Marshall had preceded him to Benning, and concluded that Stilwell was the man to support his reform efforts there. He distinguished himself there as an instructor and leader of men, but also as intolerant of incompetence, gaining the sobriquet "Vinegar Joe." Stilwell was still a lieutenant colonel at the age of fifty-one in 1933, assigned to training duties in California. Before boredom drove him to early retirement, he went back to Beijing (then called Beiping) in 1935, this time as a full colonel and as the military attaché.[9] He was fully aware of the situation he was heading into, and was rightfully pessimistic of the prospects for peace. There did not seem to be any way to stop the Japanese as they gradually took over China, and the Nationalist

---

[8] Stilwell subsequently met with Feng repeatedly over the years in China. Feng even paid a condolence call on Mrs. Stilwell in Carmel shortly after Stilwell's death. Tuchman, *Stilwell and the American Experience in China*, 82–83. His close ties to Feng no doubt caused him to downplay the Communists' "innovation" in their training.

[9] Tuchman, *Stilwell and the American Experience in China*, 139–141.

government under Chiang Kai-shek based in Nanjing appeared to be corrupt and incompetent.

Japan was pressing its military and political advantage in 1935, trying to separate northern China from direct GMD rule. Chiang Kai-shek was unwilling to fight an almost certainly losing battle against the Japanese army, and there was little that the foreign powers could do. Chiang focused instead on destroying the remnants of the Communist forces. His forlorn hope of forestalling the Japanese while he took care of the Communists relied upon American and British pressuring the Japanese to back off. Chiang's plans were deeply flawed on many levels, and they made a very poor impression on Stilwell. As Tuchman recounts the Chinese overture to Stilwell:

"America can stop Japan if she takes action," Stilwell was told, but if she failed to act Japan would gain control of China's resources to America's detriment. Stilwell commented in his report, "It looks like another manifestation of the Chinese desire to get somebody else to do something they are afraid to do themselves," and he added shrewdly, "possibly an intimation that they have no intention of offering resistance unassisted."[10]

Stilwell felt that Chiang was simply unwilling to act boldly and do what was necessary to save his country. Unfortunately, he also saw that there was no other leader of Chiang's standing available. This inaction was attributable in some sense, he believed, to the Daoist idea of "inaction" (wuwei).

There was no small irony in watching Chiang build a German-trained army while also imagining that he was practicing inaction. Perhaps one of the reasons why Western military methods ultimately became so discredited in the American view of modern Chinese history was because Chiang, for all his Chinese culture, was shown dressed as a Western general, used German- and then American-trained troops, and lost badly. Whatever the merits or force of circumstances compelled Chiang to act as he did politically within China, he looked like a poor prospect to the American government. America's continuing support, though minimal at that time, was due to the lack of any alternative. Stilwell went to Taiyuan and Shanxi in March of 1936 to gather information on the Communists. Their resources were limited, and, consequently, so were their military activities, but they were winning the propaganda war by claiming to resist Japan actively.

Stilwell recognized that the Communists were attempting to push Chiang into opposing the Japanese and thus, perhaps, to his destruction.

---

[10] Tuchman, *Stilwell and the American Experience in China*, 156.

Like many foreign observers in China, Stilwell did not believe that the Chinese Communists were really communists,

Carrying their burdens of famine and drought, heavy rent and interest, squeeze by middlemen, absentee landlordism ... naturally they agitated for a readjustment of land ownership and this made them communists – at least that is the label put on them. Their leaders adopted the methods and slogans of communism but what they were really after was land ownership under reasonable conditions. It is not in the nature of Chinese to be communists.[11]

Other American and foreign diplomats and officers also noted that the Communists treated their soldiers far better than the Nationalist troops did. Communist troops were poorly equipped, but orderly, motivated, and tough. The contrast between them and the Nationalist armies was stark. This positive view of the Communists was spread in America and the world by Edgar Snow's *Red Star over China*. Snow went to Bao'an and interviewed the Communist leadership, which resulted in an extremely sympathetic portrayal.

Snow was at least acquainted with Stilwell, quoting him in his discussion of the Communist military leadership:

Casualties among Red Army commanders were very high. They customarily went into battle side by side with their men, from regimental commanders down. Joseph Stilwell once said to me that one thing alone might explain the fighting power of the Reds against an enemy with vastly superior resources. That was the red officers' habit of saying, "Come on, boys!" instead of, "Go on, boys!"[12]

When Snow first published the book in 1937, and certainly by its reprinting in 1944, there was no need to explain who Joseph Stilwell was. By the 1968 edition, however, he felt it necessary to insert a note explaining that "Joseph W. Stilwell was in 1937 US military attaché in China. He became commander-in-chief of US forces in the China–Burma–India theater during the Second World War. See *The Stilwell Papers* (New York, 1948)."[13]

With the Japanese invasion of China in 1937, the defeat of the Nationalist Army at Shanghai, and the subsequent withdrawal of the Nationalist government from Nanjing up the Yangzi to Hankou, Japanese imperialism reached the logical limits of its existing strategy in China. The Japanese leadership, however, either didn't realize that was the case, or was unable to formulate a new strategy. The Japanese invasion prevented Chiang Kai-shek from placating the Japanese as he had

---

[11] Tuchman, *Stilwell and the American Experience in China*, 158.
[12] Edgar Snow, *Red Star over China*, New York: Grove Press, 1973 (revised and enlarged edition), 260. It was first published in 1937.
[13] Snow, *Red Star over China*, 1973 edn, 435.

planned in order to buy time to destroy the Communists, since he could not maintain his position as paramount leader of China in the face of a direct assault without going over to formal resistance.

As the Nationalists and Chiang Kai-shek were failing in their conventional, Western-style defense against Japan's conventional, imperialist, Western-style offense, the Communists were perceived to have at least partially succeeded with guerrilla, Maoist, non-Western strategy and tactics. This comparison is, however, unfair on many levels because the Nationalist government bore the full brunt of the Japanese military, fighting in densely populated cities and economically productive areas, while the Communists were neither a major threat nor a major target for the Japanese army, and occupied rural areas with dispersed populations. Chiang's strategy was to endure until the Japanese gave up from exhaustion, which in formal terms might be seen as opposing the Japanese strategy of annihilation, which would defeat China's military in order to defeat its government, by employing a strategy of attrition that would deny the Japanese decisive battles or a quick resolution by combat. This was not very different than the strategy the Communists employed against both Chiang and the Japanese, and it could easily be seen as an indirect strategy that avoided a direct test of army strengths.

The Nationalist government began retreating up the Yangzi to Sichuan in 1938 as it became clear that the Japanese would advance on Hankou. They were now cut off from the coast, and reliant upon a tenuous road through Burma for outside supplies. In December, the Japanese essentially declared their invasion over, and the areas of China under their control to be part of their empire. Chiang survived in Chongqing, and the Communists in Yan'an. Stilwell personally watched the massive operation moving people and materials up the river. Before Stilwell's departure from China on May 1, 1939, he made a trip up to Chongqing and met Chiang Kai-shek and Madame Chiang in December of 1938. "Chiang Kai-shek," Stilwell reported, "is directly responsible for much of the confusion that normally exists in his command."[14]

The China that Stilwell left in 1939 was in crisis, and Stilwell was pessimistic about his own career. But George Marshall interceded again to advance Stilwell's career, promoting him to brigadier general. Stilwell himself would demonstrate in war games tactics similar to what Germany used in reality at virtually the same time. His stellar performance during the war games in Louisiana beginning on May 10, 1940, demonstrated that the Germans were hardly the only ones interested in mobile maneuver warfare (what was subsequently called blitzkrieg). Indeed, one of the

[14] Tuchman, *Stilwell and the American Experience in China*, 197.

functions of that war game was to evaluate the possibilities of this new kind of warfare. The war games also showed Stilwell to be one of the best generals in the US Army. His performance there and consequent standing in the minds of the army's leadership put him on track to be one of America's great generals of World War II. If events had turned out differently, and he had not been sent to China, he might have ranked with Patton, Eisenhower, or Bradley. Both because of where he was sent, and the limited results achieved (followed by the Communist defeat of Chiang Kai-shek in 1949), the man believed by many, including Marshall, to be America's best corps commander would be remembered as neither an innovative tactician nor a terribly successful general.[15]

Although Chiang would repeatedly raise the possibility of making peace with the Japanese while trying to get more money and materials from America, it was never clear whether that was a realistic option for him politically. The Japanese, for their part, had still not resolved the problem of Chinese resistance to their ongoing attempt to subjugate China. Roosevelt tried to placate Chiang Kai-shek to keep the Chinese government viable and tie down Japanese troops, while not provoking the Japanese into a direct fight that America was unprepared for. The fundamental clash of war aims and strategies, combined with a history of slights between the Western powers and China, led to considerable (and justified) bitterness on the part of the Chinese. America planned to train and arm thirty divisions of Chinese troops in order to fight the Japanese. The Chinese government knew that America's main goal was to occupy Japanese armies with fighting in China.

This complicated knot of politics, diplomacy, and military resources was cut by the Japanese attack on Pearl Harbor on December 7, 1941. While the strategic wisdom of this act by the Japanese can be debated, its immediate effect was to remove any constraints on provoking Japan into war with America or Great Britain. It also transformed a looming problem into an immediate crisis. Neither America nor Great Britain was prepared to fight Japan in December of 1941, making it all the more remarkable how quickly the United States Navy and Marine Corps reversed the course of the war at the Battle of the Coral Sea (May 4–8, 1942), Midway (June 4–7, 1942), and Guadalcanal (August 7, 1942–February 9, 1943). These battles derailed Japan's strategic plans even before the United States was able to develop a material advantage over the Japanese Navy. This is to say that

---

[15] See Robert Lyman's foreword to David Rooney's *Stilwell the Patriot*, London: Greenhill Books, 2005, 12, "History and historians have tended to treat Stilwell, as is often the case with enigmatic characters of his ilk, with passion, prejudice and precious little balance. Stilwell, like that other aberrant personality Orde Wingate, seems fated to attract the extremes of comment, and a full consideration of his contribution to the ultimately successful prosecution of the war against the Japanese can too easily be lost."

it was superior American strategy, operations, and tactics, rather than material advantages, that initially turned the tide of war.

As that tide shifted, however, and as the American Navy and Marine Corps began to roll back the Japanese positions in the Pacific, China began to be less important to American war aims. One of the reasons why Stilwell would be mostly forgotten, or at least not gain the longer-term historical reputation he arguably deserved, was that by the time he achieved the limited successes he did, they were essentially unimportant for the outcome of the war.

In the immediate aftermath of Pearl Harbor, Chiang Kai-shek imagined that he could suddenly achieve everything he wanted. He was soon disabused of his hopes, with China not being invited to the First Washington Conference (also known as the Arcadia Conference) held in Washington, DC from December 22, 1941, to January 14, 1942. This meeting of American and British military leaders, as well as Churchill and Roosevelt, set out all of the major strategic and planning decisions exactly contrary to what Chiang hoped for. A meeting in Chongqing on December 23 with representatives of the Allies showed him how isolated he was. Roosevelt did worry that Chiang might make peace with Japan, and sought to placate him. This involved sending a sufficiently high-ranking general to assist Chiang, who had been offered the official desig-nation of supreme commander of Allied forces in China. There were no non-Chinese Allied troops in China, but at least it gave the appearance of treating him like the head of a great power.

After General Drum turned down the position, Stilwell, then a two-star general and corps commander, was the obvious choice. Unable to find anyone else suitable, Marshall had to suggest Stilwell. Marshall had intended to use Stilwell in Europe or Africa, but the logic of sending someone of Stilwell's experience and language ability was undeniable. Stilwell did believe that he could succeed in the position if he were given actual command of the Chinese troops. He respected the qualities of Chinese soldiers, but he was wary of Chiang and the GMD leadership. Stilwell combined hope and realism as he took up a role that required him to balance a myriad of mutually antagonistic goals, while supported to a greater or lesser extent by allies whose individual plans diverged, and who were generally pessimistic that anything could be done.

China–Burma–India (CBI)

Stilwell focused his immediate mission on driving the Japanese out of Burma. If that could be accomplished, the next phase would be to drive the Japanese out of China, followed by using Chinese bases to attack

Japan. In order to do that, he had to train Chinese troops in India, and build a road across Burma connecting with India. He faced tremendous resistance from both his Chinese and British allies in carrying this out. His only leverage in negotiations with Chiang Kai-shek was his control over Lend–Lease supplies, and this was also, consequently, a tremendous point of friction. To make matters worse, by the time Stilwell reached Burma, the British had been dealt a series of crushing defeats in Southeast Asia. Stilwell himself would soon be forced to walk out of Burma through the jungle at the head of his staff and a collection of other people fleeing the Japanese. The Japanese conquest of Burma cut the land route for supplies into China, forcing Chongqing to be supported by dangerous flights over "the Hump," an air route over the Himalayas.

The mismatch in priorities among the Allies, along with growing mutual contempt, made an already difficult situation far worse. Stilwell grew increasingly disgusted with Chiang, whom the British had long dismissed, but there was nothing he could do except vent his feelings to Marshall and Roosevelt. Chiang was, in turn, furious at Stilwell for undermining his authority and position, and for not giving him the supplies and respect he thought were his right.

Stilwell's long-planned offensive began in April 1944, finally capturing the town of Myitkyina on August 4, 1944, after a prolonged siege. The 4,600 Japanese soldiers put up a fierce resistance, fighting during the monsoon. Although it was a great victory for Stilwell and his Chinese units, it destroyed both British (Chindits) and American (Merrill's Marauders) unconventional forces. Stilwell had vastly overestimated the ability of these lightly armed units to attack directly conventional Japanese forces, or to continue operating in the jungle for long periods without rest and refitting. The capture of Myitkyina also proved both British and the Chinese wrong. Stilwell had overcome months of resistance and doubt to carry the war to the Japanese, showing that properly led Chinese troops could beat the Japanese, and that a road could be built in northern Burma.

In April of 1944, while the Burma campaign was proceeding, the Japanese launched a major offensive, Operation Ichi-Go, in southeast China. Ichi-Go's goal was to open a route to Indochina and destroy the air bases Claire Chennault had been using to attack the Japanese. This was exactly what Stilwell had feared would happen if air bases unprotected by ground forces launched bombing raids on the Japanese. The collapse of Chinese defenses precipitated a crisis in leadership. Chiang Kai-shek clashed directly with Stilwell over the response to advancing Japanese forces. As far as Stilwell was concerned, Chiang was utterly incompetent in military matters, and he hoped that the crisis would force Chiang to give him full command over Chinese forces. Stilwell wrote to Roosevelt, who, also frustrated by years of dealing with Chiang, wrote an ultimatum that demanded that Stilwell be placed in charge.

Stilwell triumphantly delivered the letter to Chiang in 1944, feeling he had finally achieved the political victory that would allow him to do what needed to be done. It was a mistake on both Roosevelt's and Stilwell's parts, for Chiang could not accept such a loss of face. He demanded Stilwell's recall, and his replacement by another American general. Roosevelt had to comply with Chiang's demand. Stilwell, a four-star general since August, immediately departed without waiting to welcome his replacement. He was ordered not to discuss the matter when he got back to America for fear of the ugly publicity that the clash with Chiang would produce. While Chiang had gotten rid of Stilwell, Stilwell remained a respected figure in the army, in the government, and among the general populace. He continued to serve in the United States for the rest of the war and after, dying from stomach cancer on October 12, 1946.

Chiang could not have acted otherwise in response to Roosevelt's ultimatum, but he paid a great price in having Stilwell removed. Stilwell's military successes with Chinese troops were in sharp contrast to Chiang's failures. He was also very much a model American general, reflecting American values and attitudes. Stilwell's removal confirmed in the minds of many Americans that Chiang was, in fact, the corrupt, incompetent despot they suspected him to be. Moreover, Chiang became much less important as the United States Navy and Marines advanced across the Pacific toward Japan, and the army returned to the Philippines. In the later stages of World War II the US was able to send far more supplies to Chiang just as there was less and less value in doing so. Many journalists continued to write negative portrayals of Chiang and the GMD, contributing to a significant weakening of support for the Nationalist government.

Theodore White, Barbara Tuchman, and the Interpretation of Stilwell

Two books shaped Stilwell's public image after World War II: Theodore White's *The Stilwell Papers* and Barbara Tuchman's *Stilwell and the American Experience in China*. White (1915–1986), who knew Stilwell in China and had reported extensively on China during World War II, produced *The Stilwell Papers* at the behest of Stilwell's widow. *The Stilwell Papers* was published in 1948, and was based entirely on Stilwell's own diary and correspondence, with White adding some context and explanation. As such, it was clearly a description of events and personalities told from Stilwell's perspective, and in many respects a personal, exaggerated perspective that he wrote down rather than expressing publicly (he had, of course, also written scathing evaluations of Chiang in his official reports and correspondence with Marshall and other US government and military officials). White had reported from China during World War II, working for a time as the China correspondent for *Time* and befriending Henry Luce, before breaking with Luce professionally (but not personally) over controls and alterations of his stories. Luce was an important supporter of Chiang Kai-shek, and White had concluded, like many foreigners in China, that Chiang and the GMD were thoroughly corrupt and despotic.

White, with Annalee Jacoby, published *Thunder out of China* in 1946, of which Robert Gale Woolbert said in his 1947 review,

It was not written in a judicial spirit, but in the angry tone of a crusader. In their review of recent Chinese history and in their suggestions for American Far Eastern policy, Mr. White and Mrs. Jacoby tread on many toes, personal and ideological. Perhaps their strictures on the Generalissimo and the old guard in the Kuomintang will sound less extravagant today, after the Marshall report, than they did when first published in the fall of 1946.[16]

By 1947, then, distaste for Chiang Kai-shek was widespread in certain circles, including the upper reaches of the American government. Marshall was certainly no supporter of Chiang, having personally tried and failed to broker an agreement between the GMD and the Communists after World War II, and seen Stilwell's difficulties during the war. *The Stilwell Papers* was also published before Chiang and the GMD lost the civil war with the Communists and fled to Taiwan in 1949. The catastrophic failure of the Nationalists in 1949 made both *Thunder out of China* and *The Stilwell Papers* seem prescient. And they were not the only negative accounts of what happened. Paul K. T. Shih (Paul Kwang Tsien, 1910–1978, professor of history and director of the St. John's University Center for Asian Studies) also included in his foreword two reports by the United States Department of the Army, *Stilwell's Mission to China* and *Stilwell's Command Problems*, published in 1953 and 1956 respectively, as influential works that were one-sided and needed to be rebutted in Chin-tung Liang's book *General Stilwell in China, 1942–1944: The Full Story*.[17]

---

[16] Robert Gale Woolbert, capsule review of *Thunder out of China*, *Foreign Affairs*, April 1947, 531.
[17] Chin-tung Liang, *General Stilwell in China, 1942–1944: The Full Story*, New York: St. John's University Press, 1972, x.

The point here is not that *The Stilwell Papers* and *Stilwell and the American Experience in China* accurately portrayed Stilwell and Chiang Kai-shek, but rather what the perception of these two figures was in the decades after World War II. Apart from Liang's forlorn attempt to change that perception, which was stimulated as much by Tuchman's book as by White's, in America Stilwell was seen positively and Chiang negatively. It is only recently that Rana Mitter, Jay Taylor, and Hans van de Ven have argued convincingly for a more balanced view of Chiang, and, by extension, of Stilwell.[18] There was nothing to recommend Chiang because he had been defeated on virtually every level, militarily and politically, from grand strategy down to tactics. His only accomplishment was to survive with a rump regime in Taiwan until his death in 1975. Stilwell's military accomplishments were also hard to praise as anything more than competent, conventional generalship under difficult political and material conditions. He was a good general who was noteworthy because of the political battles he fought, rather than for a great strategic or tactical victory. There were no strategic lessons to be learned from either man.

Barbara Tuchman instead used Joseph Stilwell's life to frame America's involvement in China in the early twentieth century. As such, she was not trying to be fair to Chiang Kai-shek, but rather to see China in that period as ordinary Americans would, though Stilwell was far from ordinary. She was also searching for a simple way to explain the Nationalists' poor military performance. The fundamental question that most Americans could not understand with respect to Chiang and his Nationalist regime was why they didn't fight as hard as they could against Japan. From the American perspective, it appeared obvious that the military and political unity that Chiang sought could only be obtained by wholeheartedly fighting the Japanese. The Communists at least created the impression that they were fighting as hard as they could against the Japanese. Mao Zedong had clearly gotten his strategy right, and his strategy, it was asserted by Griffith, grew out of or was heavily influenced by Sunzi. Tuchman could have absorbed this view either from reading Griffith's translation, or from direct conversation with Griffith, or from both.

It thus seemed reasonable and important to include some reference to Sunzi in the discussion of strategy in China. Tuchman concluded her opening section on Stilwell's term as military attaché by bringing up Sunzi: "Sun Tzu, a fifth century B.C. writer on military theory and practice who anticipated much of Clausewitz and more of Napoleon,

[18] Rana Mitter, *Forgotten Ally: China's World War II, 1937–1945*, Boston: Houghton Mifflin Harcourt, 2013; Jay Taylor, *The Generalissimo: Chiang Kai-shek and the Struggle for Modern China*, Cambridge, MA: Belknap Press, 2009; and Hans van de Ven, *War and Nationalism in China: 1925–1945*, London: Routledge, 2003.

could be read by Stilwell and his professional colleagues with profit."[19] The mention sits somewhat awkwardly in the text, raising the important, but likely unanswerable, question why she chose to place it there. Her only other explicit citation of Sunzi concerned Chinese tactics, and resistance to Stilwell's tactics on the part of Chinese commanders in 1943:

> The 18th Division was thus to be netted and annihilated in sections as the NCAC advanced. Owing to a variety of malign and unexpected obstacles, practice frequently failed to live up to the design, the more so as the Chinese, inheritors of Sun Tzu's dictum, "To a surrounded enemy you must leave a way of escape," were averse to closing the net. They preferred a U-shaped ambush with a well-advertised escape route to avoid a savage fight to the death by trapped Japanese.[20]

This came directly from Griffith's Sunzi translation, combined with Stilwell's own account of his frustration at the unwillingness of his subordinate Chinese commanders to encircle and annihilate Japanese forces. Relating Sunzi to Clausewitz and Napoleon came from Liddell Hart's foreword; it had no place in either Calthrop's or Giles's translation. The issue of leaving a clear path of escape for an enemy comes from Chapter 7 of the Sunzi. Griffith renders the passage directly: "To a surrounded enemy you must leave a way of escape." But he includes Du Mu's commentary: "Show him there is a road to safety, and so create in his mind the idea that there is an alternative to death. Then strike."[21] By contrast, Giles incorporates the commentary into his rendering of the main text: "When you surround an army, leave an outlet free. This does not mean that the enemy is to be allowed to escape. The object is to make him believe that there is a road to safety, and thus prevent his fighting with the courage of despair."[22]

This was an entirely facile use of Sunzi to explain the reticence of the Chinese Nationalist Army to accept casualties in order to destroy Japanese units. The point here is not the actual influence of Sunzi, or lack thereof, on the Nationalist Army during the war, but rather that Tuchman felt in 1971 that it was important and useful to bring up Sunzi. It would be hard at present to imagine a discussion of Chinese military history in the West for any period not mentioning Sunzi, even if only to note that Sunzi was not relevant in that particular time and place. Had the Nationalists under Chiang and Stilwell won great victories over the Japanese, and subsequently the Communists, Griffith's Sunzi translation would have been either forgotten, or interpreted very differently.

Stilwell was well aware that his Chinese units lacked the confidence to face Japanese units without overwhelming numerical superiority.

---

[19] Tuchman, *Stilwell and the American Experience in China*, 177.
[20] Tuchman, *Stilwell and the American Experience in China*, 418–19.
[21] Griffith, *The Battle for Guadalcanal*, 109–110.   [22] Giles, *The Art of War*, 35.

Chinese officers had no incentive to sacrifice their units and were in fact admonished by their superiors to preserve them as much as possible. Sunzi was quite beside the point and, indeed, if you understood Sunzi as Du Mu did, the point was not to let the enemy get away, but only to more easily destroy him because he did not *believe* he had to fight to the death. Nationalist Chinese forces were not focused on destroying Japanese units because it was not in their interest to do so at the strategic level. Stilwell was fighting to defeat the Japanese Army in order to win World War II. Chiang Kai-shek, in contrast, knew that he was fighting for control of China with other Chinese forces, particularly the Communists. The Japanese were a temporary problem, and when they left the real contest would begin.

The negative view of Chiang Kai-shek was partly based in reality – the Nationalists were deeply corrupt, for example – and partly based in very different strategic visions of the contest in China. American priorities during the war focused on the immediate Japanese military problem, rather than the longer-term issue of the political control of China. Depending upon how the war developed, China might have become a base to launch attacks on Japan. Chiang's perspective was similar in some ways to that of Great Britain in Burma. Stilwell rightly suspected that although the British were reluctant to expend scarce military resources in men and material in a secondary or even tertiary theatre, they were also unwilling to undertake offensives during the war that would undermine their colonial interests after the war. Yet the British reticence could hardly be attributed to Sunzi.

At least in the case of Tuchman, then, the essentialization of the Chinese way of fighting to Sunzi was used to encapsulate the problems facing Stilwell and to excuse his inability to do more. One of the central messages of her account of Stilwell in China is that he accomplished the limited amount he did despite ferocious resistance from Chiang Kai-shek and the GMD. He was heroic because he achieved anything at all, defeating the Japanese Army at Myitkyina and building an impossible road through Burma. Yet in retrospect it is hard not to see Stilwell's mission, like the American engagement with China more generally, as a failure. America could not overcome the reality of China under Chiang Kai-shek. China was "lost" to the Communists, who, it was seemingly forgotten, were also Chinese. Mao Zedong won by using Sunzi, but Chiang Kai-shek lost by using Sunzi. Of course, Chiang did not produce military writings validated by victory like Mao. And, as the experience of the Marine Raiders would show, it was success in war against the Chinese Nationalists and Japan that would make Sunzi important.

5   The China Marines

Joseph Stilwell's military career was a conventional success, but his historical place is more ambiguous. The height of his military career was entangled in political events that continue to shape the world, yet there was no specific battle or military accomplishment upon which to base a reputation as a "great" general. Even his capture of Myitkyina did not register as a very significant accomplishment when contrasted with other battles in late World War II. China was significant for the Americans during World War II as part of the fight against Japan. As US forces advanced across the Pacific, the war in China, let alone Burma, became far less important. Very few American troops fought in Burma, and the battles they did take part in did not generate the heroic imagery of the United States Marines fighting for islands in the Pacific, or the great naval battles involved in destroying the Japanese fleet. Moreover, the US Navy and Marine Corps campaigns were perceived as retribution for Japan's attack on Pearl Harbor. They were therefore important in ways that Stilwell's efforts in China could never be.

Barbara Tuchman's account of Stilwell tied his reputation firmly to that of Chiang Kai-shek, at least from the American (and GMD) perspective.[1] This increased the stakes in the evaluation of Stilwell. If he was a good general, then Chiang Kai-shek was not, Claire Chennault was wrong about air power, and much of the reason why the GMD failed was due to its own corruption. If Stilwell were less competent, then Chiang, Chennault, and the GMD could be seen more favorably. Regardless of where the truth lay, even before 1949, Chiang and the GMD were unsuccessful militarily and politically. Stilwell could not have changed Chiang's fortunes because the fate of the Nationalist regime was in the hands of Chiang and the GMD, not America or Joseph Stilwell. Even well

---

[1] Chin-tung Liang, *General Stilwell in China, 1942–1944: The Full Story*, New York: St. John's University Press, 1972, was explicitly written in response to Tuchman and White. It came out in 1972, just as the United States was switching diplomatic recognition of "China" from the Nationalist government in Taiwan to the Communist government on mainland China.

into the Cold War, however, very few people in the United States government accepted the notion that American money and military aid could not overcome the personalities, politics, and social realities of other states. Part of the reason for that blindness was the immense power at the disposal of the United States at the end of World War II.

The Chinese Communists had frustrated American conventional power in China just as they had frustrated Japanese conventional power from the 1930s until 1945. One of the pillars of American Army doctrine was attaining material superiority over an enemy. This was certainly an effective approach as American industry began to out-produce the Axis powers. Properly trained and supplied troops were believed to be able to overwhelm any opposition. Commando raids and small-unit actions were heroic and glorious affairs, but the major land campaigns in Europe were vast actions involving thousands of tanks, hundreds of planes, and tens of thousands of infantry. The sheer logistical effort necessary to wage those campaigns was itself an astonishing organizational achievement. While the effectiveness, if it could be achieved, of material superiority as a military advantage was clear, it did not display much in the way of clever strategy. The military question that so many sought to answer after World War I was precisely how to avoid a head-on struggle of men and material in a war of attrition. The tactical renown of German mechanized, mobile warfare defeating the Maginot Line was the paradigmatic example of a relatively small, elite force achieving a disproportionate victory over a more numerous, static opponent. Everything that followed tended to resemble that maneuver warfare rather than the static, positional fighting of World War I. That was why the German generals were so admired after the war.

World War II in the Pacific was a very different environment, with the most innovative warfare coming from the shift to aircraft carriers dominating naval warfare, and Chinese Communist guerrilla warfare surviving conventional Japanese attacks and defeating (American-trained) Chinese armies. Chinese guerrilla warfare would become connected to the United States Marines in two ways: the association of China marines with Chinese military methods through Evans Carlson and Samuel Griffith, and the use of lightly armed, but highly motivated, marine units fighting in "guerrilla" style. In the year or so following the Japanese attack on Pearl Harbor a materially inferior United States Navy and Marine Corps managed narrowly to seize the initiative in the Pacific. Material inferiority required, and highlighted the need for, intelligent strategy as a force multiplier. In this early stage of the war, for a number of idiosyncratic reasons, a new marine unit, the Raiders, was created to strike back at the Japanese. The Raider Battalions, which would exist for only two years, had three notable military actions: the Makin raid, Edson's Ridge, and the Long Patrol. As the Marine Corps expanded, and the war shifted, the Raiders were dissolved. Guerrilla warfare gave way to island hopping and amphibious assaults. The brief history of the Raiders was glorious, but, apart from Edson's Ridge, of questionable value.

Unlike Joseph Stilwell, the Raider Battalions took part in the battle for the Pacific that mattered to Americans. The behind-the-scenes politics were all American, and while that drove the formation of the Raiders in the first place, it did produce military glory. The Raiders were part of the success story of the Pacific war. A further fillip for the Raider reputation, and that of Evans Carlson, was that the Makin raid is considered the first special-operations action of the modern American military. The Battle of Edson's Ridge, which was a far more important action, was fought conventionally. Merritt Edson was very much the paradigmatic example of the conventional marine, who successfully fought a conventional defense of Henderson Field on Guadalcanal. Carlson's subsequent Long Patrol on Guadalcanal was an impressive feat that had real military value, but it was far less critical than Edson's defense of the airfield. Griffith took part in both the defense of Henderson Field and the Long Patrol.

The story of these three US Marine officers is united not just by the Raiders, but also by China. They all served in China before the Raiders were formed, and that service gave them status and cachet. All three also conceived deep dislikes or hatreds of the Japanese as a result of what they witnessed in China. Griffith appears to have overcome his wartime feelings and solicited and received help (for which he was very grateful) directly from Japanese officers and scholars after the war. All of them had also served in Nicaragua, along with other colonial duty. Yet China was the significant marker for their reputations and careers. Their times in China brought them into contact with the Japanese Army before World War II began for the United States, and connected them to the outcome of the later Chinese Civil War.

Evans Carlson imported Communist military methods into the Marine Corps and the Raiders legitimized those methods by their successes. This also coincided with a turn toward studying strategic thought in America, which, as Edward Mead Earle pointed out in his efforts to create *Makers of Modern Strategy*, had hitherto been lacking. Samuel Griffith was perfectly placed to unite Mao Zedong's military thought with Sunzi. He had served in China, translated Mao's *On Guerrilla Warfare*, fought as a Raider, and then earned a doctorate at Oxford translating Sunzi. Liddell Hart put the final touch on Griffith and Sunzi, by drawing them into the new, postwar study of strategy.

None of this would have been possible without Evans Carlson. Stilwell's "Captain Courageous" was indeed a romantic figure who lived an extraordinary life. Carlson was responsible for bringing Communist military practice into the Marine Corps, and Carlson was responsible for the establishment of the Raiders. Merritt Edson began the actual establishment of the Raiders, what would become the 1st Raider Battalion, on the East Coast before Carlson set up training for the 2nd Battalion on the West Coast. Griffith began as the executive officer for the 1st Battalion, having been in touch with Carlson beforehand. After Griffith took command of the 1st Battalion, following Edson's promotion, he brought the gung ho practices of the 2nd Battalion into the 1st.

Evans Carlson

Evans Carlson (Figure 5.1) was born in Sidney, New York, in 1896, and joined the army in 1910, having run away from home two years before. He was sent to the Philippines, and left the army in 1916 as a first sergeant, before returning to serve in Mexico. Carlson then fought in World War I,

Figure 5.1 Evans Carlson. US National Archives

where he was wounded, subsequently being commissioned as a second lieutenant, and then promoted to captain. He left the army again in 1921, and then enlisted with the marines the following year, and received his commission as a second lieutenant in 1923. He served in Puerto Rico and on the West Coast, followed by a failed attempt at training to fly airplanes in Florida. Carlson was posted to China from 1927 to 1929 as an intelligence officer, where he, like Stilwell, became fascinated with Chinese culture.[2]

Carlson next found himself in Nicaragua, where he learned a great deal about leading small units against guerrillas and rebels in difficult terrain. He also sympathized with the plight of the farmers and the poor people oppressed by the ruling class. Carlson's ability to speak Spanish and to adapt to the local culture helped him work with the Nicaraguan troops. He was also physically brave, almost to a fault. While commanding a small force of twelve men, he defeated a much larger rebel force through the use of concentrated firepower and maneuver.

It was upon his return to the United States in 1933 that Carlson made one of the most momentous connections of his career. He was assigned to be the executive officer of the marine detachment guarding President Roosevelt while on vacation in Warm Springs, Georgia. Not only did he develop a strong personal relationship with the president, he also became friends with James Roosevelt, the president's son. This connection would be key to the creation of the Marine Raiders. The President was so impressed by Carlson that he asked him to write to him about conditions in China when he left for Beijing in 1933 to study Chinese. Carlson was to write directly to the president, though the letters were addressed to his secretary, Missy LeHand, for the sake of secrecy. Roosevelt therefore obtained a direct source of information about China from outside official channels. Carlson's direct line to Roosevelt would cut both ways, of course, as it allowed him to circumvent the command hierarchy to get what he wanted, but it naturally generated immense hostility with many officers in the Marine Corps.

Carlson returned to the United States in 1936 for study at the Marine Corps and George Washington University before being sent back to Beijing (Beiping) in 1937 to study Chinese language. As he said of his arrival in Shanghai in August,

When I had sailed from Seattle three weeks before it had not been with the expectation of attending a war, though all who had lived in the Orient during the past decade realized that ultimately China and Japan must fight, for no nation

---

[2] John Wukovits, *American Commando*, New York: NAL Caliber, 2009, 5.

can, with either honor or safety, permit repeated invasions of its sovereignty. My object was to undertake the formal study of the Chinese language.

Even before he landed in Shanghai, however, the Japanese invasion of China had reached Shanghai, where Chiang Kai-shek was forced to take a stand. "I had come out then [presumably referring to his earlier, 1927–1929, posting] with a regiment of marines, sent to protect the lives and interests of Americans against the Kuomintang armies of Chiang Kai-shek which were moving up from the south." But the Japanese invasion had dramatically shifted his plans:

Destiny had taken a hand in the direction of my affairs, and although I did not know it, there would be no poring over ideographs in a language school at Peip'ing for me. Instead I would tramp the hinterland of China during the next eighteen months, accompanying the armies as an official observer for the United States Navy, and witnessing at first hand China's efforts to preserve her independence.[3]

Stilwell, of course, had encountered the extreme antiforeignism that the GMD's Northern Expedition had amplified. The American government was concerned enough about its citizens in China to send troops to secure their safety. In 1937 the United States saw the main threat to Americans in China to be the GMD, not the Japanese. The Japanese were still trying to maintain good relations with the foreign powers at that time, though as Stilwell, Carlson, Griffith, and Edson made clear in their respective accounts, the Japanese authorities made sure to insult and slight any non-Japanese in China, including, of course, the Chinese, at every possible chance.

It did not seem a productive use of Carlson to send him up to Beijing now that the Japanese had invaded China proper, not just Manchuria. Carlson met with Admiral Harry Yarnell, the commander-in-chief of America's "Asiatic" Fleet, who said, "It seems to me that you could be more useful here than in Peip'ing right now. Do you know anything about the language?"[4] Since Carlson had studied Chinese for two years (1933–1935) in Beijing he was assigned to the naval attaché's office in Shanghai. As a military observer, it was his job to explore the positions of the respective belligerents, and evaluate their capabilities and intentions while fighting. The GMD was not immediately receptive to his presence on the battlefield, but Carlson was eventually able to get a pass to move through the Chinese lines. He was present for the escalating battle for Shanghai, and his perspective was extremely similar to Stilwell's – the ordinary Chinese troops were good men fighting for their country with

[3] Evans Carlson, *Twin Stars of China*, New York: Dodd, Mead and Company, 1940, 2.
[4] Carlson, *Twin Stars*, 6.

inadequate weaponry and limited training. He was also able to travel to Nanjing, before returning to Shanghai and witnessing its fall to the Japanese.

As Carlson saw it,

Two important conclusions could be drawn from the battle of Shanghai: (1) China was determined to fight for her independence, and her army possessed the ability to absorb, as well as give, a terrific amount of punishment; and (2) the Japanese military machine, which had been regarded as formidable since its victory over Russia in 1904–05, was revealed as a third-rate army, when judged by European standards.[5]

Carlson went on to list a number of Japanese military deficiencies in doctrine, training, and performance, particularly inflexible leaders who lacked initiative, and formulaic tactics. Casualties were heavy on both sides, though much more so on the Chinese troops, as well as Chinese civilians. More to the point, Carlson heard about Communist Chinese victories over the Japanese in the north, based upon a different set of tactics and indoctrination.

This was the old Red Army of civil war days, and it had developed what was known as the Partisan type of warfare. Guerrilla tactics and strong popular support were said to be basic elements in this type of resistance . . . Perhaps the leaders in the north were . . . using Chinese initiative and ingenuity to neutralize the Japanese superiority in fire power and mechanized equipment.[6]

This was Carlson's justification for his journey to the north to gain intelligence of the Chinese Communists and their military methods in person.

Shortly thereafter, Carlson got the requisite permissions and traveled up to Yan'an, Shaanxi, where the Chinese Communist leadership was based. He met and talked extensively with the Communist leadership, accompanied Communist soldiers in action, and traveled throughout the area under Communist control. While Carlson was careful to avoid criticizing Chiang Kai-shek and the GMD, it was clear in his account that he truly admired the Communists. He was particularly struck by the equality in the army between the officers and soldiers. One of the main aspects of Communist mobilization, for both civilians and soldiers, was political indoctrination. It was crucial to explain to everyone why they were fighting in order to justify the hardships of resistance, and to create support for the political leadership.

Carlson was deeply troubled by America's continued economic support for Japan, even as the Japanese invaded China, and committed

---

[5] Carlson, *Twin Stars*, 31.   [6] Carlson, *Twin Stars*, 33.

atrocities on the Chinese people. As a serving marine, he was not allowed to express his opinions freely, so he resigned his commission on April 30, 1939, in order to take his case directly to the American people. The resignation of his commission (and subsequent reinstatement) irritated other marines, like Merritt Edson, who felt that Carlson constantly received special treatment and undeserved recognition. In addition to lecturing across America, Carlson wrote his account of his recent trip in China and time with the Communists, *Twin Stars of China*, to build support in America for helping the Chinese against the Japanese. In so doing, he became a very public figure, though one tainted for many by his association with the Chinese Communists. Carlson could not restrain himself from speaking his mind publicly, and he seemed not to under-stand, or at least accept, that Roosevelt and the American political lead-ership were well aware of the costs and benefits to continued commerce with the Japanese. Carlson saw the costs to the Chinese people, and felt that others, including the Roosevelt administration, did not see that the Japanese threat to China would eventually lead to war with the United States.

He returned to China in 1940 as a private citizen, where he saw that the Japanese were turning their attention toward America. Carlson was not alone in this, and it was glaringly obvious to many in the government, but Roosevelt was severely limited in 1940 and for most of 1941 in how far he could go in preparing the country for war with Germany and Japan. Although Carlson visited the White House and was in contact with Roosevelt, he seems never to have grasped the larger strategic issues in the Pacific, let alone globally. Nevertheless, he applied for, and received, reinstatement in 1941, to the disgust of many marines. Carlson was back in service as a major when the Japanese attacked Pearl Harbor.

The Marine Raiders

The ultimate responsibility for the creation of the Marine Raiders lies with President Roosevelt, and, for the most part, the concept was much more romantic than really effective in battle. Samuel Griffith, when asked whether Carlson played a "paramount" role in creating the Raiders, said,

No, I don't think it was paramount; of course he had something to do with it. But I can't say precisely who conceived the idea of the raider battalion, because at the time that this idea was still in the formative period, I was in England with Wally Greene – he and I were on detached duty from the United States with the British Commandos for about five months, that is during late 1941 and early 1942. In fact Wally and I were in Inverary, Scotland, when the Japanese hit Pearl Harbor, and when I came back from my trip which was in the spring of 1942, I was informed that Col. Edson (Merritt Edson), was forming a new organization, the 1st Marine Raider Battalion, in Quantico, and had asked for me as his executive officer, and so I was assigned as Col. Edson's executive officer early in April ...[7]

Griffith had been sent to England to bring back the lessons of the British Commandos, and, as it happened, he took them to Carlson, in California, first. "When I came back from England, my first job was to go out and spend a week with them. Carlson had asked for me to come out there and spend a week with him, and to conduct classes; I gave a half a dozen lectures in commando methods of training."[8]

What Griffith was unaware of was that Churchill had been trying to convince Roosevelt that he needed an American commando unit like that of the British. Churchill was enamored of his commandos, even though their actual military utility was, at best, marginal. Roosevelt was eventually convinced that he needed an unconventional unit that could launch raids into enemy territory for romantic reasons as well as the pragmatic need to strike back at the Japanese when he had very few viable military options. In real terms, the Raiders were a stopgap measure that functioned as conceived. It would take years to develop the conventional forces necessary to defeat Japan, but for reasons of morale something had to be done much sooner. That was why the Raiders were quickly established and sent into action, and also why they were abolished only two years after they were formed. The Raiders were formed under very specific circumstances, and through the intersection of very specific people.

Roosevelt had, in fact, proposed sending Carlson to Scotland along with Griffith and Greene, but Carlson demurred because he felt that his previous experience in Nicaragua and China had taught him all he needed to know about that mode of warfare. While Carlson was focused on commando operations, writing to officials and officers, including Joseph Stilwell, to see if he could be so employed, his refusal to undertake further formal training, even (especially?) in commando operations, showed a certain reluctance to subordinate himself to the military command structure.[9] His connection with the Roosevelts, father and son, allowed him to operate partly outside the chain of command.

The peculiar place of the marines in the American military establishment contributed to the unique circumstances that gave rise to the Raiders. If the marines were more than just a separate army subordinate to the navy, then what were they? From the marine command's

---

[7] Samuel Griffith interview transcript, 51.   [8] Samuel Griffith interview transcript, 52.
[9] George W. Smith, *Carlson's Raid: The Daring Marine Assault on Makin*, New York: Berkeley Publishing Group, 2001, 37.

perspective, the commando warfare Roosevelt was suggesting could be carried out by any marine unit. It wasn't necessary to create a new kind of unit, or a specialized "elite" group of marines. James Roosevelt wrote up Carlson's ideas into a proposal that, under his name, would be taken seriously in Washington. It was called "Development within the Marine Corps of a Unit for Purposes Similar to the British Commandos and the Chinese Guerrillas," and it called for all of the aspects of unit organization, like equality between officers and men, that Carlson had been so impressed by among the Chinese Communists. The connection between the commandos and Chinese guerrillas is telling, as it equates special operations and guerrilla fighting.

Since the president wanted a commando force, however, the question was what form it would take, and who would command it. Carlson was a marine, James Roosevelt was a marine, and the marines' history of flexible, small-unit deployments argued for a force made up of marines. Carlson was obviously closest to the concept, but he was by no means the most qualified man for the job. If the commander were a marine, the obvious choice would be Merritt Edson, the paradigmatic marine officer – skilled, brave, smart, also experienced and distinguished in warfare in Nicaragua, and already training marines in landing in inflatable boats. From a more special-operations perspective, the best choice was William "Wild Bill" Donovan, a man who had already won the Medal of Honor for his service in World War I, and who was heading the creation of a new intelligence service, which would later become the OSS, the precursor to the CIA. Even setting aside Donovan's other astonishing accomplishments, he was a friend and adviser of Roosevelt.

Marine Major General Holcomb was faced with a critical institutional problem. He could not prevent the creation of a commando force since the president wanted it, and he did not want the entire Marine Corps to become an unconventional appendage to the army. Donovan actually proposed a separate force that would aid clandestine activities and support local guerrillas. Unfortunately, from Holcomb's perspective, a separate force might take men from the marines, likely the best men, and absorb a marine function, thus diminishing the corps's range of responsibilities. In order to thread this bureaucratic needle, Holcomb needed to keep the commandos in the Marine Corps, but limit their scope. He kept the commandos away from Donovan by focusing them on the Pacific, rather than Europe, where Donovan was mostly concentrated. An underlying goal was either to take a position that would, by according with the president's wishes, allow the commando concept to be proven wrong, or to take credit for it if it were proven right. All of these factors, combined with the need to get the force up and running quickly, led to the redesignation of the battalion Edson already had in training as the 1st Raider Battalion, and the creation of the 2nd Battalion on the West Coast. Since Carlson, and James Roosevelt, also had to be employed, the 2nd Battalion was placed under them.[10]

One of the less obvious values of a small elite group of marines in the early stages of the war was the severe limitation available in materials, weapons, and transport. Even if the marines had been able to arm and train large numbers of men in 1942, they would have been hard-pressed to transport them to the Pacific. The raiding concept opened the possibility of striking with a small group of men at a vulnerable spot, and achieving a disproportionate effect with limited means. Paradoxically, they would, in fact, achieve a disproportionate morale effect, while the real military effect was minimal. The press was far more interested in the maverick, unconventional 2nd Raider Battalion, and in Carlson, than their activities warranted.

The most notable aspect of Carlson's Raiders was the gung ho spirit he promoted in training. In 1945, Carlson explained that

in Chinese the word *gung* meant "work," and *ho* meant "harmony." Thus, the phrase "Work in harmony" guided his operations. "Fundamentally, *Gung Ho* is an ideal, the ideal of complete cooperation and mutual trust and respect between men. *Gung Ho* is tolerance, cooperation and equality. It is democracy at work."[11]

In functional terms, this meant a great degree of equality between officers and men in the Raiders. Because Carlson could choose his men and train them as he saw fit, he was able to push them extremely hard and have them qualify with a wide variety of weapons.

His retrospective 1945 comments on gung ho, however, also contained an important political argument. While Carlson had curtailed his criticism of Chiang Kai-shek and the GMD in his 1940 writings, his advocacy for the Communists was clear. And like many pro-Chinese Communist Americans in the 1940s, he genuinely saw the Communists essentially as progressive, nationalistic, agrarian reformers rather than real communists. Carlson's gung ho was an expression of ideal American values projected onto the Chinese Communists. And arguably, to the extent that the word has been adopted into the Marine Corps and American culture, it has come to be an American expression, though not of its original meaning.

The Makin Raid

In the aftermath of the Japanese attack on Pearl Harbor, President Roosevelt felt it was important to strike back at the Japanese in some way as soon as possible. This led to the Doolittle raid on April 18, 1942,

---

[10] Wukovits, *American Commando*, 30–32.   [11] Wukovits, *American Commando*, 52.

where sixteen B-25 medium bombers launched from the USS *Hornet* and dropped bombs on Tokyo, Kobe, Nagoya, and Osaka. This symbolic act, with thirteen planes bombing Tokyo, and each of the other cities being bombed by one plane each, was a huge morale boost in the United States, and deeply embarrassed the Japanese military and government. The only real military value that could be claimed was that the demonstrated need to protect Japan's home islands diverted resources from other operations. While most of the planes crashed in China, except for one that landed in Vladivostok, the Japanese did not know where they had actually launched from. The raid also convinced the Japanese to shift their planned southern offensive, aimed at cutting Australia off from the United States, to an attack on Midway.

The 2nd Raider Battalion under Carlson, now a lieutenant colonel, and his executive officer, James Roosevelt, now a major, sailed to Pearl Harbor in early May. Part of the battalion was sent to Midway in anticipation of a Japanese invasion that never happened. With the Japanese defeat at Midway, the navy was preparing to take the offensive and seize Guadalcanal. The 1st Raider Battalion would take part in the early Guadalcanal operations (see below), leaving the 2nd Battalion to launch an attack from submarines somewhere else. Wake Island was initially considered, the Japanese having captured it on December 23, but it was too strongly held. The desire to launch an amphibious attack from submarines limited the possible targets. This was an example of how the urge to carry out a spectacular and innovative attack overrode real military considerations. The 2nd Battalion became a solution looking for a problem. The navy was stretched impossibly thin, and could only make available two submarines to transport the Raiders. Space limitations further constrained the number of men that could be employed to a total of 211 – not even two full companies.

The military justification for the submarine-launched raid would be to divert attention from Guadalcanal. After considering all of the possible targets, the logistical limitations, and the goal of supporting the Guadalcanal operation, they chose to attack Makin Atoll. It was believed that Makin was the right distance away to draw attention from Guadalcanal, and was lightly enough defended to be vulnerable to a small force. Every other consideration argued against the operation. They had very little information about Makin, there was almost no opportunity to train with the submarines and the inflatable boats, and most of the equipment was unreliable. The outboard motors on the boats, for example, tended to fail in heavy seas. To make matters even riskier, James Roosevelt was going to be part of the assault. Moreover, the 1st Marine Division invaded Guadalcanal on August 7, with the 1st Raider Battalion capturing nearby Tulagi as part of the operation.

Nonetheless, the 2nd Raider Battalion launched from Hawaii on August 8 amid great secrecy. The assault force launched from the submarines at 12 a.m. of August 17, planning to land on Makin Island, where a Japanese garrison estimated at seventy-one armed soldiers was based. Things went awry almost immediately with engine failure and more difficult seas than expected. The main force under Carlson reached shore about 5:13 a.m., after Carlson had consolidated the landing onto one beach due to the problems of getting the boats underway from the submarines. One twelve-man squad, under Lieutenant Oscar Peatross, had not received the order to change plans, and landed on the beach they had originally been assigned. Peatross successfully attacked the main Japanese headquarters, killing the garrison commander, and destroying the radios, though at a high cost in casualties, with three dead and two wounded. Still out of contact with Carlson, Peatross continued to follow the original plan and successfully returned to the submarines at dusk.

Carlson's attack initially bogged down in the face of Japanese resistance, but repeated Japanese counterattacks allowed the Raiders to kill most of the Japanese soldiers. He was fortunate in having the help of local islanders, who had been poorly treated by the Japanese. At 1:30 Japanese planes arrived, two of which were flying boats with reinforcements, which the Raiders shot up when they tried to land. The Raiders' real difficulties began when they tried to leave the island. Since the Japanese knew there were American forces on the island, they had to leave before a more determined counterattack was launched. Only ninety-three men were able to make it out to the submarines through the heavy surf on the night of the 17th, with several more boats making it out the following morning. Carlson was stuck on the island with exhausted men, most of whom had lost all of their weapons in trying to get through the surf, and the president's son. He didn't know how many Japanese soldiers were on the island, or where they were. A brief firefight with some Japanese troops that night convinced Carlson that there were still significant Japanese forces on the island, possibly reinforcements.

Although it was covered up afterward, Carlson wrote a surrender note and sent two men to take it to the Japanese commander (he didn't know who that was; the original garrison commander had been killed by Peatross's squad). They managed to hand it to a Japanese soldier, who was shortly thereafter killed by another Raider (two conflicting reports obscure the exact event). Carlson's attempt at surrender was thus inadvertently stopped, though the note was later recovered by the Japanese on the body of the dead Japanese soldier. Roosevelt was likely unaware of Carlson's attempt to surrender, and it became a controversial issue. Some people absolutely rejected the possibility that Carlson had tried to surrender, but, particularly in light of the recovery of the actual note, it seems most likely that he had done so. The accounts of other participants make it clear that he had done so, and Captain Coyte, who had actually delivered the note, was told by Carlson that Admiral Nimitz had told him to have the officers' reports rewritten, removing any mention of the note.[12]

At dawn on the following day the submarines came in as close as they could to the beach and Carlson was able to start getting the rest of his men past the breakers. Roosevelt was sent on one of the first boats out, relieving Carlson of a huge responsibility. Japanese planes appeared again before everyone had been able to leave the island, and the submarines had to dive. Carlson and the remaining men retreated back to the Japanese headquarters on the lagoon, having killed a few Japanese troops, and scrounged some supplies and weapons. They then cobbled together a larger raft, partly with native boats, managed to communicate with the submarines, and departed the island. The submarines returned to Pearl Harbor on August 25.

Carlson and Roosevelt were made into heroes in the press, but the mission, apart from the publicity, was at best unimportant and, more objectively, a costly failure. None of its stated military objectives were achieved, and its planning and execution were botched from beginning to end. Nine men had been accidentally left behind, and were later captured and executed by the Japanese. Nineteen Marines were killed in action, and two missing remain unaccounted for. Carlson stated that he had counted eighty-three dead Japanese bodies, and guessed that 160 had been killed. The actual number, based on Japanese documents, was forty-six killed, with an unknown number on the flying boats. While Carlson had performed well at some points in the battle, he also signally failed at others. The attack alerted the Japanese to the vulnerability of their outposts, which they then took precautions to protect. The raid served President Roosevelt's political and morale purposes, but it called into question the value of raids on peripheral targets of limited value. Despite that reality, Carlson and the Raiders were now celebrities.

The Long Patrol

The "Long Patrol," "Carlson's Patrol," or "Carlson's Long Patrol," was an extended operation on Guadalcanal by the 2nd Raider Battalion from November 6 to December 4, 1942. Following the United States' seizure of what became Henderson Field on Guadalcanal on August 8,

---

[12] Smith, *Carlson's Raid*, 153–157.

as well as some small nearby islands, both the United States and Japan began increasing their forces on the island. The Japanese 17th Army began arriving by August 19 to drive them off the island, and made an initial failed attempt on August 21, followed by a larger effort by 6,000 troops on September 12–14 to capture Henderson Field that was defeated at Edson's Ridge. The survivors of that attack regrouped to the west and were reinforced by a further 15,000 troops in the first weeks of October. United States forces had also reached about 20,000 by that time. A major, two-day Japanese attack on the perimeter of Henderson Field beginning on October 24 resulted in more than 1,500 Japanese killed to sixty Americans killed, and made absolutely no progress against the defenses.

As the Japanese force fell back from Henderson Field, part of it went east toward Koli Point. An American offensive in early November aimed at pre-emptively destroying Japanese forces near Koli Point before they could attack Henderson Field again. Carlson and the 2nd Raider Battalion were sent to get behind the Japanese and prevent them from escaping encirclement by the main attack. It was in this campaign that the Raiders' training would come into its own. Carlson's relentless marching, morale building, and emphasis on small-unit tactics proved, with native guides, regular resupply, and artillery support, extremely effective in the dense jungle. The Raiders harried the escaping 2,000–3,000 Japanese troops, destroying small units and pre-empting Japanese attempts to regroup as they fell back. That task was essentially done by November 15, and the Raiders' mission was shifted to finding and destroying the Japanese artillery that continued to shell Henderson Field. This was successfully accomplished by December 2, and what remained of the Raiders returned to Henderson Field.

Carlson claimed that his Raiders had killed or captured 488 Japanese soldiers during their thirty-one-day patrol, while losing sixteen killed, and seventeen wounded. The rigors of jungle campaigning, however, effectively destroyed the unit. Malaria, dysentery, ringworm, and jungle rot, in addition to sheer exhaustion and inadequate food, rendered the battalion unfit. Virtually all of their equipment was destroyed by weeks in the jungle. It was still a great success, and showed the value of rigorous training and highly motivated troops. Less clear was whether Carlson's Raiders had fought in guerrilla style, or simply in conformity with jungle warfare and difficult terrain.

The Long Patrol received an enormous amount of news coverage, as did Carlson and the 2nd Raider Battalion. This further exacerbated the hostility to Carlson, though whether it hastened the effective end of the Raiders as constituted by Carlson is arguable. The Marine Corps had grown vastly in men and equipment since the Raiders were formed, changing the nature of the way the Marine Corps and the navy, which had also grown, prosecuted the war. In March of 1943 the now four battalions of Raiders were placed under the new 1st Raider Regiment, which Carlson became second in command of, and the 2nd Battalion received a new commander. The new commander rapidly returned the battalion to standard Marine Corps practice, as did the Raider Regiment. Carlson was sent back to the United States in the summer to recover from all of the diseases he'd endured in the jungle, and also to end his experiment in organization and command. As if to confirm the belief in many parts of the Marine Corps that Carlson was a publicity hound, he was retained as an adviser to the movie *Gung Ho! The Story of Carlson's Makin Island Raiders*, which came out in December of 1943.

Carlson returned to the Pacific in November 1943 as an observer at the Battle of Tarawa. He was caught in a picture talking to Merritt Edson and the commander of the Tarawa assault, which was published with the caption "leaders of the assault." This infuriated Edson, who had been deeply involved in planning the assault, and who had long disliked Carlson. Carlson would also observe the Battle of Saipan in 1944, where he was wounded while trying to rescue a wounded man from the front line. In early 1944, the new marine commandant officially disbanded the 1st Raider Regiment, transforming it into the 4th Marines. The 1st, 3rd, and 4th Battalions were kept intact in the new regiment, and Carlson's 2nd was broken up. Carlson never commanded again, and retired in 1946. He died on May 27, 1947.

In the Marine Corps, Carlson left two legacies. The first, which was most important to him, was the idea of the gung ho spirit. While the term "gung ho" has changed considerably from his usage, the idea of political indoctrination, of explaining to the soldiers why they were fighting, has retained some currency. The second change he brought was the adoption of the ten-man squad composed of three three-man fire teams and a squad leader, as opposed to the previous eight-man squad.[13] Outside the Marine Corps, Carlson was the model of an unconventional, guerrilla, or raider warrior, who used indirect Chinese Communist methods to defeat larger Japanese forces. His successes, for the general public, were the successes of the Chinese Communists and Mao Zedong, which was also why he was anathema to much of the Marine Corps command. The

[13] This was, perhaps not surprisingly, very similar to Chinese Communist military practice. See Alexander L. George, *The Chinese Communist Army in Action: The Korean War and Its Aftermath*, New York: Columbia University Press, 1967.

effectiveness of Mao's methods would be reinforced after Carlson's death during the Chinese Civil War, and in the early stages of the Korean War.

The reverse of the marine coin was Merritt Edson, the "conventional" marine who created what would become the 1st Marine Raider Battalion. And while it is hard to argue that a man who won the Medal of Honor was overlooked, Edson certainly felt that Carlson had won more than his fair share of the accolades for fighting on Guadalcanal. Edson was not the romantic figure that Carlson was, and his career provides an important counterpoint to the idea that it was revolutionary, Chinese Communist methods that made the Raiders successful. While President Roosevelt and the press were invested in lauding Carlson, almost in spite of his Communist taint, the conventional marine success of Edson seems hardly to have counted.

Merritt (Red Mike) Edson

Merritt Edson (Figure 5.2) was born in Vermont in 1897, and, after a brief stint at college and in the National Guard, joined the Marine Corps Reserve in 1917. He went to France as a second lieutenant, but was not involved in combat. Back in the United States, he became a pilot

Figure 5.2 Merritt Edson. US National Archives

until a series of crashes convinced his superiors to revoke his flight status.[14] By 1927 he was a captain and, while serving in Nicaragua from 1928 to 1929, took part in fighting guerrillas that earned him a Navy Cross. In 1929 Edson returned to the United States, where he would teach tactics, and coach the Marine Corps rifle and pistol teams to several championships, among other duties. He always stressed marksmanship as a basic marine skill, something that carried over into his training of the 1st Raider Battalion. He believed that marines should be highly trained in all fundamental combat skills, including knife fighting.

In 1937 Edson, now a major, was posted to the 4th Marines in Shanghai.[15] He was there for only a month before the Japanese invasion of China reached Shanghai. The International Settlement, while officially off-limits to the Chinese and Japanese, was nonetheless caught between the two armies. Marine strength was soon bolstered for a defense that proved unnecessary; the Japanese captured the city on November 9 after determined resistance by Nationalist troops. At least at that time it appeared that Chiang Kai-shek would fight if he could. Edson's initial dislike of the Japanese was fanned by the victory parade they insisted on holding through the International Settlement,[16] followed by their "accidental" bombing of the *Panay*, a United States gunboat on the Yangzi. The Japanese apologized after the *Panay* incident, though all concerned were clear that it was more of reflection of Japan's awareness that it was not yet ready for war with the US than an act of real contrition. Edson reacted much as Stilwell had; he felt that it was an act of war.

Edson returned to the United States in 1939 just as the Marine Corps was beginning to expand in anticipation of war. Interestingly, one of the tasks he was assigned was writing a new *Small Wars Manual* for the Marine Corps (keeping in mind that "guerrilla" means "small war"). His experiences in Nicaragua and in troop training made him a good choice to suggest various innovations in tactics. Like many successful small-unit commanders at that time, he had new ideas of how small units should fight. "New" must be understood in the relative sense of what he had been taught before. Edson was a serious tactician and trainer with sufficient experience of guerrilla-style warfare and conventional warfare

---

[14] The reasons for Edson's crashes remain unclear. Doctors had noticed problems with his depth perception, but the exam results were inconsistent. Jon T. Hoffman, *Once a Legend: "Red Mike" Edson of the Marine Raiders*, Novato, CA: Presidio Press, 1994, 43–44.

[15] The 4th Regiment of Marines first went to Shanghai in 1927, though its designation changed to the "4th Marines" in the early 1930s. Hoffman, *Once a Legend*, 113.

[16] Edson watched and photographed the parade in civilian clothes. Hoffman, *Once a Legend*, 117. I have not had the opportunity to see if those photographs are part of the archive of several thousand in Edson's collection at the Library of Congress.

to offer alternative approaches to combat. His *Small Wars Manual* was in some sense immediately superseded by the new circumstances that the Marine Corps found itself in. Of course, his deep understanding of tactics and command would serve him and the Raiders well on Guadalcanal.

The expansion of the Marine Corps not only opened up positions for officers; it also threatened to degrade the quality of training of marines. Edson's long-standing commitment to marksmanship placed him squarely in the middle of debates over the extent of rifle training and which new rifle the Marine Corps should acquire. The long-running battles he fought to maintain or increase the number of rounds a marine would fire in training may well have exacerbated his predilection for emphasizing that the effectiveness of a marine was based upon his skill with a rifle. It also meant that when he had the chance to train a handpicked, elite unit, he would insist upon core skills. Ironically, that would make him "conventional" in comparison to Carlson's "unconventional" approach, when he got to carry out the sort of training he had been fighting for in opposition to general Marine Corps practice.

Edson's next command was critical to the future operations of the Marine Corps in the Pacific. He was appointed commander of the 1st Battalion, 5th Marines, which had just been given the responsibility of working out how to land small units amphibiously. The challenge was how to transfer troops from APDs – destroyers (D) converted to troop transports (AP) – to inflatable boats and then land them in the correct place on shore. Apart from the technical difficulties of carrying out a landing, the battalion had to be reorganized to fit its respective units aboard the available APDs. A further difficulty was that it was entirely unclear what the purpose of this unit was. Based on its unit size, the only function could be raids, reconnaissance, and feints.[17] The newly expanded 1st Marine Division was working on larger-unit landing exercises at about the same time.

As with any new operation, everything went wrong in training. The ships were poorly set up to house the troops, and bad weather made life and landings difficult. Edson was simultaneously training his officers and men, and figuring out how to carry out his unclear orders. Larger exercises showed Edson that there was a fundamental contradiction between the normal organization and equipment of a battalion and a battalion transported aboard the APDs. It was simply not possible for a battalion landing from an APD to be as heavily armed as a regular battalion (initially Edson's battalion was actually more heavily armed than a regular battalion) because of the limits of space on the ship. To add to the difficulties, his battalion was

---

[17] Hoffman, *Once a Legend*, 132.

supposed to land in inflatable boats, precluding larger pieces of equipment. Even heavy weapons like mortars created contradictions since any space or carrying capacity allotted to the weapons came at the cost of ammunition. A further problem was that it was impossible to guarantee that the smaller tactical units would land in the proper order or place, or that the headquarters element would be able immediately to take command once ashore.

Edson concluded that firepower had to be traded for mobility, since the battalion could rationally only function as light infantry once ashore. What he had envisioned was very much a guerrilla-style force that would carry out tasks to aid the main division objectives. On the more concrete level, he worked very hard to raise his men's training and physical conditioning. He believed strongly in practicing night landings, extensive marches, and marksmanship. His grueling training actually resulted in the death by heart attack of one of the captains under his command.[18] By the time of the attack on Pearl Harbor, he and his unit were finally in good shape, even though none of the issues respecting the organization or intended role of the APD battalion had been officially resolved.

It was at this historical moment that Evans Carlson's ideas, dovetailing with President Roosevelt's, led to the creation of the Marine Raiders, as discussed above. Edson's battalion, designated the 1st Marine Raider Battalion on February 12, 1942, was already operational, but caught between two stools respecting its function. On the one side was the conventional, amphibious assault function, where the battalion would be the first to assault a beach and establish a toehold, allowing heavier forces to follow, and on the other was a commando or guerrilla warfare function, where the battalion would launch raids. The nature of the original, vague instructions given to Edson had set up this contradiction from the beginning. It was the limitations of the APD transport and the rubber boats for insertion that created the material reality of what became the Raiders. Because their weaponry and equipment were severely limited, their role had to be similarly limited. Edson had responded by reconfiguring the organization and equipment of the battalion, and rigorously training his men. It would be Edson's organization that would form the basis for both Raider battalions. The major difference in training was that Edson felt that rigorous selection and training were sufficient to develop elite marines, and Carlson felt that political indoctrination, the gung ho spirit, had to be included as well.

Edson was ordered to send nearly 200 officers and men to the 2nd Battalion on the West Coast, to help it get started. The requirement was

---

[18] Hoffman, *Once a Legend*, 143.

the beginning of Edson's deep hostility to Carlson. To add insult to injury, not only did Carlson take a significant number of well-trained men, but he also rejected three-quarters of them as unsuitable. Those deemed unsuitable were then distributed to other units on the West Coast, rather than being sent back to Edson, as many of them desired. Edson angrily objected to the implication that he had somehow failed to train his men well, arguing that the rejection of those men was, in fact, a negative reflection on Carlson.[19] Given that some of those rejected men would later perform heroically in other units, there is likely merit in Edson's criticism of Carlson's selection methods. There was also no obvious difference in effectiveness between the 1st and 2nd Battalions. They were both elite units with extremely high *esprit de corps*. Indeed, the 1st Battalion was likely better trained in operating inflatable boats, night maneuvers, and knife fighting, all things that Edson relentlessly trained his men to do. The 2nd Battalion was almost destroyed during the raid on Makin by severe shortcomings in operating their inflatable boats and co-ordinating their attacks in the dark.

Most of the 1st Battalion shipped out for the Pacific on April 1, 1942, reaching American Samoa four weeks later. Edson immediately resumed intense training to bring his men back to condition after the long train and boat trip. The remainder of the battalion, under the command of his executive officer, Major Samuel Griffith, caught up on July 7. Between April and July 1942, the Japanese advanced onto Tulagi in the Solomon Islands chain, but the United States Navy crushed the Japanese Navy near Midway. The Battle of Midway, coming on the heels of the Battle of the Coral Sea, suddenly shifted the initiative in the Pacific War, blunting the Japanese naval offensive six months after the attack on Pearl Harbor. The destruction of four Japanese aircraft carriers still left a Japanese Navy superior in number and capability to the United States Navy, but it was a shocking and unequivocal defeat for the Japanese, unlike the Battle of the Coral Sea, which was conceivably a draw. It would take until the end of the year for new United States aircraft carriers to begin to address Japanese material superiority.

Midway also made island-based airfields even more important. The Japanese had begun to build an airfield on Guadalcanal that would have significantly expanded the range of Japanese reach in the Pacific. Despite limited naval and ground forces, it was nevertheless decided to attack Tulagi, Florida, in the Solomon Islands, and the airfield on Guadalcanal to push the Japanese back in preparation for eventual offensives against the Japanese base at Rabaul. Operation Watchtower was launched on

---

[19] Hoffman, *Once a Legend*, 157–158.

August 7, 1942; the Raiders would seize Tulagi. A rehearsal of the landing in late July revealed serious problems, which were only partially addressed in a second rehearsal before the real attack. The Raiders made it ashore on August 7 with some confusion, but fundamentally in good order. The defenders put up a strong resistance from prepared positions, effectively using snipers and camouflage to take a toll on the marines.

Tulagi was also the first experience the Raiders would have of Japanese night attacks. After dark, the Japanese would shout and make noise to unnerve their opponent, as Edson had seen in China, before launching an attack on the enemy line. One of the reasons for the initial noise making was to elicit a reaction from enemy machine guns, revealing their locations. The concept of the running charge at night, from the Japanese perspective, was to overwhelm their enemy with the moral force of their superior bravery.[20] While the first Japanese attack did briefly penetrate the Marines' line, it quickly petered out. A second assault ran directly into a strongly held position and failed. At the same time, the Japanese also infiltrated troops through the American lines. This sort of night fighting, dealing with both noisy assaults and infiltration, would become a regular part of the marine experience in the Pacific.

Unbeknownst to the Raiders, the defenders on Tulagi were members of the Imperial Navy's elite Special Naval Landing Force, the Japanese version of the marines. Both Edson and Griffith were surprised by the determination of the Japanese there, where the force that landed on Guadalcanal encountered mostly construction workers (though overly cautious leadership had managed to make very slow progress in the face of light resistance). Cleaning out the remaining Japanese forces on Tulagi entailed a great deal of grenades and dynamite to dislodge them from caves, and hand-to-hand fighting at night with knives and grenades. Night fighting with knives and grenades would later be a leitmotif of the defense of Henderson Field. Firing a rifle at night gave away one's position, and could temporarily blind you with the flash. Instead, men would try to roll or throw a grenade in the direction of any noise they heard. Anyone who was too close for a grenade had to be killed with a knife. Japanese infiltrators used knives in order not to alert the marines that they were there.

While the initial landings were successful, the United States did not have full control over the sea. The Japanese Navy sortied from Rabaul almost immediately and inflicted severe damage on the US surface fleet covering the landing forces. The surface fleet was forced to withdraw without dropping off all of the supplies or troops to maintain the newly

[20] Hoffman, *Once a Legend*, 179.

captured positions. This balance between Japanese and US forces would continue for the next six months, highlighting how precarious the American position was. The navy could not risk its remaining aircraft carriers to cover the positions except episodically, and the Japanese surface fleet was both superior in strength and based nearby. What became Henderson Field provided its own air cover for the force on Guadalcanal and the surrounding area during the day, but the Japanese Navy controlled the surrounding waters during the night. The stakes were too high for either side to easily yield control, because the airfield was such a crucial strategic position.

By late August it was clear that the Japanese were concentrating their efforts on Guadalcanal, and that there were insufficient US forces there to maintain the position. Edson, the Raiders, and the Parachutists were therefore transported over to Guadalcanal to reinforce the airfield. Edson immediately dispatched units to reconnoiter the nearby smaller islands. The greater threat was a Japanese buildup of forces on Guadalcanal in preparation for an assault on Henderson Field. The Americans had some intelligence from native scouts of the size and location of the Japanese force under Major General Kiyotaki Kawaguchi, but the higher command discounted either the numbers (2,000–3,000 men) or their condition. Edson was therefore allowed to launch a pre emptive amphibious raid on the village of Tasimboko (to the east of Henderson Field) in early September.

While the Raiders were somewhat hobbled by limited transport, they were fortunate in that the Japanese initially believed there was a much larger American force landing. The Japanese force defending the landing area fell back into the jungle toward Tasimboko. As Edson and Griffith led the Raiders inland, it was clear that the scouts' estimates were correct and that the Japanese force was well supplied. Without further support, however, and the likelihood that the Japanese would soon re-form and counterattack, they pulled out soon after capturing Tasimboko. The raid gained them accurate intelligence of the Japanese force, and allowed them to destroy some of their supplies. It confirmed that some 3,000 Japanese troops were preparing to attack Henderson Field.

Edson's Ridge

The limited manpower available meant that the entire perimeter sur-rounding Henderson Field could not be protected. The Americans would have to guess where the Japanese would attack. Edson reasoned, correctly, that the Japanese would attack from the south, and that the defenses would have to be established along a bare ridge in that area.

A large Japanese force would have to choose a clear enough area to allow its men to advance in an organized assault, which precluded the thick jungle areas along the water. It was certain that they would attack at night, because this could be co-ordinated with the frequent Japanese naval shelling from the water, and because the American planes based at the field could not provide air cover in the dark. Edson was unable at first to convince the base commander, General Vandegrift, that they should establish their main defenses along the ridge, however, because the general still believed that the Japanese were more likely to attack from the water. Edson therefore chose to achieve his tactical aim by deceiving his commanding officer. He asked if he could move his men to the ridge as a way to rest them after their recent raid. This request was granted, and while he and Griffith reconnoitered the area, he ordered his men urgently to entrench their positions. They did the best they could with inadequate tools, digging through the shallow layer of soil before hitting solid coral. To add to their difficulties, the Japanese suddenly began bombing the ridge. This at least confirmed that they were planning to attack through that area.

Vandegrift now agreed as to the likely direction of a Japanese attack and allowed for a redeployment of men for that eventuality on September 11. It was a tactically difficult position defended by an inadequate number of men. The ridge ran roughly from northwest to southeast, but the attack would likely come from the south. To the west of the ridge was the Lunga river, which provided some semblance of a covered flank, and there was a lagoon in between the river and the ridge that further divided the area into two defense zones. Edson's units were thus broken up by the terrain, with almost no defense in depth anywhere. A Raider company covered the position from the river to the lagoon; another Raider company filled the position from the lagoon to the ridge. To the immediate south and lining the ridge on its east side Edson placed the Parachute Battalion. Two more Raider companies were on the west side of the ridge, where they could bolster either the Parachutists on the ridge or the Raiders to the south. Edson himself was on the top of the ridge, close to the front, where he could direct the battle.

Kawaguchi's plan for the evening of September 12 was too complex for the terrain and conditions. His men had great difficulty moving through the jungle, their intelligence was poor, and the Americans knew they were coming. The attack on the first night was piecemeal but made some progress on the positions between the river and the lagoon. The marines there were forced to withdraw back north and toward the ridge. Still, the Raiders were familiar with Japanese night tactics, fought well, and did not collapse. Kawaguchi's men held their positions at daybreak, and began to consolidate and re-form their units. Edson was unable to dislodge them, and was forced to pull all of his units back to the north to establish a continuous front. There was no question that the Japanese would resume their attack the following night.

After an initial attack on the weak forces between the lagoon and the ridge on the 13th, the main Japanese attack focused on the ridge. The Parachutists and Raiders were forced back along the ridge, leaving a hole between the Raiders covering the space between the river and the lagoon, under Griffith, and those on the ridge. Kawaguchi did not exploit that hole, either because he was unaware of it, or because his main attack on the ridge appeared to be going well. While the Raiders and Parachutists desperately held their lines against repeated Japanese attacks, marine artillery and machine guns took their toll of the attackers. The fighting was brutal and desperate, lasting until the afternoon of the following day. Japanese soldiers had infiltrated throughout the American positions, and still held on throughout the morning. Daylight allowed American planes to strafe Japanese positions, forcing them back. When Kawaguchi finally retreated, he left nearly 700 dead, with the majority of the 500 wounded who retreated dying in the jungle as they fell back. The Parachutists suffered 128 casualties, by Griffith's count, and the Raiders 135, fifty-nine of whom were killed or missing in action.[21] It was a clear, but costly, victory, and it was not the end of the Japanese threat on Guadalcanal. The importance of the airfield had not changed, nor the central place of Guadalcanal in the struggle for the Pacific.

Edson had been promoted to colonel shortly before landing on Tulagi, and with the continuing expansion of the Marine Corps, colonels were needed for higher command. He was moved to command the 5th Marines, his old regiment based on Guadalcanal. The 5th were known to be a poor-performing regiment when Edson took over, but he really had no time to re-form or retrain the 5th before leading them into battle. With the arrival of the 7th Marines, the Americans were able to begin limited offensive operations against the Japanese. The first attempt went poorly, as the separate units ran into large numbers of well-prepared Japanese troops. Griffith, now in command of the 1st Raider Battalion, was wounded during the operation. Subsequent operations were more successful in pushing back the Japanese, but the American base at Henderson Field was still severely threatened. The Japanese Navy was still able to land more troops, and to continue naval bombardment.

---

[21] Hoffman, *Once a Legend*, 205.

It was not until November that the 5th Marines began to perform well. Continual campaigning, and the gradual removal of substandard officers, noticeably improved the regiment. By November the tide had turned in favor of America with greater naval control of the surrounding waters, and multiple airfields on Guadalcanal covering the land and sea. The 2nd Raider Battalion under Evans Carlson arrived on November 4, where it would carry out what was later known as "the Long Patrol." Edson and the 5th's time on Guadalcanal was over on December 9 as the army took over from the Marine Corps. He was subsequently awarded the Medal of Honor for his actions during the Battle for Lunga Ridge, which was more popularly known afterward as "Edson's Ridge."

In 1943 Edson became chief of staff for the 2nd Marine Division, where he was involved in planning the amphibious invasion of the Tarawa atoll, and was promoted to brigadier general and moved up to assistant division commander ahead of the invasions of Saipan and Tinian. After serving in the Pacific through the end of the war, he returned to the United States, retiring as a two-star general in August 1947. In civilian life, he became commissioner of the Vermont State Police, followed by president of the National Rifle Association (NRA) from 1949 to 1950, and executive director of the NRA to promote marksmanship in the United States. He was still working for the NRA when he committed suicide in 1955. The reason or reasons for his suicide were unclear, but his personal life had been unhappy even before World War II, and he had always had significant concerns over money. For all of his accomplishments as a leader in battle, his career in the Marine Corps had not progressed as he had wanted, and his civilian career was similarly a series of personal disappointments. He would have been even more disappointed if he had known how little he would be remembered after his death.

Jon T. Hoffman, Edson's biographer, noted, "In the first few years after his death, Red Mike maintained a place of importance in the hearts of fellow Marines," with a destroyer named after him, as well as a firing range, a building at Quantico, and a reserve center; however, "Despite these physical commemorations of Red Mike, modern Americans are only vaguely familiar with the man and his deeds. Several dictionaries of military biography take note of Carlson and Puller, but not Edson." His counterinsurgency fighting at the beginning of his career paled in comparison to the Vietnam War, and he gets no credit in discussions of guerrilla warfare despite his *Small Wars Manual*. He was not in quite the right places at the right times, so his accomplishments were over-shadowed by other, larger battles where he was not the commanding officer. "Only Red Mike's heroics on the Ridge generate some recognition, but he too often appears as a one-dimensional figure, the stereotypical leader who instills courage by screaming at his men about 'guts.'"[22]

Hoffman concludes, "History has not treated Edson kindly." Chesty Puller enhanced his reputation after World War II by fighting in the Korean War. Carlson had written a book about the Chinese Communists who went on to take control of China. Edson's skills as a tactician, steadfast courage, and organizational capabilities were extraordinary, but those were functionally ephemeral. Like many great soldiers, he was a giant during war, and comparatively less important during peace. But it is his contrast with Carlson and even Griffith that is most pronounced. Edson was perceived as a successful conventional warrior, not an innovator. His great success at Edson's Ridge was a conventional defense, rather than a guerrilla raid. Once he left the Raiders he was "only" a highly accomplished marine general. Perhaps if he had written his own account of Guadalcanal, or offered up his own ideas of warfare he might have had more influence. Yet it was his former subordinate, Griffith, who made a greater impact, and Carlson, whom he loathed, who was retained in historical memory.

Samuel Griffith

Samuel Griffith's life story ties together several strands of Chinese influence on the American military, and, through that, on American ideas of strategy. China connects Stilwell, Carlson, Edson, and Griffith, as did the war against the Japanese. Griffith studied Chinese in the same school in Beijing that Stilwell and Edson had, traveled in the same circles in China, and knew Carlson personally. Griffith was Edson's executive officer in the 1st Marine Raider Battalion, though they were not personally close. The one thing that truly distinguished Carlson and Griffith in their influence on post-World War II America was that both men published books that capitalized on their military reputations and reached a wider audience. Griffith was the least famous or decorated as a soldier, though his achievements and awards were extremely impressive, but it was his education and publication after the war which truly distinguished him. Yet without not only his own experiences, but also the publicly lauded exploits, Carlson, the results of the Chinese Civil War, and the Korean War, Sunzi, through Griffith's translation, would not have had the impact in the West that it did.

---

[22] Hoffman, *Once a Legend*, 414–415.

Figure 5.3 A young Samuel Griffith. US National Archives

Griffith was born in 1906 in Lewistown, Pennsylvania, making him about a decade younger than Carlson and Edson, and more than twenty years younger than Stilwell. In terms of age alone, he was better placed to have an impact after World War II, though Carlson died relatively young. Griffith went to the Naval Academy and studied electrical engineering, before serving in Nicaragua, China, and Cuba. He enjoyed living in Beijing from 1935 to 1938, though unlike Stilwell or Carlson he was more content to study during his posting there, rather than looking for reasons to go out into the countryside. He nevertheless spent a good deal of time as an attaché observing Chinese and Japanese troops. As he recounted in a later interview,

in fact when I was on this trip with the Japanese army, when Carlson and I later compared notes, during the days that I was up in Shansi, Carlson was very close with Red Army patrols to several of the places I was: he was within 15 or 20 miles of these places on those particular days.[23]

After his posting to China, he returned to the United States for further training, which he found quite boring.

---

[23] Samuel Griffith interview transcript, 50.

In 1940, Griffith was almost sent to Chongqing, which would have brought him into direct contact with Stilwell, were it not for a blunt assessment of the Chinese Nationalist government. In April of 1940,

I had received orders to go to Chungking, in China, and my wife was to come to Hong Kong. At this time, you remember, China was fighting the Japanese, and the government had been pushed out of Nanking and Hangkow, and had retreated to Chungking, and I was ordered to Chungking as an assistant naval attaché. I really don't want to go into this in too much detail because it could be rather embarrassing to some people. But at a dinner party I had made some remarks that an admiral who was present considered indiscreet, about Chinese prospects. I had been asked the question directly by him, what I considered Chinese prospects to be, and I said that I considered them to be next to zero, that I had no faith in the government in Chungking, that the Chinese armies were useless as they were then organized and led, the command was inept, the government was corrupt, and I didn't expect to see it last.[24]

As this anecdote demonstrates, disgust with the GMD was widespread among Americans who had lived in China. Had Griffith gone to China at that time, he likely would not have ended up in the Raiders or fighting in the Pacific.

Despite the efforts of a different admiral, Griffith was told that he was not to go to Chongqing. As he later discovered, there was a battle over whether or not to send him. Although he was disappointed at the time, in retrospect, however, "This turned out to be about the best break I ever got in my life, and I am deeply indebted to the admiral who at that time caused me all that embarrassment."[25] Griffith was subsequently sent to Great Britain to learn about the British commandos. His training, experience in Nicaragua and China, and excellent reputation made him an obvious choice for executive officer for Merritt Edson as he was developing the 1st Raider Battalion. Griffith served in that role through the Battle for Edson's Ridge, and then as commander of the battalion in the subsequent fighting on Guadalcanal after Edson was promoted. He was wounded while leading his men, but returned to command when he recovered.

After World War II, he commanded the 3rd Marine Regiment in Qingdao in China as part of the US occupation of north China from 1946 to 1947. He was subsequently at the Navy War College as a student and then teacher from 1947 to 1950. Griffith served as chief of staff of the Fleet Marine Force, Atlantic, from 1951 to 1952, and then on the staff of the US commander in chief, Europe, until his retirement in 1956. Upon

---

[24] Samuel Griffith interview transcript, 64.   [25] Samuel Griffith interview transcript, 64.

retiring, he went to Oxford University to pursue a D.Phil. in Chinese studies.

The details of Griffith's postwar career are central to this book, and will be discussed in great detail in later chapters. But the impact of his work as a scholar and translator cannot be understood without reference to the backgrounds of several notable American officers. Griffith gained credibility not just because of his own accomplishments, but also because the American public were well acquainted with Joseph Stilwell, Evans Carlson, and Merritt Edson. There were other famous American officers who were associated with China, but these three were also connected to Chinese ways of fighting, or to "unconventional" warfare. Moreover, they were part of the American victory over the Japanese, and the definitive emergence in the public mind of America as a Pacific power. At least in the American mind, the defeat of Japan was almost a solely American project. And it was Midway and Guadalcanal that the navy and Marine Corps turned the tide through superior strategy and fighting spirit.

6 The Captain Who Taught a General

Colonel Samuel Griffith (Figure 6.1) retired on March 1, 1956, and was promoted to the rank of brigadier general in consideration of his distinguished service in combat. He then became, in his own words, "The first grandfather ever to be admitted to New College, Oxford as a freshman."[1] His initial contact with Liddell Hart has not left a record, but a letter from Liddell Hart to Griffith dated August 20, 1957, extends an invitation to Griffith and Robert Asprey, "for lunch as suggested." Where or when this was suggested is unknown, but it was clearly early or at the very beginning of their relationship as Liddell Hart opens the letter, "Dear General Griffiths," showing both formality and his mistaken spelling of Griffith's surname. He also includes directions to his house, and that "we," presumably he and his wife, looked forward to meeting Griffith's wife.[2] It seems it was not until November that Liddell Hart realized he was spelling Griffith's name wrong, crossing out in pencil the extra "s" in both the opening and closing to a letter, a letter in which he got Griffith's rank wrong, "major general," even though he'd gotten it correct in the earlier letter. He acknowledged receiving Chapter 2 of Griffith's thesis, promising to get to it soon, and closing, "Our best wishes to you both."[3]

Chapter 2 had been accompanied by a letter dated November 12, in which Griffith said he was "in the middle of your 'Strategy – The Indirect Approach', and enjoying it indeed." Griffith addressed the letter to "Captain Liddell Hart," and Liddell Hart's return letter of the 14th opened with "Dear Griffiths." Griffith closed the letter, "my best regards to you and Mrs. Liddell Hart." Within the letter itself, he disagreed with some of Liddell Hart's discussion of the American Civil War in *Strategy: The Indirect Approach*. Griffith mentions that Robert Asprey helped him on the chapter, and that Asprey was pleased with a note that Liddell Hart had sent him. Liddell Hart had apparently agreed to read and comment

[1] Samuel B. Griffith, "Some Chinese Thoughts on War," *Marine Corps Gazette*, April 1961, 40–42.
[2] Liddell Hart to Griffith, August 20, 1957, LHA.
[3] Liddell Hart to Griffith, November 14, 1957, LHA.

Figure 6.1 Samuel B. Griffith II. Alamy Stock Photo

on Griffith's thesis: "I can't tell you how much I appreciate your advice and help on this work. I hope you will not find the task that you have so generously assumed too boring or demanding of your time."[4]

Sometime between November of 1957 and January of 1958, Griffith discovered a way to repay Liddell Hart's help. Liddell Hart had had, or had been planning to have, pipe cleaners sent from the United States. Griffith wrote to him in a letter dated only "Sunday," opening, "Dear Captain Liddell Hart," "About the pipe cleaners – it just happens that we had planned to go to Upper Heyford tomorrow, and I will certainly be glad to procure a supply and mail them off to you in the afternoon."[5] He also set out for Liddell Hart his plan for the eventual book that would come out of his doctoral thesis, and how he hoped Liddell Hart might help him in choosing what to include in the book,

---

[4] Griffith to Liddell Hart, November 12, 1957, LHA.
[5] The United States Air Force Strategic Air Command was located at RAF Upper Heyford, a former Royal Air Force base, located in Upper Heyford, Oxfordshire. By an interesting coincidence, the land the base was built on was originally owned by New College, Oxford.

As to the passages underlined in my Chapter II. These are the passages that I should want to put into my book. Naturally no publisher would take the whole thing, and my purpose in the underlining was to indicate first, everything Sun Tzu said, and second, the comments that I consider most relevant or most interesting. If you think that some of the comments I have underlined are <u>not</u> of sufficient pertinence or interest, I wish you would draw a line beside them and put a minus sign in the margin. On the other hand, if you think that some should be included which I have failed to include, you should indicate your feeling by putting a plus sign in the margin.[6]

From the very beginning of his doctoral work, Griffith was planning to produce a book, and he logically sought and accepted the help of the foremost strategist in the world, a man who wrote books for the general audience.

They were still on a somewhat formal basis in January when Griffith wrote again. Addressing him, "Dear Captain," Griffith assured him that he could keep him supplied with the desired pipe cleaners, though he was unsure of the "unit of fire."[7] This would become a long-running aspect of their relationship. Liddell Hart replied to "My Dear Griffith,"

I much appreciate your offer to maintain my supply of Dill's pipe cleaners – which will be very helpful. Although my rate of "fire" is rather high, as with tobacco itself, the scale of supply you suggest would amply keep up with the need, even when I am working at top pressure.

Liddell Hart was then working on his two-volume history of the tank, but hoped that Griffith and his wife would drive over when he was done with Chapter 3 of Sunzi. As was now usual, Liddell Hart and his wife both sent their good wishes to the Griffiths.[8]

Ten days later, Liddell Hart wrote to "Sam," thanking him for the Dill's pipe cleaners.[9] By March, not only was the flow of pipe cleaners continuing, but also everyone was on a first-name basis. Griffith wrote to "Basil" as he informed him that he was "going to inflict Chapter IV on you when we come out Sunday. It was so nice of you and Kathy to ask us, and we will of course pick up your friend."[10] Griffith would send another letter the following day with Chapter 4, in which he noted that there were only a few parts that he had red-lined for special note. Some handwritten notes at the bottom of this note (dated March 30), presumably by Liddell Hart, list "Gave him" with a few barely legible words including

---

[6] Griffith to Liddell Hart, undated letter, LHA, original emphasis.
[7] Griffith to Liddell Hart, January 13, 1958, LHA.
[8] Liddell Hart to Griffith, January 18, 1958, LHA.
[9] Liddell Hart to Griffith, January 28, 1958, LHA.
[10] Griffith to Liddell Hart, March 24, 1958, LHA.

"Ardennes" and "Patton," and "To Send him" which possibly includes "Sherman Foreword."[11]

The friendship between the two couples was now quite strong, as was the intellectual exchange between the two men. Griffith's adviser, Norman Gibbs, was also close with Liddell Hart; Gibbs and Liddell Hart are noted as driving off together from Paris on holiday in May of 1958.[12] After mentioning a piece that will be published in the *New Yorker*, and that he is enclosing Chapter 5 of Sunzi plus commentators, Griffith clarifies,

> Please note that this time I have underlined in red only what Sun Tzu said, and hope you will indicate marginally, as you have done in the past, the comments that you think particularly relevant or interesting. Again, I will not bother you with the notes, most of which only identify people, places, events, etc.
>
> I am trying to leave out of the full manuscript all comments that are purely repetitious, or paraphrases of Sun Tzu. This explains why every now and then there is a blank after a commentator's name. (All these omissions will be duly noted in the manuscript submitted to the University, but the Book Version will contain Sun Tzu plus only the comments you are so kindly helping me to select.

He adds that he was including a copy of Chapters 3 and 4, with only the Sunzi along with what he and Liddell Hart felt were the "cream of the comments."[13]

It is clear from Griffith's letter that he was translating Sunzi with the canonical eleven commentators. This would explain what would have been a slow pace of translation were he only rendering the main text. The small number of commentaries that made it into the published version of the translation at first seems quite random. On the contrary, the selected commentaries were chosen in discussion between Griffith and Liddell Hart. While it might make sense to exclude those commentaries that repeated what other commentaries said, or paraphrases of Sunzi, in the end, most of the commentaries, including those that were neither repetitious or paraphrases, were not included. This shows the level of engagement in the work on Liddell Hart's part especially in molding the thesis for eventual publication. Between the two of them, they cut out most of the commentaries from what would become the manuscript for the book. At a minimum, it was clear that neither man imagined the Sunzi

---

[11] Griffith to Liddell Hart, March 25, 1958, LHA.

[12] The relationship between Gibbs and Liddell Hart was not without friction. Robert Asprey later confided to Griffith that Gibbs had opposed Michael Howard's appointment to All Souls College because he saw him as Liddell Hart's protégé. Asprey to Griffith, October 15, 1969, BU archive.

[13] Griffith to Liddell Hart, May 23, 1958, LHA, original emphasis. The lack of closing parenthesis is in the original.

translation as an academic book. Clarity of presentation and ease of understanding were paramount in the book, if not in the thesis.

Their mutual focus was on the translation of Sunzi and the selection of commentaries. One of the areas either that Liddell Hart offered to advise Griffith on, or that Griffith most sought Liddell Hart's input on, was the rendering of Sunzi into English. Their discussions of the translation highlight three interlinked issues: accurate understanding of what the text meant, rendering that accurate understanding into felicitous and precise English, and placing Sunzi into the general discussion of strategy. None of these concerns were historical. Griffith and Liddell Hart assumed that there was a true or original meaning in Sunzi. As a classic, Sunzi had a single, correct meaning that could be discovered or excavated. They sought to choose a single line of interpretation among the commentaries, rather than demonstrate the disagreements among the commentaries. The commentaries were not seen as chronologically distinct moments in Sunzi interpretation. Like Griffith and Liddell Hart, each commentator sought to explain the parts of Sunzi that appeared to require further elaboration. The point of Griffith's translation was to present a clear, understandable, English version of Sunzi, not to render ambiguous classical Chinese passages into ambiguous English.

Griffith's reading of the classical Chinese text, as well as of the literary Chinese commentaries, was subject to his biases and those of his Chinese tutor, Wu Shih-ch'ang. As with any translator, even when the meaning of a text is completely and accurately understood, the choice of words and use of language used to render that meaning are filtered through the translating process and, in this case, the understanding of English military and strategic terms. Griffith was highly qualified to understand the English military and strategic terms, but he also believed that Chinese strategy was fundamentally different from Western strategy. The possible exception to that was Liddell Hart's work. As he had mentioned, he was actually reading Liddell Hart's *Strategy: The Indirect Approach* as he was translating Sunzi. Moreover, he had translated Mao Zedong's *On Guerrilla Warfare* (*Youji Zhan*) twenty years earlier, and would reaffirm the connection between Mao and Sunzi in his thesis and book:

Mao Tse-Tung has been strongly influenced by Sun Tzu's thought. This is apparent in his works which deal with military strategy and tactics and is particularly evident in *On Guerrilla Warfare*, *On Protracted War*, and *Strategic Problems of China's Revolutionary War*; it may also be traced in other essays less familiar to Western readers.[14]

---

[14] Samuel B. Griffith (trans.), *The Art of War*, Oxford: Oxford University Press, 1963, 45.

Yet Griffith went beyond the direct connection of Mao Zedong's writings or thought and Sunzi's *Art of War*; he asserted that Sunzi had been fundamental to Communist Chinese warfare from the beginning: "Some years before Chairman Mao took his writing-brush in hand in Yenan, Red commanders had applied Sun Tzu's precepts to their operations in Kiangsi and Fukien, where between 1930 and 1934 they inflicted repeated defeats on Chiang K'ai-shek's Nationalists whose object was to exterminate the Communists."[15] Since Griffith was well aware that the Nationalists had been armed and trained by Western military advisers both before and during World War II, he implies that the true Chinese way of warfare used by the Communists based on Sunzi was superior to Western strategy. It was not that Mao had injected Sunzi's principles into the Red Army by his military writings, but rather that those principles were available and practiced in China before him. It was only in 1933–1934 that the Communists were driven out of Jiangxi by Chiang Kai-shek's Fifth Annihilation Campaign, sending them on their Long March to safety in Yan'an. As Griffith describes it (after pointing out that the Nationalist campaign had been organized by German advisers), Mao then took to writing up the lessons of the Communist defeat.[16] The defeat was a failure to follow Chinese, Sunzi-based strategy, rather than a success of Chiang Kai-shek's army.

China's recent history, some of which Griffith had been part of, was marked by the defeat of a series of conventional, Western-style armies by less well-equipped Chinese Communist forces. By the time Griffith was writing his thesis, Communist forces had survived the Japanese Army's occupation of China, defeated Chiang Kai-shek's Nationalists in the Chinese Civil War, and fought the United States-led UN forces in Korea to a stalemate. From his point of view, the Communists were doing something right strategically or operationally that allowed them to overcome Western military methods. It is worth emphasizing here Griffith's own background as an unconventional soldier. Eliding the significant differences between guerrilla and mobile warfare, the Chinese Communist approach was obviously not to *directly* engage Western or Western-style forces, making their approach *indirect*.[17] And

---

[15] Griffith, *The Art of War*, 45.

[16] Mao and his faction blamed the CCP defeat on Otto Braun, the CCP's German military adviser. The politics of the assignment of blame is, of course, quite complicated.

[17] The issues of direct and indirect approaches applied most strongly to the higher levels of fighting. At the tactical level, a unit might try to attack the flanks and rear of an enemy, but more likely would, at some point, have to directly attack that enemy. Hence, in Korea, there were many instances of the People's Liberation Army, the name of the Red Army after the conquest of China, launching "short attacks," where large numbers of Chinese soldiers tried to overwhelm UN troops in frontal assaults.

since that approach, so fresh in his mind from reading and talking to Liddell Hart, used by the Communists, was directly connected back to Sunzi, Griffith tended to see reflections of that indirect method in Sunzi. This is not say that Griffith's translation was wrong, only that in unifying the influence of the commentaries into clear English, as almost every translator of Sunzi has done,[18] he chose wording consistent with Liddell Hart's indirect approach. Just as he saw Sunzi in Mao, he saw Mao in Sunzi, and even there, a particular view of Mao and Communist Chinese warfare. Griffith may well have held the view, widely prevalent in the West until recently, though likely still not entirely gone, that the Chinese Communists won the Chinese Civil War with guerrilla tactics. He certainly believed that Mao was the strategic brains behind the Communist success. Ironically, while Mao's military writings were instrumental in creating the myth of Mao's military genius, he was, in fact, much less involved in directing the military aspects of the battles against the Nationalists. For a number of political and propaganda reasons, the Communist leadership promoted Mao's image as a great political and military leader. This downplayed the critical leadership of military commanders like Zhu De and, particularly in the civil war, Lin Biao. It was Lin Biao's brilliance during the Manchurian campaign that defeated the Nationalists in Manchuria, leading directly, and unexpectedly quickly, to the collapse of the Nationalists.[19] It is, however, unlikely that Griffith was aware of these aspects of the Chinese Communist successes.

Both Liddell Hart and Griffith were also interested in establishing Sunzi in the context of Western strategic thought. This was outside the historical context of either China or the West. Griffith believed that Liddell Hart was much less interested in the explanatory notes. This may well have been not because Liddell Hart was uninterested in the identification of "people, places, events, etc." but because he was not in a position to advise or comment on those matters of Chinese history. Griffith invested considerable work in the intellectual and military background to Sunzi. The field of strategic thought was, however, a Western realm even though neither of them recognized it as such. The Sunzi translation had to use Western strategic terms that had automatic, specific

---

[18] The most notable exception to this is John Minford's translation of Sunzi that includes most of the commentaries. John Minford (trans.), *Sun-tzu The Art of War*, New York: Penguin Books, 2002.

[19] Harold Tanner, *The Battle for Manchuria and the Fate of China: Siping, 1946*, Bloomington: Indiana University Press, 2013; Harold Tanner, *Where Chiang Kai-shek Lost China: The Liao–Shen Campaign, 1948*, Bloomington: Indiana University Press, 2015; Christopher Lew, *The Third Chinese Revolutionary Civil War, 1945–49: An Analysis of Communist Strategy and Leadership*, London and New York: Routledge, 2009.

implications for a Western reader. In making the translation felicitous, Griffith also introduced shades of meaning into the text that aligned or opposed Sunzi to the canon of Western strategic thinkers.

Of course, the second area that Griffith and Liddell Hart were mutually concerned with was Sunzi's relationship to Clausewitz. Liddell Hart's own struggles with Clausewitz effectively narrowed the question of Sunzi's place in Western strategic thought to whether Sunzi agreed with or opposed Clausewitz. Both Griffith and Liddell Hart were well read in the other works of the Western strategic canon, but the question they faced in the late 1950s and early 1960s was Sunzi's relationship to Clausewitz. One of the most tantalizing questions was whether Clausewitz had read Father Amiot's Sunzi translation. It was certainly possible.

Consequently, Griffith wrote to Professor Doctor Werner Hahlweg at the University of Münster on July 13, 1959, "Both Captain Liddell Hart and Mr. Peter Wachter-Paret have suggested that I write you in relation to a question that has arisen in my mind concerning the possible sources of some of Clausewitz' thoughts on the theory of war."[20] Hahlweg was the editor of the 1952 edition of *On War*, which reprinted the original text, and was, as a consequence, appointed to edit a two-volume collection of Clausewitz's work.[21] He was regarded as the foremost authority on Clausewitz when Griffith wrote to him. After introducing himself and his thesis project, and sketching out the history of Amiot's Sunzi translation, Griffith came to the point:

Certainly this must have been widely read in military circles in Europe, and while I feel Clausewitz must have seen it, it is only a conjecture. I wonder if you know what Clausewitz did read? Probably this Amiot translations was [sic] in the library at Berlin while he was there? Or he may have read it while a prisoner of the French during part of 1806?

Is there anything known of the contents of Clausewitz' own professional library? Or by chance did he, in correspondence, ever mention Sun Tzu, or refer to any Chinese military writer?[22]

If Professor Hahlweg replied, his letter is no longer available. Griffith does not mention a response or lack of response from Hahlweg. He did, however, include a copy of his letter to Hahlweg in a letter he wrote to Liddell Hart. Liddell Hart said that he would be interested in his reply, but, "To me it seems doubtful whether Clausewitz had Sun Tzu's 'Art of

---

[20] Griffith to Hahlweg, July 13, 1959, LHA.
[21] Peter Paret, review of Werner Hahlweg (ed.), *Schriften-Aufsätze-Studien-Briefe (Volume II, Parts 1 and 2)* by Carl von Clausewitz, Göttingen: Vandenhoeck and Ruprecht, 1990, *Journal of Military History*, October 1, 1991, 55/4, 536–537.
[22] Griffith to Hahlweg, July 13, 1959, LHA.

War'. For Clausewitz's own 'On War' would have been a better book if he had. It could hardly have failed to have had an influence on his thought." He did press Griffith on the question whether Amiot's translation was the first into a European language, as well as why he'd pushed Sunzi's likely date to *c.* 350 BCE instead of the previously accepted 500 BCE.[23]

Griffith spent considerable effort in tracking down Sunzi's first appearance in Europe, and the effects of Sunzi on European military thought. As can be seen from Liddell Hart's question, and prompting of Griffith, it was of great interest to Liddell Hart as well. Griffith responded on August 3, in a detailed five-page letter, laying out the state of his knowledge about translations into Western languages, and the evidence for Sunzi's later date. Most of that information would later appear in the published version of the translation. As far as Griffith was able to tell, Amiot's translation was, indeed, the first into a Western language.[24] No earlier translation has been discovered in the intervening years to overturn Griffith's evaluation. He was unable to prove that Amiot's translation had any effect on strategic thought in Europe, and neither had any of the translations up until Griffith's. Either Sunzi's ideas were too similar to European works after being fit into the European intellectual framework, or they were too exotic in origin to be accepted. The intellectual conditions were not right to absorb a Chinese work on strategy until the 1960s. Liddell Hart seemed to be so taken with Sunzi that he found it hard to believe it hadn't had any intellectual impact. As Adam Parr showed, however, Sunzi via Amiot's translation was both more profound and less apparent than he could have imagined.

Liddell Hart's offhand query regarding Griffith's change in the dating of Sunzi elicited several pages of historical notes, capped by Griffith mentioning,

I have a long letter signed by Doctor Kuo Mo-jou, who is President of the Academia Sinica in Peking in which he adduces some of the reasons I have given in support of his contention that the book was written in about 350 B.C. As a matter of fact, this has been suspected ever since the Sung Dynasty, but classical Chinese scholars only dared mention it and did not really attack the traditional view until the last twenty or thirty years.

He had originally accepted the traditional, earlier date but come to change his mind. As to the possibility that *The Art of War* was in fact written by Sun Bin, Griffith thinks it is possible, given that it would not have been uncommon for someone to attribute a book to an earlier writer.

[23] Liddell Hart to Griffith, July 16, 1959, LHA.
[24] Griffith to Liddell Hart, August 3, 1959, LHA.

The real key for both Griffith and Liddell Hart, and the reason why Liddell Hart raised the issue of the later dating of the text came down to precedence and legitimacy: "None of the foregoing detracts from the worth of this classic, which remains the first coherent exposition of war that has been written and which still antedates Clausewitz by almost twenty-two hundred years – and as you suggested is a better piece of work."[25] Both men had reached intellectual agreement about the value of Sunzi, particularly in relation to Clausewitz. Just as significantly, both simply accepted Clausewitz as the paradigmatic Western strategist with whom to compare Sunzi. The champions of their respective "cultures," using the term here advisedly, were used to represent the traditions of strategic thought in the West and China in their entireties. Sunzi was classical, having set out the principles of strategy and war in China, and Clausewitz was modern, reflecting and reducing warfare in the West to an unsophisticated test of strength on strength.

Liddell Hart's *Strategy: The Indirect Approach* had presented Western examples of the indirect approach in warfare. One of the main criticisms of Clausewitz was that his stress on the direct clash of armies in a climactic battle blinded European generals to any other possible strategic goal. European strategists under Clausewitz's influence believed that campaigns and the fates of nations were determined by great battles. They discounted the possibility that any other operational goal would produce significant military, and hence political, results. By contrast in China, not only had Sunzi early on laid out the superiority of the indirect approach, but Chinese strategists had followed that without break through the twentieth century.

Griffith and Liddell Hart had functionally constructed a clash between classical China and the modern West. In both cases, the long histories of military writing were ignored, though Griffith did include a translation of Wu Qi, the second most important classical Chinese strategist. The issue of the commentators, however, highlighted a very significant difference between the Western and Chinese intellectual traditions of military thought. There was no tradition in the West of commentary on military texts. Later writers might refer to earlier ones, but even canonical works like Vegetius were not the subject of a commentarial tradition. In China, by contrast, beginning in the third century CE with Cao Cao, educated men directly addressed the problems of understanding Sunzi. Sunzi was, in this sense, truly a "classic" that could only be discussed, but not surpassed. No one in Chinese history discounted Sunzi among military thinkers, even if some, most notably the Kangxi Emperor, felt there was little practical value to reading strategists, or even canonical histories.[26]

---

[25] Griffith to Liddell Hart, August 3, 1959, LHA.
[26] See Spence, *Emperor of China*, 22.

Griffith was translating the thirteenth-century compilation of Sunzi with eleven commentaries. There were subsequent commentaries, but the thirteenth-century edition functionally became the canonical text with commentaries. As with the text of Sunzi itself, those commentaries were flattened out historically into a synchronic explanation, rather than a diachronic development of different thinkers in different times. Griffith repeated his explanation to Liddell Hart for his selection of comments:

You will recall that everything I have underlined in numbered paragraphs is SUN TZU. All his words of course go into the book. The additional under-lining is what I personally think is the best of the comments – either because they are explanatory (where explanation is needed) or because they seemed to me interesting, or amusing (sometimes both), or because they are as appropriate to affairs now as when they were written so many hundreds of years ago.

After some discussion of the notes, which he was not sending to Liddell Hart, he continued on the topic of the commentary,

If you recall, what you were good enough to do before was to make a light check in the left margin where you agreed with my selection of comments for inclusion in the book, and an "X" where you did not. Additionally, you indicated other not underlined comments with a checkmark when you thought them particularly apt, and worthy of inclusion.[27]

Griffith's instructions and his process with Liddell Hart were consistent from the beginning of their discussions. Liddell Hart indeed followed this, writing Griffith on September 29,

Since I wrote to you last I have unearthed your Chapter XIII of the Sun Tzu translation, which got buried under a pile of stuff that poured in while I was away. I found it of great interest and return it herewith, having marked with plus or delete signs the passages which seem to me worth adding, not worth adding, or borderline in either respect.[28]

A letter from Griffith on November 7 mentioned Liddell Hart's marking up of the text. The same letter also says,

As I know how busy you are, and how kind you are to everyone, I really feel rather hesitant about sending on any more of this Sun Tzu. I do, however, send this chapter because it is relevant to so many of your own thoughts. I am sure you will enjoy reading Verses 31, 32, 34, 35, 36, 37; also Verses 5, 6, 15, 16, 17, 22 and 23. This is one of the best chapters in Sun Tzu.[29]

---

[27] Griffith to Liddell Hart, August 28, 1959, LHA.
[28] Liddell Hart to Griffith, September 29, 1959, LHA.
[29] Griffith to Liddell Hart, November 7, 1959, LHA.

Due to the inconsistencies of editions, it is not immediately clear which chapter of Sunzi Griffith sent Liddell Hart.

Liddell Hart's letter of November 12 clarifies the matter:

I have now squeezed time to go through your latest chapter (VII) on Maneuver/ (I hardly recognized the term in your way of spelling!) – and fully agree with you that this is one of the best chapters in Sun Tzu. I return it with my markings, and also your notes, which I was interested to see.

   I am so behindhand with urgent and overdue work that I <u>ought not</u> to go on turning aside to read your remaining chapters – but I am so interested in them that I cannot forebear [*sic*] to do so.[30]

Quite offhandedly, Griffith and Liddell Hart hit on the core of Sunzi's resonance with Liddell Hart's work, or, seen another way, the greatest influence of Liddell Hart's strategic thought on Griffith's translating. In Griffith's translation, Chapter 7 is titled "maneuver," a rendering that is not supported either by the actual title or by the contents of the chapter itself.

Chapter 7 and the Matter of Interpretation

The Chinese title of the seventh chapter of Sunzi is "Junzheng" (軍爭). *Jun* is the word for an army in general, or a military unit of a specific size. *Zheng* means to contend or struggle. In modern Chinese, the word for "war" is *zhanzheng* (戰爭), which might literally mean "fighting and contending." John Minford renders *junzheng* as "The Fray," Victor Mair as "The Struggle of Armies," but, quite interestingly, Lionel Giles uses "Maneuvering." Griffith was well aware of the literal meaning of the title, however, explaining in a footnote, "Lit. 'struggle' or 'contests of the armies' as each strives to gain an advantageous position."[31] Mair accepts this view of the general thrust of the chapter: "The main topics of this chapter are how to forestall the enemy by securing the conditions for victory and by setting up a superior situation from which to do battle. Essentially, it is a question of jockeying for advantage." While this partially explains the contents of the chapter, it narrows the conception of what is being discussed to the movement of armies and downplays those passages that do not fit the question of maneuvering an army with respect to another army.

Chapter 7 presents a collection of strategic anecdotes mixed in with both sides of operational or tactical circumstances. For example, early in the chapter Sunzi suggests tempting one's opponent with advantage, and

---

[30] Liddell Hart to Griffith, November 12, 1959, LHA, original emphasis.
[31] Griffith, *The Art of War*, 102, fn. 1.

later in the chapter says that in waging war one does not take troops dangled as bait. Much of the chapter is taken up with how to control one's own troops, provide their supplies, maintain order, and make sure troop morale is high when attacking the enemy at a time when his troops' morale is low. It is only by stripping out all of these passages in a fairly short chapter that the issue of maneuvering an army becomes central.

There are a few critical passages that highlight the way Griffith translated certain terms in keeping with Liddell Hart's strategic vision. The first one is passage 3: "Thus, march by an indirect route and divert the enemy by enticing him with a bait. So doing, you may set out after he does and arrive before him. One able to do this understands the strategy of the direct and indirect." Giles: "Thus, to take a long and circuitous route, after enticing the enemy out of the way, and though starting after him, to contrive to reach the goal before him, shows knowledge of the artifice of deviation." Mair: "Therefore, take a circuitous route to reach the enemy, tempt him with advantages. Though I set out after him, I reach my destination before him. This is the planning of one who knows how to make the circuitous straight." Minford: "Take a roundabout route, and lure the enemy with some gain; Set out after him, But arrive before him; This is to master the crooked and the straight."

The second critical translation comes in passage 16: "He who knows the art of the direct and indirect approach will be victorious. Such is the art of manoeuvring." Giles: "He will conquer who has learnt the artifice of deviation. Such is the art of maneuvering." Mair translates this same passage: "He who is the first to know the planning of how to make the circuitous straight will be victorious. This is the method of the struggle of armies." Minford: "Victory belongs to the man who can master the stratagem of the crooked and straight."

At first, Griffith's translation does not appear to be a significant stretch from the underlying terms of "crooked" and "straight," particularly with respect to the chapter's larger argument. However, when coupled with his chapter title, and the deeper implications of the terms "direct" and "indirect" in the Western context, a passage that was somewhat similar to Liddell Hart's concept of maneuvering becomes exactly consonant with that concept. The ambiguities of the underlying text open up the broad variation demonstrated in the four translations of the same passage, variations that could be multiplied by listing other translations. Only Griffith reads *yu* 迂 as "indirect," drawing from the concept of an indirect route, rather than one of the meanings of the term "circuitous," or "winding." Mair's translation is much closer to what would appear, in light of the rest of the chapter, to be the real meaning of the passage. Someone who knows how to "plan" can make the circuitous straight. The term *ji* 計, which Mair renders as "plan," can also mean "to calculate," either of which would be consistent with the focus in the chapter on effectively moving an army on campaign. Someone who knows not only how to plan or calculate, but also the terrain and the nature of armies on campaign, can make an apparently less direct route the faster route. The faster march between two places may not, in fact, be a straight line. A knowledgeable commander would see that the circuitous route is faster, and hence "straight," or could clear his own path by luring his opponent out of the way.

Chapter 7 also repeats the core Sunzi concept that, "war is decided by deception," or variations of that phrasing. In Chapter 1, translated by Griffith as "Estimates," the same term *ji* 計 discussed above, Sunzi states, "War is the way of deception," or, for Griffith, "All warfare is based on deception."[32] Many earlier concepts are repeated in Chapter 7, raising the question of why both Griffith and Liddell Hart thought it a particularly good chapter. Chapter 1 discusses in much greater detail all of the topics in Chapter 7, but perhaps they also felt that Chapter 1 was good. At least in their letters, however, they do not stress the importance of deception in warfare. While it is impossible to explain a lack of discussion, it may well have been that since Liddell Hart's focus was generally on speed and maneuver, he was less interested in issues of deception.

Griffith does not, in fact, use the terms "direct" and "indirect" anywhere else in the main text of his translation (though he does in the notes; see below).[33] The obvious reason for this is that Sunzi does not use those terms or concepts. Chapter 7's discussion of the circuitous and straight was really the closest point, and Griffith stretched to make the most of it. That said, in Chapter 5, "Position *shì* 勢," which Griffith, following Giles, translates as "energy," he does bring up "direct" and "indirect" in a footnote. The passage reads, "That the army is certain to sustain the enemy's attack without suffering defeat is due to the operations of the extraordinary and the normal forces." The footnote to that passage then says,

The concept expressed by *cheng* (正), "normal" (or "direct") and *ch'i* (奇), "extraordinary" (or "indirect") is of basic importance. The normal (*cheng*) force fixes or distracts the enemy; the extraordinary (*ch'i*) forces act when and where

---

[32] Li Ling feels that the original title of the chapter was simply Ji 計, not Shǐji 始計, the "shi" being a later addition, Li Ling, *Sunzi Yizhu*, Beijing: Zhonghua Shuju, 2012 (2nd ed.),1.

[33] Griffith would have closely connected Sunzi to Liddell Hart if he had used "direct" and "indirect" more freely, but he would also, perhaps, have made his own translation more similar to that of Giles. There is no direct evidence that Griffith was concerned about this, though it is hard to believe that he wasn't aware of that his translation would be compared to that of Giles.

their blows are not anticipated. Should the enemy perceive and respond to a *ch'i* manoeuvre in such a manner as to neutralize it, the manoeuvre would automatically become *cheng*.[34]

Unfortunately, *zheng* and *qi* do not mean "direct" and "indirect," even, or particularly, with respect to maneuver. Slightly further into the chapter it continues, "Generally, in battle use the normal forces to engage; use the extraordinary to win. Now the resources of those skilled in the use of extraordinary forces are as infinite as the heavens and earth; as inexhaustible as the flow of the great rivers." Sunzi's point is that the components of an army should shift between the regular and irregular as circumstances dictate. Benjamin Wallacker's linguistic connection between *zheng* (正) "regular" and *zheng* (征) "fixing," "spiking," yields a more convincing explanation of "fixing and toppling" for *zheng* and *qi*.[35] The regular and irregular forces are not inherently so, they are only regular and irregular based upon their positions relative to the enemy forces. This is consistent with other places in Sunzi where good generals are supposed to respond to what the enemy does, or conform to the enemy's formation. With respect to tactics, this is a description of trying to get around an opponent's flanks to defeat him. Should he turn and strongly defend that flanking attack, then what was originally the frontal attack itself might become a flanking attack. These qualities are relative to each other, and to the enemy, rather than inherent in the forces employed. This is also consistent with the chapter itself, which concerns itself with position. One tries to achieve an advantageous position, but that is never static because things are always changing. It is also always relative to the enemy.

There are only two other places in Sunzi that show some similarity to Liddell Hart's thought, near the end of Chapter 6 (empty and solid), and near the beginning of Chapter 8 (nine changes). Close to the end of Chapter 6, which Griffith translates as "weakness and strength," it says,

Now an army may be likened to water, for just as flowing water avoids the heights and hastens to the lowlands, so an army avoids strength and strikes weakness. And as water shapes its flow in accordance with the ground, so an army manages its victory in accordance with the situation of the enemy. And as water has no constant form, there are in war no constant conditions.

It was this likening an army to water which prompted Sir John Duncan to write to Liddell Hart in 1927. Duncan saw a similarity between this passage and Liddell Hart's "expanding-torrent" idea. There are real similarities to Liddell Hart's expanding torrent, but Sunzi's observation

---

[34] Griffith, *The Art of War*, 91.
[35] Benjamin E. Wallacker, "Two Concepts in Early Chinese Military Thought, *Language*, April–June 1966, 42/2, 298.

does not pair particularly well with Liddell Hart's advocacy for operational and tactical movement after forcing a breech in the enemy line.

At the beginning of Chapter 8, translated by Griffith as "the nine variables," Sunzi makes an important strategic and operational point: "There are some roads not to follow; some troops not to strike; some cities not to assault; and some ground which should not be contested." This almost seems like a further refinement of his much-misunderstood dictum in Chapter 3: "The worst policy is to attack cities. Attack cities only when there is no alternative."[36] Sunzi is actually making two very different points, though Liddell Hart would likely have agreed with both. The first point is that there are some operational or tactical targets that would be so costly to pursue that they would not be worth the gain. One might even use the example of World War I to prove that exact point. Rather than calculate the costs and consequently reject offensives against heavily defended positions, the generals instead focused on the benefits of taking a position and downplayed the costs, resulting in strategically pointless slaughter. Liddell Hart was very much reacting to that evaluation of World War I in his advocacy of avoiding strongpoints.

The second point made by Sunzi concerning attacking cities is often taken as a prohibition against attacking cities. Sunzi's point was actually that of all the ways to succeed in a struggle for power between states, attacking cities was the least good. As he describes it, the best way to bend an enemy to your will is to do so without the costs of an actual armed conflict. The most skillful and least costly technique is to defeat an enemy's plans in the planning stage. This is not to say that one does not use violence to defeat those plans, only that one changes the conditions that would have allowed those plans to proceed before they commence. If one cannot disrupt the planning stage, diplomacy should be used to undermine his alliances. Failing all of those possibilities, one attacks the enemy's army. This is far costlier and riskier, but might prevent the enemy's plans from succeeding. Attacking cities is the last possibility, and the least good, but Sunzi does allow that there might be no alternative to doing so.

Liddell Hart would have agreed that attacking cities, or fortifications, was an extremely bad idea. Indeed, much of his concept of mobile warfare was predicated on the notion that cities or fortifications could be bypassed by fast-moving armies, and their defensive power rendered moot by deep penetrating attacks. Entire armies could be paralyzed by faster-moving opponents striking at their command centers rather than trying to destroy combat units. It is less clear whether Liddell Hart would have accepted

---

[36] Griffith, *The Art of War*, 78.

that there were circumstances under which a strong defensive position or city would have to be attacked. More generally, however, these ideas matched, if somewhat imperfectly, Liddell Hart's. Sunzi certainly accepted, as did Liddell Hart, that it might still prove necessary to fight another army, but that was neither ideal nor something that demonstrated strategic skill.[37]

A close look at Griffith's translation shows that while he did stretch his terms at a few points to bring Sunzi more in line with Liddell Hart, he did not consistently bias his reading in unsupportable ways. There was no way to force Sunzi into the mold of Liddell Hart without mistranslating the source text, something Griffith did not do. There was, however, one other place in the published book where Griffith had the opportunity to inflect his understanding of Sunzi with Liddell Hart, Chapter 5, "Sun Tzu on War." That chapter carried over from his thesis, and interpreted Sunzi in a way much more consistent with Liddell Hart. Griffith did not misinterpret Sunzi, so much as emphasize in his analysis aspects of Sunzi that matched Liddell Hart's strategy.

There were three areas that Griffith, perhaps inadvertently, related to Liddell Hart's thought: non-destruction of the enemy's army, aiming at the mind of the enemy, and explicitly characterizing Sunzi as advocating an indirect method. Griffith explains, "this ancient writer did not conceive the objects of military action to be the annihilation of the enemy's army, the destruction of his cities, and the wastage of his countryside."[38] Sunzi makes it very clear that in the ideal world one defeats one's opponent without fighting, which saves both you and your opponent from destruction of people and goods. If one does fight, one ideally captures the enemy army intact and incorporates it into one's own; failing that, one should capture intact as much as possible. Once again, Sunzi presents possible methods for conducting war in a graded system of best to least-good outcomes. He argues that one should try to achieve the best outcome while well aware that one is likely to fall short. Of course, few, if any, military writers have advocated for the annihilation of an enemy army, as distinct from defeating an enemy army. Attacks focused on the enemy army aim at defeating rather than annihilating it, and there are very few battles where a large army was annihilated or nearly annihilated, even if

---

[37] Both Liddell Hart and Clausewitz proceeded from the point at which fighting had become necessary. Clausewitz felt that once that point had been reached, despite any efforts to the contrary, a military decision required a climactic battle between the main forces of the respective sides. Liddell Hart felt that the war could be decided without that climactic battle, an idea Clausewitz would likely have seen as naïve. Sunzi's point was that a good general would have achieved his goals without fighting; if he were fighting, then he was not good general, so there was nothing to be proud of even if he won.

[38] Griffith, The Art of War, 40.

a part of an army did suffer that fate. World War I might have loomed large in Griffith focusing on Sunzi's non-emphasis on annihilating an army.

The mind of the enemy commander was very much the focus of Sunzi's strategies. This is why "all warfare is based on deception." Deception is useful for the general because his "primary target is the mind of the opposing commander; the victorious situation, a product of his creative imagination. Sun Tzu realized that an indispensable preliminary to battle was to attack the mind of the enemy."[39] Liddell Hart's strategy of mobile warfare was aimed at disrupting the enemy's command system, thus paralyzing the enemy army. Unexpected moves undermined the enemy commander's plans and operations, causing a mental failure that obviated the need for the destruction of his army.

Griffith's most explicit connection to Liddell Hart is his assertion that the expert

approaches his objective indirectly. By selection of a devious and distant route he may march a thousand *li* without opposition and take his enemy unaware. Such a commander prizes above all freedom of action. He abhors a static situation and therefore attacks cities only when there is no alternative. Sieges, wasteful of both lives and time, entail abdication of the initiative.[40]

Not surprisingly, this summation of Sunzi paraphrases the passages from Chapter 7 that Griffith and Liddell Hart found so praiseworthy. That was also the passage that Griffith stretched to render as "the art of the direct and indirect approach." He goes on to characterize the wise general as one who "conducts a war of movement; he marches with divine swiftness," focusing again on not just indirect, but mobile, warfare. The wise general understands that a lengthy war is bad for his country.[41] This was an important point to emphasize for someone who had lived through two world wars.

In the final analysis, Griffith went as far as he could to interpret Sunzi in line with Liddell Hart. At no point in his letters, however, does he explicitly say that he was doing so, or that it was his intention to do so. He may genuinely have felt that Sunzi and Liddell Hart were in general agreement. Of course, he was not only reading Liddell Hart's books; he was also in direct conversation with him on questions of strategy, military history, and writing. Griffith pushed Sunzi slightly closer to Liddell Hart in his summation of Sunzi's thought, and this may have had a more significant influence on the general reading of the work. Particularly following Liddell Hart's own claims of similarity, Griffith's summation

[39] Griffith, *The Art of War*, 41.   [40] Griffith, *The Art of War*, 41.
[41] Griffith, *The Art of War*, 41.

firmly pushed a particular reading of Sunzi that has persisted until today. A selective emphasis on certain aspects of Sunzi over others, or the suggestion that good strategy pursues certain ideals, without tempering that by pointing out that Sunzi also clearly understands that those ideals may not obtain in reality, supported a reading of Sunzi in line with Liddell Hart and Western military thought.

Western Military Philosophers

Griffith sent two chapters to Liddell Hart on October 21, 1960, one on "Sun Tzu and Mao Tse-tung," and the other on "Sun Tzu and Western Military Thought." The former was mostly complete, and the latter was, "a semi-final draft."[42] Liddell Hart provided detailed stylistic comments on the Mao chapter, and substantive ones on the chapter on Western military thought. The "Sun Tzu and Mao Tse-tung" chapter made it in to the published book, but "Sun Tzu and Western Military Thought" was cut. Liddell Hart may have felt it should have been included in the book (Griffith thought so), but his critique of Griffith's characterizations of Western strategists, particularly his list of great strategists, was the result of extensive reading and thought. Their candid discussions reveal their overall understanding of Western military thought, and of how Sunzi related to it. One of Liddell Hart's greatest strengths as a writer was his inclination to take clear positions on issues. This is amply revealed in his views of Western military thinkers.

Liddell Hart's attention to detail, and the significant time and effort he put into Griffith's thesis, were impressive. He also well knew that Griffith was planning to publish the thesis in short order. In response to Griffith's letter of October 21, including the two chapters, he writes, concerning the Mao chapter, "This is very interesting, but in a few places you seem to 'expose your flank' to critical historians – and it might be wise to cover yourself a little more carefully by a slight revision of wording." He then proceeds to work through bad phrasing and logical contradictions line by line. In a very perceptive note he points out that, "The critic may wonder whether you have tended to accept the 'Mao myth' in some respects." He then goes on concerning a later section, "There is an important truth here, but not complete truth – the commander who forfeits the initiative is not always lost, nor has the one who possesses it always won." Of the following page, he comments, "Those who adopt a static attitude are often 'fools', but they are hardly ever 'megolomaniacs' [*sic*]." And on the next page, "The word 'modestly' appears dubious in application to Mao."

---

[42] Griffith to Liddell Hart, October 21, 1960, LHA.

His last comment on that chapter is: "One can never be 'sure' that anyone has learned from experience."[43]

Taken together, Liddell Hart's comments show both care and intelligence, even excluding the recounting of the purely stylistic or rhetorical points. He was sensitive to the construction of the Mao myth, an aspect of Mao that would, of course, become more pronounced leading up to and through the Cultural Revolution (1966–1976). And Mao was many things, but modest was not one of them. Overall, Liddell Hart was a good editor, with many useful things to say.

Liddell Hart then turned to the chapter on "Sun Tzu and Western Military Thought." He made no comment on Griffith's framing of the chapter as the relationship of a single, canonical Chinese thinker to the entirety of the Western tradition of military thought. Liddell Hart, of course, was unaware of the large corpus of Chinese military writings other than Sunzi and Mao Zedong. He presumably became aware at some point of the second great Chinese strategists, Wu Qi, when he read Griffith's translation of Wu Qi in his thesis, and of the existence of the other five books in *The Seven Military Classics*. Sunzi would still stand alone as a work and as a representative of Chinese military thought. All of the comments Liddell Hart had to make on the chapter, after saying it was "excellent," regard Western military thought.

He began by arguing that Pericles, Brasidas, Lysander, and Xenophon qualified as military strategists who pre-dated Philip of Macedon, contrary to Griffith's assertion that Philip was the first Greek military strategist. He also suggests reading the Greek Wars section of his book on strategy. To Xenophon, whom Griffith had described as "possibly" the only Greek to qualify as a military thinker, Liddell Hart advised adding Polybius, mentioning that Pyrrhus had composed a no-longer-extant military textbook, and removing the "possibly" regarding Xenophon. Liddell Hart disagreed with Griffith's statement that "[t]he Romans, who inherited Alexander's art of warfare, produced no generals of his caliber." Scipio Africanus was superior to Alexander "in many respects," he felt, and this list neglected Onasander and Polyaenus. Continuing his ranking of texts and generals, he rates Maurice's *Strategicon* superior to Leo's *Tactica*.

These were functionally antiquarian arguments about ancient history, unconnected to Sunzi per se. Liddell Hart finally engages the comparative issue by disputing Griffith's statement that, "Machiavelli's approach to the problems of war was <u>essentially</u> quite different from Sun Tzu's." This was not wrong, but excessive. What Liddell Hart meant by this is hard to

---

[43] Liddell Hart to Griffith, October 24, 1960, LHA.

ascertain. Did he mean that it should simply read that Machiavelli's approach was "quite different" or just "different" than Sunzi's? And, if so, was this merely an issue of writing style, or a substantive issue of whether and to what extent Machiavelli differed from Sunzi?

In a much more self-serving and recondite turn, Liddell Hart disputes Griffith's idea that Bourcet influenced Sherman. Moreover, "Although Bourcet's thought was introduced to a small circle of military students by Spenser Wilkinson, neither Bourcet nor Guibert were widely known in the modern world until my book The Ghost of Napoleon." Liddell Hart's possessiveness about the field of military thought is telling here, as is his sense that he alone was responsible for bringing to light Pierre-Joseph Bourcet (1700–1780) and Jacques Antoine Hippolyte, Comte de Guibert (1743–1790) in the modern world. Presumably by "modern world" he meant the twentieth century, and by "widely known" he meant outside the scholars and strategists who knew of and studied their works. As is sometimes the case, the knowledge upon which a popular writer builds their own work is discounted because it is only known by scholars. A journalist or popularizer then "discovers" this hitherto unknown information among the academic research of isolated scholars. Liddell Hart's work had always been easy to read and insightful, but he relied almost entirely on the work of scholars to write his books. He used history to support his theories, and chose events to argue his points, but he was not usually a researcher.

Liddell Hart continued in this vein, arguing that Guibert was more important than Bourcet, before turning back to flog Clausewitz again, "I would not describe Jomini or Clausewitz as 'strikingly original military thinkers'. On the other hand I would regard the books of both of them as systematic treatises." And continued immediately afterward, "Here again I would qualify the term 'originality' as applied to Clausewitz."[44] Liddell Hart genuinely disliked Clausewitz, and had little regard for Jomini as well. Of course, he could be more nuanced in his comments on some occasions. This contradiction may well have been a product of the tension between his desire to take a clear position and his actual reading of Clausewitz. Liddell Hart tended to categorize thinkers, making value judgments about them, before discussing the finer points of their writing. He was very careful to demonstrate that he had, in fact, read all of the earlier military writers in order to establish his own authority, so that he could then make clear that his own work was a break from the earlier tradition.

Liddell Hart was extremely self-conscious of his reputation and how he might be perceived. A final issue that arose in Griffith's list of great

---

[44] Liddell Hart to Griffith, October 24, 1960, LHA.

military philosophers was the place of Liddell Hart himself. Liddell Hart's direct involvement in Griffith's work might have left him vulnerable to criticism for the final product. He wrote in response to Griffith's list, "While I appreciate your inclusion of my name in this all-time 'hierarchy of military philosophers', and ^{when you} should say that 'Mahan and myself are the 'only two produced by the English speaking community' I would strongly urge that Fuller's name should be included also."[45]

J. F. C. Fuller's inclusion in Griffith's discussion of twentieth-century military thought remained on Liddell Hart's mind. As he wrote in a subsequent letter on November 2, the last letter before Griffith turned in his thesis, "Fuller's realization, and mine, of the 'need for a statement of general principles' started almost simultaneously but independently, in 1916–17 – was developed more fully in 1919, and continued in company from the time of our 'get together' in 1920." This followed a criticism of Ferdinand Foch's work for failing to "derive or formulate a clear list of principles."[46] Liddell Hart was careful both to credit Fuller and also to insist that his own work had developed independently. His relationship with Fuller, and the close connections and similarities between their ideas, created a great deal of tension in his claims of primacy for those ideas. As his letters to Griffith show, Liddell Hart was very concerned with questions of originality and systematic thinking. Fuller's proximity overshadowed absolute claims of either and, indeed, despite Liddell Hart's grudging concession that Jomini and Clausewitz had written "systematic treatises," he was himself neither very clear with his principles nor systematic.

Near the end of that letter, Liddell Hart made an extraordinary statement: "Without disputing the general truth of your statement here about the neglect of Sun Tzu in the West, I would remark that I have long emphasized his outstanding significance."[47] While it was true that Liddell Hart emphasized in the Foreword he wrote for Griffith's translation that he had been alerted to Sunzi's work in 1927, there does not appear to be any record of him "emphasizing" Sunzi's significance before that Foreword. Even if there are as yet undiscovered instances of him discussing Sunzi before 1960, they were not prominent. Perhaps the most that can be said of this is that Liddell Hart was trying to impress Griffith with his complete grasp of military thought, and that his characterization was hyperbolic.

---

[45] Liddell Hart to Griffith, October 24, 1960, LHA. The errant quotation before Mahan is in the original. The superscripted text was written in with pen in the original.
[46] Liddell Hart to Griffith, November 2, 1960, LHA.
[47] Liddell Hart to Griffith, November 2, 1960, LHA.

From 1957 to 1960, Samuel Griffith and Liddell Hart, along with their wives, formed a deep friendship. Both men were extremely accomplished and successful by 1957, though Liddell Hart was a far more famous and public figure than Griffith. Their mutual admiration and vigorous intellectual exchange were an important influence on Griffith's work on Sunzi. Both men wrote about strategy and war with the intention of affecting actual military practice. Griffith was the more accomplished soldier and scholar, and Liddell Hart the more influential writer. Neither man needed the other professionally. Certainly, Liddell Hart's reputation was in no way enhanced by his association with Griffith and his Sunzi translation. Griffith, in turn, could have written his thesis and gotten it published without Liddell Hart.

Without Liddell Hart's Foreword, however, and his influence on Griffith, it is hard to see how the indirect strategy would ever have been attributed to Sunzi. The term barely occurs in the translation, and Griffith's strongest argument for it is in his overview. It is possible that his overview of Sunzi might have been the same without Liddell Hart; however, to not only read Liddell Hart's work but also engage directly with him about strategy made it far more likely that Griffith's language would come to resemble Liddell Hart's. By introducing Sunzi with Liddell Hart's Foreword, which placed the Chinese text in Liddell Hart's own intellectual framework, a reader would be hard pressed to avoid seeing Sunzi in terms of indirect strategy. One of Liddell Hart's greatest skills was clarifying (or simplifying) complex and nuanced topics into understandable arguments. The writing of that Foreword and its nuances is itself something in need of clarification.

7   "The Concentrated Essence of Wisdom on the Conduct of War"

Liddell Hart's foreword to Samuel Griffith's 1963 translation of Sunzi is the locus classicus for the interpretation that Sunzi advocated an "indirect approach" to strategy.[1] It is therefore important to examine carefully what Liddell Hart did and did not say in that Foreword. Liddell Hart asserted that Sunzi is the greatest military thinker, with only Clausewitz comparable, if dated, and that much of the suffering caused by World War I and World War II would have been avoided if planners had absorbed some of Sunzi's "realism and moderation" to balance Clausewitz's theoretical emphasis on "'total war' beyond all bounds of sense." He goes on to say that the first Sunzi appeared in Europe with a French translation in the late eighteenth century, and that, even though it appealed to the "rational trend of eighteenth-century thinking about war," it was not influential because of "the emotional surge of the Revolution." A new and complete translation was needed, particularly with the appearance of nuclear weapons, and China becoming a great power under Mao Zedong.

Having provided some historical context for reading Sunzi in the West, and justified a new translation, Liddell Hart turns to his personal connection to Sunzi. He dates his first encounter with Sunzi to a letter sent to him in 1927 by Sir John Duncan, who pointed out that Sunzi's likening an army to water sounded very much like Liddell Hart's expanding-torrent theory.[2] Liddell Hart then read Sunzi and found that it was very much in keeping with his own ideas, "especially his constant emphasis on doing the unexpected and pursuing the indirect approach." During World War II the Chinese military attaché (who was "a pupil of Chiang Kai-shek") told him that his books and J. F. C. Fuller's were the main texts in China's military academies. Liddell Hart asked about the use of Sunzi and was told that it was regarded as out of date, though seen as a classic. Liddell Hart thereupon recommended that they go back to Sunzi, since it

---

[1] The title of this chapter is taken from Liddell Hart, Foreword, in Griffith, *The Art of War*, v.
[2] John Duncan to Liddell Hart, May 7, 1927, LHA.

"embodied almost as much about the fundamentals of strategy and tactics as I had covered in more than twenty books."

For purposes of analysis, the Foreword can usefully be split into two parts: Liddell Hart's contextualization of Sunzi in Western military thought, and Liddell Hart's connection to Sunzi. Before turning to that analysis, however, I will first provide the background for how Liddell Hart came to write his Foreword. Fortunately, the writing of the Foreword, and its contents and perspective, are the subject of a number of extant letters between Liddell Hart, Griffith, and the editors at Oxford University Press. All the parties were aware that at least one competing translation was being produced, and that Liddell Hart would possibly be asked to write a Foreword for it. The fact that Griffith was not the only person producing a Sunzi translation in the early 1960s, and that Liddell Hart was an attractive possibility as the author of a Foreword on such a work, suggests that there was a broader confluence of historical trends and personality bringing Sunzi and Liddell Hart together.

The Background to the Foreword

Given Liddell Hart's extensive involvement in Griffith's translation of Sunzi, and, even more importantly, their deep friendship, it was natural that he would write a Foreword for the published version of Griffith's dissertation. As detailed in Chapter 6, Liddell Hart's influence on Griffith's translation was both personal and intellectual. Griffith read Liddell Hart's *Strategy: The Indirect Approach* while he was translating Sunzi, and was strongly influenced by Liddell Hart's work in general. Griffith relied heavily on Liddell Hart's extensive and extremely careful criticism of his work. Judged solely from their extant letters concerning first Griffith's doctoral thesis, and then his book manuscripts, Liddell Hart invested an extraordinary amount of time in reading drafts of his work. This is particularly striking when we realize that Liddell Hart had no formal role in Griffith's doctoral committee.

It is important to keep in mind that, in the eyes of many people, including Samuel Griffith, Liddell Hart was the most eminent strategist of the twentieth century. His interest in Griffith's work, and his detailed responses to his thesis and book chapters, were a sign of his commitment to the work itself and of his friendship with Griffith. Liddell Hart actively supported and pushed Griffith's translation. In a letter of November 16, 1960, Griffith relates that he had submitted his thesis, "Sun Tzu, First of the Military Philosophers," to his examiners, Norman Gibbs and Geoffrey Hudson. He goes on to say that he will be meeting with Mr. Sutcliffe from Oxford University Press on November 21, and that he would be grateful if Liddell Hart would indeed write to someone at the press in support of the work, as he had previously offered.

Griffith concludes the formal part of the letter by saying, "There is no way I can adequately express my gratitude for your constant interest and encouragement while I have been labouring on this project, and for your offer to write a Foreword if a book is to be published." The last part of the letter then reverts to a very personal discussion of when he and his wife will leave England. Belle (Griffith), he says, will write to Kathy Kathy (Kathleen Liddell Hart) to work out when they will visit before leaving. In a postscript, Griffith then alludes to "logistic support," which was their code term for supplies of pipe cleaners and paper clips for Liddell Hart, though that would require a trip up to Upper Heyford.[3]

Liddell Hart's involvement in the book that would eventually be produced was profound. Griffith continued to keep Liddell Hart up to date on the progress of his degree, and of the book. On December 18, 1960, he wrote a much less formal letter to Liddell Hart that began on the topic of pipe cleaners:

I enclose enough pipe cleaners to keep you going for a few months, I hope. If you have been like the wise virgin or the provident squirrel you will have been storing up pipe cleaners so I hope that you will have enough to last you until I get back and can resume normal supply.

Liddell Hart scribbled a note next to that paragraph: "I have!" On the very bottom of the letter, a further handwritten note added, "24 dozen pipe cleaners (8 packets) (not acknowledged)."[4]

Griffith reports that he took his viva on December 16 and, although he thought he did well, he would not hear anything officially or unofficially until after January 25, 1961, the University Senate possibly meeting on the 27th. Any news about his book from Oxford University Press would likely occur at about the same time because nothing happened around Oxford over the Christmas break.[5] It would not be until February 20, 1961, that Griffith was able to report that his degree would be conferred on April 27, and that Peter Sutcliffe, an editor at Oxford University Press, and his adviser, Norman Briggs, had both recommended that the press publish his book (subject to some changes for Briggs).[6] By March 7 Griffith was adapting his thesis for publication, editing the translation in particular, and that his introduction "will be preceded by the Foreword you have so kindly agreed to write, and a short Preface by me, which will

---

[3] Samuel Griffith to Liddell Hart, November 16, 1960, LHA.
[4] Samuel Griffith to Liddell Hart, December 18, 1960, LHA.
[5] Samuel Griffith to Liddell Hart, December 18, 1960, LHA.
[6] Samuel Griffith to Liddell Hart, April 27, 1961, LHA.

include acknowledgements." While hoping for publication in November, he pledged to send the manuscript to Liddell Hart by mid-April, if he was willing to do so.[7]

Griffith did, indeed, send Liddell Hart a typed manuscript by April 4, "for which I hope you are still inclined to write the Foreword." The thesis chapters on "Sun Tzu and Western Military Thought" and "The Principles of War" were cut from the book, and the chapter "Sun Tzu's Influence on Japanese Military Thought" was placed in an appendix. After asking for criticisms and edits, he concludes the letter,

> I am very much in your debt, as are so many others. Your criticism and encour-agement have helped provide me with the determination to bring this work to what I hope will be a successful conclusion. Whatever small contribution it may be to the general field of military writing will be due in no small measure to you.[8]

Part of the point of the changes was to keep the focus of the book on China. Liddell Hart replied to this letter on the 28th, suggesting some changes, which were not carried out, to make the work more accessible to the general reader. He reassured Griffith that, while his Preface "naturally includes some points I had in mind to say myself in the Foreword, a short Foreword will more [sic] effective."[9] Griffith justified the changes made in consultation with Oxford University Press and Norman Briggs to Liddell Hart on May 2, concluding the letter with the hope that Liddell Hart would be able to get the Foreword to the press in early June so that the book could be published by the end of 1961.[10]

There was more, however, to Griffith's justifications to Liddell Hart in his letter of May 2. Griffith included a copy of his letter to Liddell Hart when he wrote to Norman Briggs, asking his help in convincing Liddell Hart that the current structure of the book made sense. Griffith and his wife were in Spain at that time, and he hoped that Briggs, who was in England, might persuade Liddell Hart to come around. It is clear from the letter to Briggs that Briggs had also been involved in the decisions to structure the book the way they had. What Griffith suspected was that Liddell Hart did not agree with changes that focused the book on China. He feared that if they did not proceed with the manuscript as it was then structured, the book's publication would "be contemporaneous with the

---

[7] Griffith to Liddell Hart, March 7, 1961, LHA.
[8] Griffith to Liddell Hart, April 4, 1961, LHA; Griffith to Liddell Hart, April 4, 1961, MCA.
[9] Liddell Hart to Griffith, April 28, 1961, LHA; Liddell Hart to Griffith, April 28, 1961, MCA. The typo is in both copies. The copy in the LHA is cleaner, having been retyped with the corrections which were made by hand in the copy in the MCA.
[10] Griffith to Liddell Hart, May 2, 1961, LHA. Griffith to Liddell Hart, May 2, 1961, MCA.

Second Coming." To make matters worse, a different editor, Davin, had taken over responsibility for the manuscript at Oxford University Press, and was suggesting a publication date in the spring or fall of 1962, rather than late 1961 or the end of February 1962, as the previous editor, Sutcliffe, had proposed.[11]

The tension with Liddell Hart was partly due to Liddell Hart's interest in placing Sunzi within the larger field of Western military history and military thought, and partly to a very different set of values with respect to publishing. Whereas Liddell Hart made his living by publishing books and articles, Griffith did not expect to make any money off of the Sunzi translation. Griffith felt, "The publication of a good translation of Sun Tzu has been too long delayed as it is." Davin justified pushing back publication in order to do some "sales promotion." But Griffith thought this ridiculous:

For a book of this sort any talk of organized "sales promotion" is absurd. No one, least of all me, is going to make any real money out of this book, but when I get to the States I will naturally do all I can to push it. –Well, the hell with that.[12]

Liddell Hart's audience for his books was always the interested lay reader rather than academics. In many respects, his influence within military and government circles was due to his accessible books. He wrote to be understood, not to wrestle with the finer points of historical sources or methodologies. Although he wrote histories, he never sought to be a scholar, nor did he become one. Liddell Hart wrote fluent narrative histories that supported his strategic analysis, but was almost wholly dependent upon English-language sources for his information. Moreover, Liddell Hart's actual experience of war was extremely limited, both in time spent in service and in command responsibility. He was not quite an armchair general, having spent some time in service, and having a prolonged and deep engagement with military training, military policy, and political leadership, especially as a journalist. Unlike J. F. C. Fuller, who remained in the army, Liddell Hart was an outsider whose distance provided him with an important perspective on theoretical issues unobscured by day-to-day concerns. But because he had no institutional position, particularly after World War II, he needed to get as much credit as possible for his ideas in order to sustain himself financially.

Griffith, by contrast, had extensive military experience in multiple theatres, across many levels of command, and in combat. Even prior to World War II, he had served in Nicaragua, Cuba, and China. During World War II, he was a decorated combat veteran who took part in some

---

[11] Griffith to Briggs, May 2, 1961, MCA.   [12] Griffith to Briggs, May 2, 1961, MCA.

of the most difficult fighting of the war. In a further contrast to Liddell Hart, Griffith had a much better and broader education. He attended the US Naval Academy, where he studied electrical engineering. Griffith learned Chinese while posted to the US Embassy in Beijing, and then undertook his D.Phil. at Oxford after retiring from the Marine Corps as a brigadier general. It is unclear where or when he learned classical Chinese, which was necessary for translating Sunzi. He does not appear to have read or translated anything else in classical Chinese after completing his dissertation, republishing his translation of Mao Zedong's *On Guerrilla Warfare*, and writing a book on the Guadalcanal campaign, as well as many articles in various journals and magazines. For most of his adult life, Griffith was part of a larger institution, and, after his retirement, had sufficient resources from his previous service that he was not entirely reliant upon his publications to make a living. While not wealthy, Griffith and his wife appear to have been comfortable.

Just as it seems the final form of the book was coming together, Griffith's drive to get it published in 1961 was undercut again. An American publisher, Praeger, was going to reissue Griffith's translation of Mao Zedong's *On Guerrilla Warfare*, and asked him to write a 10,000-word introduction to it. Griffith wrote to Liddell Hart on June 26 to complain that he had been unable to work on the Sunzi book because Praeger wanted to publish the Mao translation in early October. He was, however, waiting for Liddell Hart's comments on the Sunzi manuscript.[13] Griffith had earlier, in May, suggested cutting his own Preface, feeling that it was superfluous with Liddell Hart writing a Foreword.[14] Liddell Hart was clear that Griffith's Preface was important, partly because, as he had said earlier, "it would be difficult for me to find time to write a lengthy one."[15] In short, both men were extremely busy, and remained extremely busy during the entire process of revising the book.

On August 13, Griffith informed Liddell Hart that the manuscript was in its final draft, and that no further substantive changes would be made. The copy of the manuscript then in Liddell Hart's hands was essentially complete, and he should feel free to write his Foreword based on that. Griffith's Oxford tutor, Mr. Wu Shih-ch'ang, was checking over the Preface, but Griffith didn't expect any significant changes. He emphasized that Liddell Hart should not write the Foreword before his

---

[13] Griffith to Liddell Hart, June 26, 1961, MCA.
[14] Griffith to Liddell Hart, May 13, 1961, LHA.
[15] Liddell Hart to Griffith, April 28, 1961, LHA.

upcoming trip to Geneva if he was pressed for time. His plan was to get the final draft to Sutcliffe and Davin by September 7.[16]

Liddell Hart's response on August 31 was encouraging, but also raised the issue of a competing translation. The trip to Geneva had been postponed because of the "European situation" (the Berlin crisis of 1961). He had been asked to be the British member of an international group formed by the Red Cross to produce rules "for the protection of the civil population in case of war." The American members, General Maxwell Taylor and Walter Lippmann, were pulled away to help deal with the crisis, as was a replacement, James Reston. Liddell Hart and his wife decided to take a vacation in Ireland. He hoped to write the Foreword before they left, but promised that if he couldn't, he would write it when they got back in early October. Before closing, Liddell Hart brought some important news:

> It may interest you to know that I had a letter yesterday from John Bright-Holmes, of Eyre and Spottiswoode, telling me that Lieut-General T. C. Tang is preparing a new edition of Sun Tzu's book, which they are considering for possible publication and would like me to write a Foreword for it. I have written back to say that I am already committed to writing a Foreword to a new edition, yours, that will be coming out much earlier![17]

Liddell Hart was an old hand at dealing with editors and publishing houses and likely knew that Griffith would put the information about a competing translation to good use. He also, no doubt, knew that telling the editor at Eyre and Spottiswoode that Oxford was about to publish a Sunzi translation with his Foreword might give them pause in their plans. Griffith responded on September 24, commiserating over the Geneva conference, and showing that Liddell Hart's letter had both reassured him and supplied him with ammunition:

> I consider myself most fortunate to have corralled you before Messrs. Eyre and Spottiswoode managed to do so. Of course this unexpected competition puts the heat on, and I feel most negligent. But on the other hand, the Press had told me the earliest possible date was the spring of 1962, so I never felt under real pressure until the news contained in the last paragraph of your letter. I have taken the liberty of quoting this to Sutcliffe.

In a postscript to the same letter, he asks Liddell Hart to send him a copy of the Foreword, for which he will send in return rust-proof paper clips

---

[16] Griffith to Liddell Hart, August 13, 1961, LHA.

[17] Liddell Hart to Griffith, August 31, 1961, LHA. The "new edition of Sun Tzu's book" appears to refer to Zi-Chang Tang's *Principles of Conflict: Recompilation and New English Translation with Annotation on Sun Zi's Art of War*, San Rafael, CA: T. C. Press, 1969. I have been unable to find further information on T. C. Tang, beyond the fact that the same person also published a translation of Tang poems, and *Wisdom of Dao*.

when he gets to Washington. He also asks for a "routine report on the Dill pipe cleaner situation."[18]

Liddell Hart duly sent Peter Sutcliffe at Oxford University Press his Foreword on October 9, after returning from Ireland. He wrote,

As you will see, I have emphasised the comparison with and contrast to Clausewitz, as that seemed to me the best way of bringing out the importance of Sun Tzu – as all likely readers of the book are likely to be familiar with Clausewitz, at least in the broad way. But if you think the passages about Clausewitz are unduly long, let me know, as they can be easily cut down.

He was also concerned that his mentions of Duncan's 1927 letter and his conversation in 1942 with the Chinese military attaché were too personal.[19]

Both Davin and then Sutcliffe wrote back to Liddell Hart in turn, praising the Foreword overall, but suggesting some minor edits. Davin's immediate purpose was to acknowledge receipt of the Foreword on October 12, since Sutcliffe was on holiday, but also to suggest a slight change in the second paragraph.[20] Liddell Hart wrote back the following day thanking Davin for his suggested change, and amending the Foreword accordingly.[21] Sutcliffe did not think Liddell Hart's references were "unduly personal," but "possibly in the penultimate paragraph your admiration for Sun Tzu might be put in more general terms rather than by saying that his view coincided with your own line of thought. ' ... I found many other points of peculiar interest ... ' might meet the case."[22] Liddell Hart rejected Sutcliffe's proposed changes on November 24, and not only requested a proof copy, but also pressed him for the book's publication date.[23]

Griffith received the Foreword and wrote back to Liddell Hart on October 13. After assuring Liddell Hart that he would send more rust-proof paper clips, he opined that the news of a possible competing Sunzi translation had spurred Sutcliffe to move more quickly.[24] Liddell Hart's letter of November 24, appears to have been an effort to add further pressure on Sutcliffe to finally publish the book. Both Griffith and Liddell Hart seemed a bit frustrated with Sutcliffe by this point, if not earlier, but the manuscript was now mostly complete and the only obstacle left was the press itself.

It was, however, about six months later, on May 5, 1962, that Griffith again wrote to Liddell Hart to tell him that he had finished the page proofs

[18] Griffith to Liddell Hart, September 24, 1961, LHA.
[19] Liddell Hart to Peter Sutcliffe, October 9, 1961, LHA.
[20] Davin to Liddell Hart, October 12, 1961, LHA.
[21] Liddell Hart to Davin, October 13, 1961.
[22] Sutcliffe to Liddell Hart, October 17, 1961, LHA.
[23] Liddell Hart to Sutcliffe, November 24, 1961, LHA.
[24] Griffith to Liddell Hart, October 13, 1961, LHA.

for the book. The press was now scheduling publication in August. Wu Shih-ch'ang was doing a final check of the bibliography. Griffith was encouraged by the success of his translation of Mao's *On Guerrilla Warfare*, and hoping that the Sunzi book might actually do well: "The present American interest in China, in Mao, in revolutionary guerrilla war, might, if sustained, considerably help the sale of the Sun Tzu. The Mao book has done very well indeed here, at least 13,500 and now in a third printing. Hope it does 15,000, anyhow."[25] In July, however, Griffith lamented that, despite their promises of an August publication, he had not heard from the press recently. They now had everything, including the index, which he sent them in June. Griffith was also about to send the finished draft of his book on Guadalcanal to Lippincott Press.[26]

Griffith was finally able to write to Liddell Hart on January 22, 1963, that the Sunzi book would be published on February 14. His new book on Guadalcanal was going to come out on August 1 with Lippincott. Admiral Nimitz had read, and was enthusiastic about, the Guadalcanal book.[27] The Sunzi book was finally published in the middle of February, and Sutcliffe reported to Griffith that it had sold 620 copies by the end of the month.[28]

Griffith's work on Sunzi, and Liddell Hart's connection to it, were further perpetuated when *Encyclopaedia Britannica* asked Griffith to write the entry on Sunzi in 1967. His instructions were to "begin with a phrase or sentence summing up Sun Tzu's chief claim to fame, to give the facts of his life and to discuss his work briefly with some critical evaluation of it, concluding with a short bibliography of one or two items."[29] Griffith composed his entry and sent it to *Encyclopaedia Britannica* in December of 1967. He claimed that Sunzi lived in the fourth century BCE, making his *Art of War* one of the earliest works on war and strategy. While allowing for the fact that when Griffith was writing, Sunzi was still widely believed to have been a real person, the claims of his next paragraph mixed the true and the entirely unsupportable: "For centuries, the Chinese have accorded to the Sun Tzu Ping Fa preeminent position in their martial canon, and throughout China's long recorded history, her military leaders have without exception been assiduous students of these succinct and perceptive essays."[30] Of course, Griffith had to sell the importance of Sunzi, and the biographical sketch was

[25] Griffith to Liddell Hart, May 5, 1962, LHA. Griffith to Liddell Hart, May 5, 1962, MCA.
[26] Griffith to Liddell Hart, July 31, 1962, LHA. Griffith to Liddell Hart, July 31, 1962, MCA.
[27] Griffith to Liddell Hart, January 22, 1963, LHA. Griffith to Liddell Hart, January 22, 1963, MCA.
[28] Sutcliffe to Griffith, March 12, 1963, MCA.
[29] Christopher Kent (*Encyclopaedia Britannica*) to Griffith, August 31, 1967, MCA.
[30] Griffith, December 15, 1967, Sun Tzu biographical sketch for *Encyclopaedia Britannica*, MCA.

a gross oversimplification, but he had no evidence to support the idea that Chinese military leaders had all studied Sunzi. He intentionally or not had reduced the entire history of Chinese warfare to one book, and had done so as the then leading expert on the subject in the West in an authoritative reference book.

In the final paragraph, Griffith invoked the authority of Liddell Hart: "Of The Art of War, Captain Sir Basil Liddell Hart, the modern strategist and historian, has written that Sun Tzu's essays on war, '-have never been surpassed in comprehensiveness and depth of understanding. They might well be termed the concentrated essence of wisdom on the conduct of war.'"[31] These were the opening lines of Liddell Hart's Foreword, thus reaffirming the importance of Sunzi, but also of Liddell Hart. Liddell Hart was at the height of his reputation at that time, and his endorsement of Sunzi legitimized it as a valid strategic text which might otherwise have been dismissed as mere oriental exotica. The only work in the accompanying bibliography was Griffith's own translation of Sunzi.

By 1967 at the latest, Samuel Griffith, with the critical support of Liddell Hart, had established Sunzi's *Art of War* as a valid strategic text. That is not to say that it was widely accepted or read in Western military circles, but it was not rejected out of hand by everyone. There was, and is, resistance to reading or taking seriously an ancient Chinese text. It was clearly and obviously outside the Western tradition of strategy, which was a positive for some people and a negative for others. Griffith's authority as both a translator and a veteran with extensive experience of China further bolstered the legitimacy of Sunzi. Yet Griffith's connection to Mao's writings, and his personal belief that Mao's military thought was based upon Sunzi, inextricably tied Sunzi to guerrilla war. As we shall see, Liddell Hart intentionally and forcefully presented Sunzi as equivalent, and superior, to Clausewitz. The highlighting of these differences, combined with contrast between the conventional warfare associated with Clausewitz and the unconventional warfare associated with Mao, and therefore Sunzi, and therefore all of Chinese culture, became a fixed idea in the West following the publication of Griffith's translation in 1963.

The Foreword: The Intellectual Context

Liddell Hart began the Foreword by establishing Sunzi's as the first military text anywhere in the world. This was and is a typical approach to legitimizing Chinese culture. One of the greatest strengths of Chinese

---

[31] Griffith, December 15, 1967, Sun Tzu biographical sketch for *Encyclopaedia Britannica*, MCA.

culture is its long, unbroken history. Being the first or having the oldest occurrence of something is an important support for anyone arguing that Chinese culture should be taken seriously. China is the quintessential "other" to the West, whose ancient, continuous history is contrasted with the West's late dash to modernity. From the classicist's point of view, China's ancient civilization did as much to define its fundamental culture as ancient Greek and Roman civilization did to define the West's fundamental culture. And indeed, Liddell Hart directly engages this issue of China's wise, continuous civilization in contrast to the West's recent and rash civilization. Less clear is whether Liddell Hart did this intentionally or unintentionally, or, perhaps more to the point, whether he was self-consciously creating a dichotomy between ancient Chinese civilization and the modern West.

Clausewitz, Liddell Hart claimed, was the only "comparable" military thinker to Sunzi, a dramatic reduction of the entire tradition of Western military thought to a single, very late, thinker. Liddell Hart was well acquainted with the tradition of Western military writing, both of military histories and of works on military thought, that he had just simplified into Clausewitz. He elevated Clausewitz to the pinnacle of Western military thinkers, a view that most scholars would support, and allowed the Prussian general's work to stand in for all of Western strategic thought. This was probably the first time that Sunzi and Clausewitz had been made into the exemplars of the military thinking of their respective cultures. They became not just strategists who had written important strategic books, but men who reflected in their writing the fundamental strategic cultures of China and the West. Liddell Hart, who had invested considerable effort in his previous work in setting Clausewitz up as a straw man containing all of the worst impulses of Western strategy, now contrasted that straw man with his new hero, an ancient Chinese general.

Liddell Hart was alert to the immediate objection to such a comparison, that Sunzi was ancient and Clausewitz modern, and so their respective works were appropriate for the times in which they wrote. He argued that, to the contrary, it was Sunzi who was timeless and classic, and Clausewitz who was "more 'dated' than Sun Tzu, and in part antiquated, although he was writing more than two thousand years later."[32] In other words, Sunzi was profound and eternal (to paraphrase Liddell Hart), and Clausewitz was shallow and historical. Liddell Hart did not mean to make a broader critique of Chinese versus Western culture, his interest was purely military, and he does not appear to have placed any particular value on other aspects of Chinese culture (if he was even aware

---

[32] Liddell Hart, Foreword, v.

of them). But Clausewitz had long been Liddell Hart's self-created bête noire, and in making Clausewitz the representative of Western strategic culture he amplified, rather than diminished, the orientalist, classical, ancient-China-versus-modern-West dichotomy. This artificial polarization would ramify throughout the field of military history, military thought, and Chinese history for the rest of the twentieth century and into the twenty-first, an issue I will return to in the Conclusion.

Liddell Hart continued his attack on Clausewitz, attributing a significant amount of the destruction of World War I and World War II to the influence of *On War*. In his view, Clausewitz's insistence on the "logical ideal and 'the absolute'" led to the concept of total war. Moderation, in this interpretation of Clausewitz, was illogical because war should logically move toward an unrestrained and complete concentration of all the means of a state to accomplish its goals. He quotes Clausewitz, "To introduce into the philosophy of war a principle of moderation would be an absurdity – war is an act of violence pushed to its utmost bounds." Liddell Hart does not, however, argue that Clausewitz should have been entirely done away with, only that he should have been "blended with and balanced by a knowledge of Sun Tzu's exposition on 'The Art of War'." Sunzi was more realistic and moderate. Here again, however, Liddell Hart created an artificial dichotomy between Sunzi and Clausewitz, attributing to Sunzi all of the positive characteristics.

Had Liddell Hart continued entirely in this vein he might easily have been dismissed as either not having read Clausewitz or not having understood him. He therefore tempered his remarks because he knew that his initial description of Clausewitz was an oversimplification, and he knew that he needed to show that. The Foreword then adds nuance to its discussion of what Clausewitz said, placing much of the blame for the failures of its strategic approach on those disciples of Clausewitz who had oversimplified Clausewitz. This was a clever rhetorical move that made Liddell Hart the better reader of Clausewitz than his disciples, and the defender of his honor, rather than an entirely hostile critic. Clausewitz had admitted that "the political object, as the original motive of the war, should be the standard for determining both the aim of the military force and also the amount of effort to be made." Even Liddell Hart had to admit that Clausewitz had, in fact, concluded that his theoretical ideal of war would not have worked, and would lead to a failure to appropriately relate ends and means.

At that point, the Foreword briefly unravels as Liddell Hart concedes that "the underlying trend of his [Clausewitz's] thought ... did not differ so much from Sun Tzu's conclusions as it appeared to do on the surface."³³ In the space of little more than a page, Liddell Hart went from condemning Clausewitz's thinking and praising Sunzi's to seeing them as fundamentally similar. This raises the important question whether or not Sunzi and Clausewitz in fact agree with each other, in which case the value of a new translation of Sunzi is less clear. Liddell Hart swerves away from this question, and untangles his somewhat contradictory stance, by blaming some of the mistaken interpretations of Clausewitz on Clausewitz's manner of writing, "expounding his theory in a way too abstract and involved for concrete-minded soldiers to follow the course of his argument, which often turned back from the direction which it seemed to be taking." Ironically, this same argument could be made for those preaching the use of the indirect approach, attributed either to Liddell Hart or to Sunzi.

Sunzi, in contrast to Clausewitz, wrote clearly, and Sun Zi's clarity would have helped people understand Clausewitz, or at least the ideas they were both explaining. Even though Sunzi was introduced to France in the late eighteenth century and fit well into the trend of rational thought at that time, the emotions of the Revolution and Napoleon's victories prevented it from being influential. Clausewitz began work during the revolutionary period, but died before revising his work. Here Liddell Hart has hazarded an entirely speculative and unprovable explanation for why Father Amiot's translation of Sunzi was not influential in Europe. He has also elided the actual course of the intellectual influence of Enlightenment military thinkers and Clausewitz's much later rise to influence in the nineteenth century.

Since the translation of Sunzi, at least from Liddell Hart's perspective, accorded with rational, Enlightenment thinking, it would not have had much influence because Enlightenment military thinkers were already inclined to be rational, moderate, and limited in their strategies. Moreover, if Sunzi and Clausewitz were more in accord, at least at the fundamental level as Liddell Hart had just argued, then Clausewitz was not the Counter-Enlightenment or German Romantic thinker he felt himself to be. In Liddell Hart's telling, again defending Clausewitz, Clausewitz was heading back toward the rational, moderate approach that characterized Sunzi and the Enlightenment military writers. The misunderstanding of

---

³³ This shift in Liddell Hart's characterization raises two, not necessarily antagonistic, possibilities on his reading of Clausewitz. One is that he had earlier in his career misread Clausewitz and subsequently read him more carefully. The other is that his earlier characterizations of Clausewitz were necessary when he was establishing his own strategic thinking and reputation, but that by 1962 he felt secure enough in his position that he no longer needed to completely disparage Clausewitz.

Clausewitz was due to his only partially revised manuscript of *On War*, which, had he not died of cholera in 1831, would have been brought into line with exactly the thinkers he was writing against. Of course, if Clausewitz and Sunzi were, in fact, saying the same thing, and they were the two greatest military thinkers in history, and Liddell Hart, as we shall see in the next section, was actually in accord with Sunzi, and also with Clausewitz, then his strategic thought was on par with theirs.

Liddell Hart also well knew that it was Jomini, an Enlightenment military thinker, who was and remained the dominant strategist until well into the second half of the nineteenth century. The officers trained at West Point who fought on both sides in the American Civil War, for example, had all studied – indeed, a few had even personally met – Jomini.[34] It was really with the rise of Prussia in the Austro-Prussian War (1866) and the Franco-Prussian War (1870–1871) that Clausewitz became an important strategist. These Prussian successes were attributed to the disciples of Clausewitz, not Jomini, suggesting that it was Clausewitz who had correctly analyzed the reasons for Napoleon's victories. It was in these conflicts that the Prussian military asserted its independence from political control. The extremist disciples of Clausewitz that Liddell Hart referred to were those Prussian military leaders who sought to run wars once they had begun as they saw fit.

The Clausewitzian extremists were dominant when newer translations of Sunzi appeared in Europe. Here Liddell Hart presumably refers to the translations of Calthrop (1905 and 1908), Giles (1910), Navarra into German (1910), a revised version of Amiot (1922), and two Russian translations by Sreznevskij (1860) and Putyata (1889). These earlier translations failed to exert much influence in military circles, partly from the prevailing focus on Clausewitz, and partly because of the translations themselves. The time was right for a new and complete translation. Of all of the things that Liddell Hart asserted in the Foreword, the correctness of the timing of the translation proved to be the most accurate. Whether that was because, as he argued, the threat of nuclear weapons and the establishment of China under Mao Zedong as a major power made it timely, or because his support of a translation done by a veteran marine and China hand gave it the credibility it previously lacked, is less certain.

---

[34] For Jomini's influence on Civil War leaders see Carol Reardon, *With a Sword in One Hand and Jomini in the Other: The Problem of Military Thought in the Civil War North*, Chapel Hill, NC: University of North Carolina Press, 2012.

Liddell Hart and Sunzi

In the last part of the Foreword Liddell Hart explained his own relation-ship with Sunzi. This was the part that he had been reassured by both the editors and Griffith was not "too personal." As with the first part of the Foreword, the last part can be read on several levels. He concluded the first part by complimenting Samuel Griffith as an ideal person to undertake the translation, but then did not mention his own direct engagement with Griffith during the translation of Sunzi or the writing of the surrounding materials. Perhaps he felt that the credibility of his endorsement would be undermined if he took some responsibility for the work; it seems less likely that he was just being humble. Liddell Hart was many things, but humble was not one of them. Alternatively, he did not want to call attention to his influence so that it would seem as if Sunzi agreed with him, independently of any bias he might have induced in the translation. Finally, he may have wanted to distance himself from his involvement in the writing of the thesis because of his very delicate relationship to Sunzi.

Just as Liddell Hart understood the stakes in his convoluted and contradictory discussion of the relationship between Sunzi and Clausewitz, he also understood the problem of the relationship between his own writings and those of Sunzi. He had to establish that his strategies had been developed before he had read Sunzi, but also that he knew about Sunzi before meeting Griffith, and that Sunzi turned out to agree with his independently created strategies. If Sunzi's strategies agreed with Liddell Hart's then there was always a danger that he could be accused of merely following Sunzi. This is also why he brings up his sometime friend J. F. C. Fuller toward the end of the Foreword. Both Fuller and Liddell Hart were actively forming their strategic thinking together after World War I. Chronology and influence are critical in the second half of the Foreword. He is also careful not to say that he learned anything new from reading Griffith's translation, or indeed any other translation.

Liddell Hart claims that Sunzi was first brought to his attention in 1927 by Sir John Duncan (1872–1948), an officer then in Shanghai who was observing Chiang Kai-shek's Northern Expedition.[35] Sir John said that he had been reading *The Art of War* and was struck by its similarity to Liddell Hart's expanding-torrent theory, and by its argu-ment that "the supreme art of war is to subdue the enemy without fighting." Having clearly established that he had published his ideas, or

[35] Major General Sir John Duncan, served in India, in the Second Boer War, and at Gallipoli during World War I. He commanded the Shanghai Military Force in China from 1927 to 1928.

at least those similar to Sunzi's, before reading Sunzi, Liddell Hart says, "I found many other points that coincided with my own lines of thought, especially his constant emphasis on doing the unexpected and pursuing the indirect approach." This anecdote not only reinforces the idea that Liddell Hart's writings pre-dated his awareness of Sunzi, but also shows that important people were reading Liddell Hart's books and articles. In the final sentence of that paragraph, he makes a play for the classic or, at least, eternal truth of his own strategic thought. Reading Sunzi in 1927 "helped me to realize the agelessness of the more fundamental military ideas, even of a tactical nature." Liddell Hart's strategic thought was thus rendered essentially scientific insofar as he had discovered basic truths about war that transcended time and space.

Liddell Hart had every reason to deny familiarity with Sunzi, particularly the Giles translation, or, as he did in the Foreword, to avoid mentioning it. Since Giles translated *zheng* and *qi* as "direct" and "indirect," acknowledging a pre-1927 familiarity would have run the risk of making Liddell Hart a follower of Sunzi, and his thoughts and terms derivative, rather than an equal who had independently reached the same conclusions. There is no evidence that Liddell Hart had read any translation of Sunzi before 1927, though, if he had, he certainly had every reason to assert, as he did in the Foreword, that he had not. The letter from Sir John Duncan is extant, and refers to the Calthrop translation, which did not use the terms "direct" and "indirect." The Giles translation was a threat to Liddell Hart's claim to have independently originated the term "indirect" with respect to strategy.

Absent the discovery of any new evidence, it is impossible to prove when Liddell Hart first read the Giles translation, let alone whether it happened before formulating his own strategic vision. In the preface to *Strategy* (1954), Liddell Hart wrote, "My original study of 'the strategy of indirect approach' was published in 1929 – under the title *The Decisive Wars of History*."[36] He wrote the Foreword for Griffith in 1961, continuing to lay claim to indirect strategy, while also attributing it to Sunzi. The Giles translation was the elephant in the room that Liddell Hart never acknowledged; Griffith's translation almost seems, though this is speculative, to avoid using "indirect" as Giles did. "Indirect" was left to Liddell Hart, even though, or perhaps because, Griffith had read Liddell Hart's *Strategy: The Indirect Approach* (1941) while he was working on his own translation. Certainly, Griffith never imagined that Liddell Hart had received the term from Sunzi.

---

[36] B. H. Liddell Hart, *Strategy*, New York: Frederick A. Praeger, 1954, 18.

In the final paragraph of the Foreword Liddell Hart's backhanded self-promotion reaches its pinnacle. He relates that when he was visited by Chiang Kai-shek's military attaché during World War II, he was informed that his books and J. F. C. Fuller's were the main textbooks in the Chinese military academies. He asked about Sunzi and was told that it was merely regarded as a classic, no longer relevant under modern conditions. Here Liddell Hart was able to admonish his Chinese interlocutor while praising himself: "I remarked that it was time they went back to Sun Tzu, since in that one short book was embodied almost as much about the fundamentals of strategy as I had covered in more than twenty books." The great Chinese classic on strategy contained almost as much as Liddell Hart's own voluminous output.

As an act of self-promotion, Liddell Hart discovered that Sunzi had emphasized an indirect method in his strategy similar to Liddell Hart's. Yet he never proved this by a detailed listing of passages; he merely asserted that it was so. Indeed, Liddell Hart claimed that he was not the first to see this; it was Sir John Duncan, who recognized the similarity in description between Liddell Hart's expanding torrent and Sunzi's strategy. These similarities were rather tenuous, but they were enough. Liddell Hart read the indirect method into Sunzi, and Sunzi absorbed the indirect method, dropping its association with Liddell Hart. It is possible that Liddell Hart took the indirect method from Sunzi, particularly through the Giles translation, and made it his own. If that is true, then Liddell Hart popularized the idea, and promoted Sunzi, as the Giles translation had not. In either case, the widespread association of Sunzi with the indirect strategy grew out of Liddell Hart's Foreword to Griffith's translation.

8   The Reaction to Griffith's Sunzi Translation

> A Chinese philosopher, Sun Tzu, 2,500 years ago, said, "Winning a hundred victories in a hundred battles is not the acme of skill. To subdue the enemy without fighting is the acme of skill."
>
> President Ronald Reagan, address at commencement exercises at the United States Military Academy, May 27, 1981[1]

Samuel B. Griffith passed away on March 27, 1983, in Newport, Rhode Island. At the time of his death, he was considered by many to be the foremost expert on Sunzi in the West. His friend B. H. Liddell Hart had already passed away more than a decade before on January 29, 1970. Earlier in 1983, Lionel Giles's translation of Sunzi was republished, this time with a Foreword by the novelist James Clavell. Clavell's fame as the author of novels set in East Asia helped to create a new wave of readers of Sunzi, just as Liddell Hart's Foreword had broadened the audience of receptive readers for Griffith's translation in 1963. The far greater recognition that Griffith's translation received outside the sinological community, as compared to Giles's translation, completely shifted the place of Sunzi in the West. The serendipitous coincidence of Griffith's credibility as a marine with experience of China, the success of the Chinese Communists under Mao Zedong in the Chinese Civil War, and the more general rise of China as a major and revolutionary power, all made the Sunzi important in the West as it had never been before.

The Western interpretation of Sunzi started from Griffith and Liddell Hart's perspective, and was then influenced by the marketing of the work, by its perceived value in military education, and its use as a window into Chinese strategic culture. In marketing terms, Griffith and everyone who followed him claimed that as a classic work of Chinese strategy it offered both profound strategic wisdom and insight into Chinese behavior. As a strategic work, a number of military and political leaders in the West called for it to be included into the curricula of military academies and

---

[1] Note that this quote from Chapter 3 comes from Griffith's Sunzi translation. It is entirely absent from Giles's translation.

officer training. And, absent any real knowledge of Chinese military history and strategic culture, the Sunzi could be substituted for a fully informed expert. This was particularly useful for academic disciplines inclined toward abstract universals that excluded culture and history as a means to understand China. Sunzi was either a classic work of universal wisdom, or it was an ancient Chinese classic that described immutable, fundamental Chinese orientations, or perhaps both.

The initial reaction to Griffith's translation was confined to the sinological community. Some scholars were unimpressed with the translation on technical grounds, others complained that it was neither scholarly enough nor popular enough, and most recognized the limitations of some of Griffith's claims for Sunzi's relationship to Mao Zedong. In other words, the book received the usual amount of scholarly ambivalence for a new work. The premodernists were primarily concerned with linguistic issues, and the modernists wished that Griffith had spent more effort tying Sunzi to Mao and Chinese Communist strategy.

The major difference for Griffith's translation took place outside the sinological community. Sunzi became a general work on strategy not only comparable to Clausewitz and Liddell Hart, but eventually beyond them. Liddell Hart had always written for a general audience, but by the 1980s he was much less widely known beyond specialist circles. Clausewitz had never been read by a casual reader, and, to the extent that nonspecialists knew of him, it was Liddell Hart's simplistic caricature as a thuggish, bloody-minded warmonger. Alessandro Corneli argues that Sunzi had attracted the attention of "Western experts" in two periods, the mid-1960s and the early 1980s, with interest in the latter period due to the republication of the Giles translation.[2] Corneli's well-informed overview of Sunzi in the West up until 1987 is a useful vantage point from which to examine the influence of Sunzi in general, as well as the Griffith–Liddell Hart "indirect-strategy" interpretation of *The Art of War*. Before turning to Corneli, however, we should first look at the sinological reception of Griffith.

Reviews of *The Art of War*

Before turning to the broader reception of Sunzi in the 1960s and after, it is also important to understand how Griffith's translation was received within the scholarly community. The earliest review was by the great sinologist and Chinese historian Michael Loewe in October 1963 for

---

[2] Alessandro Corneli, "Sun Tzu and the Indirect Strategy," *Rivista di Studi Politici Internazionali*, July–September 1987, 54/3 (215), 419.

the *Journal of the Royal Asiatic Society of Great Britain and Ireland*. Loewe was not very impressed:

The introductory chapters of this new translation of the *Ping-fa* cover a wide variety of subjects, ranging from the transmission of the text to the recent performance of the People's Liberation Army and its opponents. The treatment of such issues is poorly balanced, being too superficial for the scholar but, elsewhere, too technical for the general readers. Historians may find the account of pre-Han China to be insufficiently realistic, and the assumption that Mao Tse-tung's ideas of strategy can be traced to Sun Tzu's precepts cannot be accepted without more explicit evidence.

Loewe was also familiar with the Giles translation: "Much of the translation of the text is similar to the rendering published by Giles in 1910."[3] But, also in 1963, a brief review in *Revue bibliographique de sinologie* by Timoteus Pokora (1928–1985) called it an "exact and readable translation of the *Sun-tzu ping-fa* and of the *Wu-tzu*." Pokora noted, "Special interest is paid to warfare during the Warring States period and to the way in which Mao Tse-tung made use of Sun-tzu's ideas."[4] It is worth noting that Pokora's review of the Griffith translation was sandwiched between two reviews of Japanese books on Sunzi which had also come out in 1963, Kanaya Osamu's *Sonshi*, which contained the Chinese text, a traditional Japanese reading, and a modern Japanese translation, and Satō Kenji's *Sonshi no taikeiteki kenkyū*, which discussed Sunzi's relation to other Chinese military writers, as well as a modern Japanese rendering of the text. Quite by accident, 1963 was a good year for studies and translations of Sunzi.

Benjamin Wallacker wrote a long and detailed appraisal of Griffith in the *Journal of the American Oriental Society* in 1963, in which he began by speculating, "With the ever-growing importance of China in the present world scene, we may yet see the time when the name of Sun Tzu, the classic military thinker, is as well known in the West as the names of his Confucian and Taoist contemporaries." Wallacker mentions that quotes from Sunzi are found in the writings of Mao Zedong, "his twentieth century follower." Griffith's book would "supplant the fine version of Lionel Giles as the standard English translation"; however, "The translation itself differs from Giles's more in style than in degree of accuracy, and preference for one over the other is often a matter of taste." After a comparison of translations between Giles and Griffith, along with

---

[3] Michael A. N. Loewe, "*Sun Tzu: The Art of War* by Samuel Griffith," *Journal of the Royal Asiatic Society of Great Britain and Ireland*, October 1963, 3/4, 252.
[4] Timoteus Pokora, "*Sun Tzu: The Art of War* by Samuel Griffith," *Revue bibliographique de sinologie*, 1963, 9, 372.

careful criticisms of the finer points of translating certain passages, Wallacker concludes that "we have reason to be grateful for the appearance of Dr. Griffith's excellent work."[5]

In 1964, Scott and Howard Boorman wrote a review article titled "Mao Tse-tung and the Art of War" for the *Journal of Asian Studies* centered on "*Sun Tzu: The Art of War* Translated and with an Introduction by Samuel B. Griffith, with a foreword by B. H. Liddell Hart." The Boormans were concerned not only to review the Griffith translation, but also to relate it to contemporary Chinese military thought. They began by praising Sunzi's enduring legacy,

> Yet the durability of Sun Tzu's basic concepts is indisputable. Portions of Clausewitz are today of almost antiquarian interest; many recent books on the theory and practice of war are partially outdated. Sun Tzu, however, has been handed down for over two thousand years with reputation virtually untarnished, with text virtually intact.

As with so many promoters of Sunzi, it is presented as a classic in contrast to Clausewitz's historically circumscribed theories. Howard Boorman, at least, had corresponded with Griffith,[6] so was very much aware of Griffith's background, which is recounted in the review article, along with an overview of other translations. They chose to compare Griffith and Giles, finding that "Griffith's translation is more precise and more comprehensible and profits from his long military experience. It must be admitted, however, that the similarities between the two translations outnumber the differences, as may be expected in comparing versions of so short a text."[7]

The Boormans were primarily interested in the place of Sunzi in twentieth-century China, discussing Chiang Kai-shek's interest in and collection of editions of Sunzi, as well as the Chinese Nationalists' military theorists, Chiang Fang-chen (1882–1938) and Yang Chieh (1889–1949), who had both written commentaries on Sunzi. With respect to Sunzi's influence on the Chinese Communists, they can only speculate that the "influence may have been substantial," since research on the issue was lacking. Mao had relied on the Sunzi somewhat, and other Communists had written about it. The Boormans are clear, however, that Griffith's assertion of significant influence is an unproven theory, though the first in a Western language. To their disappointment, his

---

[5] Benjamin Wallacker, "*Sun Tzu – The Art of War* by Samuel Griffith," *Journal of the American Oriental Society*, April–June 1963, 83/2, 268–271.
[6] See Howard Boorman's letters to Griffith on October 5, 1964, and January 1, 1965, MCA. They suggest much earlier contact with Griffith.
[7] Scott A. Boorman and Howard L. Boorman, "Mao Tse-tung and the *Art of War*," *Journal of Asian Studies*, November 1964, 24/1, 129–131.

discussion of Mao and Sunzi is brief and shallow. After an intriguing discussion of passages that Mao may have copied from Sunzi, they bring up Kuo Hua-jo, a Communist military theorist who was chosen to write the introduction to the newly published edition of Sunzi in 1961. Leaving aside his Marxist-themed comments, Kuo also noted that "Sun Tzu advocated offensive strategy designed to end a war quickly rather than the indirect approach of protracted war." Mao, of course, had written an essay on protracted war.

Kuo Hua-jo's criticism of Sunzi's lack of an indirect approach highlights two important points: that Sunzi can be interpreted very differently from the twentieth-century Western reading, and that Liddell Hart's conception of indirect strategy is very specific, tied to speed and mobility rather than strategy in general. The Boormans lament that Kuo's commentary on Sunzi also does not address the relationship between Sunzi and Mao Zedong's military theories. To undertake such a task would require "a substantial body of monographic work in at least three areas: first, the study of Sun Tzu; second, the history and doctrine of the Chinese Communist forces during their insurgent period; and, third, Chinese military history." Very little progress has been made in addressing any of these issues in the subsequent fifty-five years. They continue, "The rescue of Sun Tzu from semi-obscurity constitutes a research objective of intrinsic value." In yet another aspect that hasn't changed; they complain that one of the main problems is the thicket of bad studies by incompetent writers who lack knowledge of Chinese language or history.[8]

Two Western books stood out for the Boormans in learning about early Chinese Communist military history: Edgar Snow's *Red Star over China* (1938), and Evans Carlson's *Twin Stars of China* (1940). They also acknowledge that the field of strategic studies was, at that time, producing a large number of "analytical studies of guerrilla, unconventional, irregular, and revolutionary war." Much of the Boormans' critique of the then inadequate field of studies of insurgency, at least with respect to pre-1949 China, leads up to their conclusion, agreeing with Loewe, that Griffith did not prove his thesis of a connection between Sunzi and Mao. Yet it is their more general comment with respect to the Chinese Communists and Sunzi that is most telling:

The Chinese military tradition, long obscured and discredited by generations of humanistic scholarship both in China and in the West, has now been repolished in Peking ... The reappearance of Sun Tzu as part of the canon of the People's

---

[8] Boorman and Boorman, 134.

Republic is an intriguing symbol of the admixture of continuity and change inherent in a revolutionary upheaval.[9]

Where the Boormans were mostly concerned with the place of Griffith's translation with respect to twentieth-century Chinese military affairs, D. C. Lau focused exclusively on Griffith's linguistic failures. Lau says that Amiot's translation was ignored by professional sinologists, and that the Giles translation, "though far from being satisfactory," was the most widely used after 1910. A new translation was welcome, but Griffith's "has turned out to be so disappointing." Griffith's military background established his unquestionable expertise on the art of war, "But it would seem that the task of coping with the pitfalls inherent in the language of the Classical period and with genuine textual difficulties has proved too much for Griffith." Lau goes on to criticize the edition of Sunzi that Griffith based his work on, followed by a long technical discussion of the philological problems of interpreting the text. Part of the problem in understanding the Sunzi was the lack of philological scholarship, as distinct from the extensive commentarial tradition. As a narrow philological critique, Lau stands on firm ground, though his privileging of his philologically based interpretation over Griffith's military-based interpretation is not unassailable.[10]

The variety of opinions within the scholarly community reflected the respective concerns of the scholars writing. Most had no interest in the strategic content of the Sunzi, nor did they recommend it as a work of practical use. The Boormans were the only reviewers who saw the work in the context of military history, but were more interested in the question of Sunzi's influence on Mao, and the use being made of Sunzi within Communist China. None of the reviewers suggested that the core of Sunzi was one strategy or another, though some noted Giles's use of "direct" and "indirect" for *zheng* and *qi*, where Griffith used "normal" and "extraordinary." Professional sinologists, to use D. C. Lau's term, in the 1960s did not characterize Sunzi as a champion of indirect strategy. The Boormans even cited an example of a Chinese Communist military theorist criticizing Sunzi for not having an indirect strategy. Outside the field of China specialists, however, the indirect strategy was attributed to Sunzi, and became orthodoxy. That orthodoxy would eventually pervade not only nonspecialists, but also specialists in China studies.

[9] Boorman and Boorman, 137.
[10] D. C. Lau, "Some Notes on the Sun Tzu," *Bulletin of the School of Oriental and African Studies*, 1965, 28/2, 319, 320–321 fn. 9.

"Sun Tzu and the Indirect Strategy"

The most obvious marker of the influence of the indirect-strategy inter-pretation is that in surveying Sunzi's influence Corneli takes it as a given that Sunzi advocated for indirect strategy. His article is titled "Sun Tzu and the Indirect Strategy," and it begins, "Over the last five to six years, there has been renewed interest in Sun Tzu's political and military thought, mainly by experts in strategy (particularly *indirect strategy*), international political relations and *intelligence* who are most concerned with the matter."[11] Corneli adds that Sunzi "is considered the first theoretician on guerrilla warfare, and it is certain that Mao Tse-Tung sought inspiration from him. Finally, since the last chapter of his book deals with the role of secret agents, he is also regarded as the theoretician of *intelligence*."[12] Contrary to the expert opinion among China scholars, the connections between Sunzi, guerrilla warfare, and Mao Zedong had become as unquestioned for Corneli as indirect strategy. The main add-ition to the list of Sunzi connections is his emphasis on the use of spies.

To be fair, Sunzi had gained some association with guerrilla or revolu-tionary warfare even before Griffith (keeping in mind the frequent confla-tion of those two kinds of warfare). Colonel Gabriel Bonnet knew about Sunzi, and attributed to him the earliest understanding of revolutionary war, which he saw as the combination of partisan and psychological war in his 1958 book *Les guerres insurrectionelles et révolutionnaires*.[13] As a French officer, Bonnet associated Vietnamese anticolonial warfare with the ancient Chinese thinker. Certainly, the association of Chinese commun-ist guerrilla warfare and the general worldwide wave of anticolonial guer-rilla insurgencies made this an easy connection. Less clear is whether he had any direct evidence that anti-French insurgents were reading Sunzi; it may have been enough that they were likely reading Mao, who was much more directly relevant to their immediate operational needs. What is important here is that Bonnet believed that there was some connection between guerrilla warfare and Sunzi even in 1958. Griffith's earlier Mao translation had come out in 1941 and Bonnet's stance shows that, at least among experts, the association of Sunzi with Mao and thus guerrilla warfare pre-existed the publication of Griffith's Sunzi translation.

Corneli goes on to point out that Sunzi is first mentioned in the *Encyclopaedia Britannica* in 1961, within the "Strategy" entry, only gain-ing a separate entry in the 1974 edition. That edition also mentioned

---

[11] Corneli, "Sun Tzu and the Indirect Strategy," 419, italics in the original.
[12] Corneli, "Sun Tzu and the Indirect Strategy," 419, italics in the original.
[13] Gabriel Bonnet, *Les guerres insurrectionelles et révolutionnaires*, Paris: Payot, 1958, 288, cited in Corneli, "Sun Tzu and the Indirect Strategy," 421.

Sunzi under "A Brief History of Intelligence Activities," "Methods of Guerrilla Warfare," and "Evolution of the Theory of Propaganda."[14] The evolution of the *Encyclopaedia Britannica*'s engagement with the Sunzi shows that while the Sunzi was known before 1963, it became a real topic to be explained after the publication of Griffith's translation. Sunzi's inclusion under guerrilla warfare was further confirmation of his association with Mao and insurgency, but he was now connected to intelligence and propaganda as well. Bonnet, of course, had emphasized Sunzi's influence on revolutionary and psychological war, all of which were connected to propaganda. In the late 1960s and early 1970s Sunzi was a strategist of unconventional, revolutionary war, and an exemplar of anti-imperialist, anti-Western resistance. Similar to earlier efforts to connect Sunzi to Napoleon, some people associated Sunzi with Soviet Russia. Sunzi became not just the strategist of China, East Asia, or Asia, but of the entire non-West.

In *The Craft of Intelligence*, also published in 1963, a former head of the CIA, Allan Dulles, not only includes Sunzi in his discussion of intelligence, but also refers directly in a footnote to Samuel Griffith's translation. Given the timing of both publications, it seems likely that Dulles had access to a pre-publication draft of Griffith's work. Griffith wrote to Dulles on August 12, 1961, including in that letter a pre-publication copy of the introduction to Praeger's publication of his translation of Mao's *On Guerrilla Warfare*. Griffith promised Dulles an author's complimentary copy of his Sunzi translation. Dulles thanked him for the introduction in a letter replying on August 30, 1961, said he would hold him to the promised complimentary copy of Sunzi, and, "In closing let me say that many of your old friends in the agency send their regards as do I."[15] Of course, Dulles could not have read the translation while he was serving as head of the CIA from 1953 to 1961. Writing after leaving the CIA he felt compelled to include Sunzi in his overview of the history of intelligence. He was not familiar with any of the earlier translations.

The 1968 edition of the *International Encyclopedia of Social Sciences* includes Sunzi under the category of "strategy" but states that "his 'Art of War', however, is today merely quaint." Similarly, the 1964 *Grand Larousse encyclopédique* notes that Sunzi is the foundation of military thought in China and Japan.[16] Even those who did not take Sunzi seriously as a text were aware of it, and felt that not including the work would reflect poorly on them. That is to say, *The Art of War* was widely enough

[14] Corneli, "Sun Tzu and the Indirect Strategy," 421.
[15] Griffith to Dulles, August 12, 1961; Dulles to Griffith, August 30, 1961, CIA-RDP80B01676R003500090004-3.
[16] Cited in Corneli, "Sun Tzu and the Indirect Strategy," 422.

known in 1964 that not mentioning it in an encyclopedic work would undermine the works' claims to comprehensive coverage. Sunzi had become important enough that it couldn't be ignored, though it could still be disparaged. As an unconventional work, or at least one outside the Western tradition of military thought, it was and remains often the subject of a strong resistance to reading seriously. Some of this stems from its reading as an anti-Western text, or one associated with communist insurgencies.

Field Marshal Bernard Montgomery (1887–1976) published *A History of Warfare* in 1968. Montgomery was familiar with Sunzi, commenting, "I should like to have talked with Sun Tzu; it would appear that on the subject of the conduct of war we would have much in common, and he understood the human factor."[17] As Corneli points out, the bibliography of that book only mentions the Giles translation reprinted in T. R. Phillip's anthology of 1943. When exactly Montgomery read Sunzi can therefore only be narrowed down to sometime between 1943 and 1968. Montgomery's decision to praise Sunzi may well have come from genuine admiration, but like many victorious generals writing about war after their time of glory we must be sensitive to his self-conscious interest in placing himself within the history of war. He was acutely aware of the histories of World War II being written, and of their evaluations of his work and that of his contemporaries. At a minimum, he felt it was important not only to indicate that he had read Sunzi, but also that he held similar views on warfare. This was exactly the same position that Liddell Hart had taken in 1963, connecting his views with those of Sunzi to legitimize Sunzi and, in so doing, to elevate his own status.

By 1987, when his article was published, Corneli felt it necessary to point out that Liddell Hart had written the Foreword to Griffith's translation, describing him as the "well-known expert in indirect strategy."[18] As with the title of the article, Corneli took it as a given that Sunzi advocated for an indirect strategy and that Liddell Hart as a twentieth-century expert was particularly qualified to endorse that strategy. Quoting from Liddell Hart's Foreword that the world would have been saved from the destruction of the two world wars if Europeans had been less inclined to follow Clausewitz and included more of Sunzi in their thinking, he concludes that section by saying that "Liddell Hart's warning was not to be followed for almost twenty years."[19] At least for Corneli, and

---

[17] Bernard Montgomery, *A History of Warfare*, London: Collins, 1968, 383, cited in Corneli, "Sun Tzu and the Indirect Strategy," 423.
[18] Corneli, "Sun Tzu and the Indirect Strategy," 423.
[19] Corneli, "Sun Tzu and the Indirect Strategy," 424.

unbeknownst to him, Liddell Hart had succeeded in making Sunzi a proponent of the indirect strategy.

If Sunzi was the earliest advocate of indirect strategy, perhaps even the originator of the idea, then all subsequent writers, like Liddell Hart, were merely derivative. Hence Montgomery would attach himself to Sunzi without giving Liddell Hart any credit for his successes in war. The great advantage of discussing a classical writer was that one could look educated and thoughtful without attributing any innovation to a contemporary. Liddell Hart had already claimed credit, sometimes with J. F. C. Fuller, for blitzkrieg, which was the most notable "strategy" of World War II. One of the oddest aspects of World War II historiography is how much praise the German generals received from the countries that defeated them. Liddell Hart was an important part of that evaluation and it played a significant role in restoring his reputation as a strategist after World War II.

Before continuing to the 1980s, it is important to pause in the 1970s, specifically in 1974, to examine a pivotal book that helped to cement the notion that China had a distinct method of war, *Chinese Ways in Warfare*. The roots of that volume went back to 1963, when a conference on Chinese governmental institutions was held at Harvard University, at which Professor Jung-pang Lo presented a bibliographic introduction to Chinese military history. A subsequent conference on Ming dynasty government in 1965 strongly recommended convening a military-history conference. These two meetings, the former sponsored by the Social Sciences Research Council, and the latter by the American Council of Learned Societies (ACLS), led to an ACLS and Harvard East Asian Research Center-supported meeting hosted by the Massachusetts Institute of Technology from August 24 to 29, 1969. The conference included many prominent scholars and military men, and eventually led to the publication of *Chinese Ways in Warfare* by Harvard University Press in 1974.[20] Despite such an auspicious beginning, the field of Chinese military history remained perennially nascent until 2002, with the tipping-point publication of David Graff's *Medieval Chinese Warfare, 300–900*.[21]

---

[20] Frank A. Kierman and John K. Fairbank, "Acknowledgments," in Frank A. Kierman Jr. and John K. Fairbank (eds.), *Chinese Ways in Warfare*, Cambridge, MA: Harvard University Press, 1974, vii.

[21] This is not to dismiss the important work of Bruce Elleman, Arthur Waldron, Ed Dreyer, and Ed McCord. Beyond those scholars' work on Chinese military history, Iain Johnston's work in political science, Robin Yates's tremendous contributions under the umbrella of Joseph Needham's publications on Chinese science, and Ralph and Mei-chün Sawyer's translations all laid an important foundation for the field as it finally gained some forward momentum.

Chinese Ways in Warfare explicitly recognized the need for Chinese military history, as distinct from strategic thought. The goal was to present "researches on battles and sieges, on campaigns abroad and at home, and on suppressions of invaders and of rebels that date all the way from 632 B.C. to A.D. 1556. The researchers' aims are essentially analytic, to show facets of the Chinese military style and tradition." Fairbank argued that the military circumstances confronting the world made a consideration of China's military history timely. He also detected some differences in Chinese warfare: "In the aftermath of the age of Western expansion that seems to have reached one kind of a climax in Vietnam, we may well view the Chinese style of warfare as somewhat less expansive than our own."[22] Here again we see the "West-versus-the-rest" paradigm, with China standing in for the larger non-Western world. Fairbank's claim of a "somewhat less expansive" Chinese style or way of warfare may have made sense in the wake of Western imperialism, but it was historical nonsense. It nonetheless represented a frequently held view that persists to the present that Chinese military culture is fundamentally less aggressive than Western military culture.

Fairbank then turns to the journalist Walter Millis's 1961 essay *Military History*, "The historical views of Jomini and Clausewitz," Fairbank paraphrases, "are no less outdated than the ideas of General Henry Halleck, G. F. R. Henderson, Sir Charles Oman, Alfred Thayer Mahan, J. F. C. Fuller, and others in this field."[23] He points out in the endnote that Millis made no references to Asia, which was also true of the volume Edward Mead Earle edited in 1944, *Makers of Modern Strategy*.[24] Curiously, Millis mentions Fuller but not Liddell Hart, perhaps a sign of how patchy Liddell Hart's reputation was in 1961. The list is also strange because Henderson and Oman were eminent military historians (Henderson also had a distinguished military career), Halleck was an American Civil War general, and only Mahan and Fuller were really strategic thinkers similar to Jomini and Clausewitz. Millis's goal was to move the world toward a more civil dominant society, and the nobility of that end may perhaps excuse his unsystematic approach to military history. He recognized, however, the importance of military history in shaping societies' attitudes toward war, which caused him to urge military history as a field to move away from the historical study of wars and become more engaged with politics, economics, sociology, and applied science.[25] This explains Millis's mishmash of important military figures.

---

[22] John K. Fairbank, "Introduction: Varieties of the Chinese Military Experience," in Kierman and Fairbank, *Chinese Ways in Warfare*, 1.
[23] Fairbank, "Introduction," 1.   [24] Fairbank, "Introduction," 311 n.
[25] Fairbank, "Introduction," 1.

He understood "military history" to include a wide range of people discussing military affairs from many perspectives. But he was also entirely Western in his perspective, and did not, as others would, suggest that non-Western military perspectives would fulfill his goals.

Sunzi comes up only three times in *Chinese Ways in Warfare*. Further on in his Introduction, Fairbank says that the strategy and tactics that had developed in the Warring States period were written down in military manuals like the Sunzi, which he dates to *c.* 400 to 320 BCE, and that Sunzi continues to influence Chinese and worldwide thinking up until the present. In his endnote to this statement, he cites Griffith's Sunzi translation, and Griffith's connection of Sunzi to Mao Zedong's doctrines.[26] Sunzi is mentioned a second time in Frank Kierman's chapter on "Phases and Modes of Combat in Early China," where he produces a plan for a battle based upon his assumption that the commander would have followed Sunzi's advice:

This plan is based upon a combination of inferences from the topography of Ching-hsing area, from what the text says, and from the ideas in Sun-tzu's *Art of War (Sun-tzu ping-fa)*. Quite clearly Ch'en Yü, as a solid book-soldier, would have kept the hills to his rear and right and would have constructed his entrenchments on relatively high ground.[27]

His reconstruction relies upon a number of questionable assumptions, not the least of which is that because the commander was well read, he would have been very familiar with Sunzi, and would have followed him regardless of whatever other circumstances he faced.

The third mention of Sunzi, by Charles A. Peterson, in his chapter "The Huai-hsi Campaign, 815–817," follows a logic similar to Kierman's. Recounting the unexpected forced marches of troops under Li Su, who first overran a rebel position after a twenty-mile night march, followed by a twenty-three-mile march through a snowstorm that allowed them to capture a town by surprise, he says, "By this stroke, Li Su, perhaps unconsciously but not accidentally, had acted in the highest tradition of Chinese generalship. Acknowledging Sun-tzu's precept that 'rapidity is the essence of war,' he had taken 'advantage of the enemy's unreadiness,' made his way 'by unexpected routes,' and attacked 'unguarded spots.'"[28] Peterson's references are to the Giles translation, and are part of his analysis. The primary sources for his account do not

---

[26] Fairbank, "Introduction," 311 n.
[27] Frank A. Kierman Jr., "Phases and Modes of Combat in Early China," in Kierman and Fairbank, *Chinese Ways in Warfare*, 60.
[28] Charles A. Peterson, "The Huai-hsi Campaign, 815–817," in Kierman and Fairbank, *Chinese Ways in Warfare*, 144.

mention Sunzi, nor is there any discussion of strategy with reference to texts there. Rather than merely presenting this series of surprise marches as an example of Li Su's generalship, Peterson connects his tactics to Sunzi. In this construction, even if Li Su had never read Sunzi, his tactics reflect the fundamentally Chinese way of war described in the Sunzi.

To reinforce this connection to Sunzi, he says of Li Su, "He took another lesson from Sun-tzu as well: 'At the critical moment, the leader of an army acts like one who has climbed up a height and then kicks away the ladder behind him. He carries his men deep into hostile territory before he shows his hand.'"[29] It is not surprising in a book aimed at seeking a Chinese way in warfare that the contributors should emphasize tactics or strategies that exemplified the written tradition of Chinese warfare. Equally important, in the 1960s and early 1970s there was almost nothing in a Western language on Chinese military history, and not much more in Chinese or Japanese. The single most important work on China's military past was Sunzi's *Art of War*. English translations of Sunzi by Giles and Griffith were the de facto foundation of all discussions of Chinese military history.[30]

Even before the reissue of the Giles translation, Sunzi was quoted by prominent figures involved in foreign policy. Former president Richard Nixon published *The Real War* in 1980 (in which he quoted Liddell Hart more than anyone else). As part of an extensive critique of how the Vietnam War had been waged, he lamented the gradualism and reticence to employ overwhelming force that he believed had undermined the United States' military efforts. He quoted a private conversation with former president Eisenhower, who "fumed about this gradualism," saying, "If the enemy holds a hill with a battalion, give me two battalions and I'll take it, but at great cost in casualties. Give me a division and I'll take it without a fight." Nixon himself summed up the problems:

In Vietnam during that period we were not subtle enough in waging the guerrilla war, we were too subtle in waging the conventional war. We were too patronizing, even contemptuous toward our ally, and too solicitous of our enemy. Vietnamese morale was sapped by "Americanization" of the war; American morale was sapped by the perpetuation of the war.[31]

---

[29] Charles A. Peterson, "The Huai-hsi Campaign, 815–817," 144.

[30] Although it is beyond the scope of the present work, it is worth noting that the Taiwanese military produced, at Chiang Kai-shek's order, a military history of China in eighteen volumes, in 1972, after sixteen years of work. That history, *Zhongguo lidai zhanzheng shi*, also inserted quotes from Sunzi throughout its campaign accounts, even though Sunzi was not mentioned in the primary sources.

[31] Richard Nixon, *The Real War*, New York: Warner Books, 1980, 105.

This led to Nixon's important point:

Democracies are not well equipped to fight prolonged wars. A democracy fights well after its morale is galvanized by an enemy attack and it gears up its war production. A totalitarian power can coerce its population into fight indefinitely. But a democracy fights well only as long as public opinion supports the war, and public opinion will not continue to support a war that drags on without tangible signs of progress.[32]

Nixon then felt it useful to quote two passages from Chapter 2 in Griffith's translation, "There has never been a protracted war from which a country has benefitted," and "What is essential in war is victory, not prolonged operations." These passages supported his position with respect to the United States and democracies, but not totalitarian regimes. Nixon had effectively placed Sunzi on the side of American strategy and vice versa. All of this discussion was a preamble to explaining his announcement in Guam on July 25, 1969, of what became known as "the Nixon doctrine." The Nixon doctrine centered on the idea that "countries threatened by communist aggression must take primary responsibility for their own defense." Nixon does not, unfortunately, tell us if he had read Sunzi before developing the Nixon doctrine, or if he was merely using it as a *post facto* explanation of his thinking.

Nixon also drew on Sunzi to critique the American nuclear strategy that existed before he took office. The prevailing strategy was based upon the deterrent effect of mutually assured destruction (MAD). Since the response to a nuclear strike by either the United States or the Soviet Union would result in a counterstrike, and since any nuclear strike would completely destroy the target society, a nuclear launch was tantamount to mutual suicide. Nixon raised three objections to MAD. First, the Soviet Union believed it could, with proper preparation, survive a nuclear strike. Regardless of the truth of that belief, it meant that MAD would not deter the Soviet Union. Second, MAD provided no options to the United States if deterrence failed, and lacked rational objectives, political or military, if war broke out. Third, it was simply morally wrong; "The United States should never place itself in a position where its strategy implies that the deliberate slaughter of civilians is a proper objective. Deterrence should not be based on such a threat."[33]

Nixon's connection of the moral and strategic problems of MAD led him to Sunzi's admonition in Chapter 3: "What is of supreme importance in war is to attack the enemy's strategy." He includes in his quote Sunzi's descending order of preference, disrupting alliances, attacking his army,

---

[32] Nixon, *The Real War*, 105.   [33] Nixon, *The Real War*, 162.

and finally attacking cities. Nixon used an apposite quote that showed the enduring strategic value of the Chinese text for nuclear strategy. Apart from the failure of MAD as a deterrent, Sunzi's strategy of attacking enemy strategy seems a fair description of much of the Cold War. The United States and the Soviet Union each struggled to frustrate the other's strategies and break apart their alliances, and fought a few peripheral wars, never attacking each others' cities. Unlike Kierman and Peterson's association of Sunzi-like ideas in their analyses of the Chinese past, Nixon offers direct evidence of the influence of Sunzi on his thinking. He read and thought through Sunzi enough to quote the text directly in support of a change in strategy.

His engagement with Sunzi went even deeper than just nuclear strategy, further indication that he read the text seriously. Nixon was interested in formulating a successful strategy to defeat the Soviet Union. In Corneli's telling, Nixon advocated "using an adequate dosage of strength (military strategy) and cunning and propaganda (indirect strategy)."[34] What Nixon actually wrote was,

More than 2,000 years ago the ancient Chinese strategist set forth this principle: Engage with the *ch'eng*[35] –the ordinary, direct force – but win with the *ch'i* – the extraordinary, indirect force. In his wisdom he saw that the two are mutually reinforcing and that the way to victory is by the simultaneous use of both. In our own time we have no choice but to engage with the *ch'eng* – to counterpose our military strength to that of the Soviet Union, to hold our alliances together and increase the combined strength of the West. This is the way to avoid defeat; this is the way to contain the Soviet advance. It is an essential first step, just as the tide has to stop coming in before it goes out. The next step – to go on toward victory, to win with the *ch'i* – is at once more complex, more subtle, and more demanding.[36]

Corneli adds, "we may simplify by saying that the ordinary force of *ch'eng* is the military one (direct strategy), while the extraordinary force or *ch'i* stands for all those actions which seek to bend the enemy's will without fighting: it is therefore indirect strategy."[37]

Corneli's simplification here goes too far, since Sunzi explains that *zheng* and *qi* forces can switch places as circumstances develop. Nixon grasped Sunzi's meaning very clearly, seeing that counterposing military strength to the Soviet Union was a way of defeating their strategy without necessarily fighting, and also understanding that the *qi* part of strategy was a much more difficult and less obvious, but critical, counterpart to the

---

[34] Corneli, "Sun Tzu and the Indirect Strategy," 425.
[35] This should be *cheng* in Wade–Giles romanization (*zheng* in Pinyin), not *ch'eng*.
[36] Nixon, *The Real War*, 300.
[37] Corneli, "Sun Tzu and the Indirect Strategy," 425. Corneli makes the same *cheng/ch'eng* error.

demonstration of conventional military strength. Using conventional military strength to defeat or deter enemy strategy might, in fact, lead to war, but unlike nuclear war it would be less likely to lead to suicide or atrocities. Counterposing conventional military strength to frustrate Soviet plans was contrary to the theory of MAD, and avoided all of the problems with MAD that Nixon had identified.

James Clavell's Sunzi republication did not, therefore, introduce or revive Sunzi for experts. Even Henry Kissinger, who made only a single reference to Sunzi, was clearly aware of the work.[38] It did promote Sunzi to a broader audience. Clavell's Foreword was in many respects similar to Liddell Hart's, if considerably more idealistic. He avowed that if modern leaders had read Sunzi the Vietnam War would have turned out differently, we would not have lost the Korean War, we would have skipped the Bay of Pigs and the hostage crisis in Iran, the British Empire wouldn't have collapsed, and World War I and World War II would have either not taken place or been waged more effectively. These are simply extraordinary claims which go far beyond what a military historian, general, or political leader would ever imagine. Yet Clavell was a writer and not a military expert. He also stressed that Sunzi was required reading for Soviet Russian leaders, and that it was the source for Mao's "*Little Red Book* of strategic and tactical doctrine." Here we see again the invocation of the great powers of the non-Western world to legitimize the reading of Sunzi. Clavell believes that those opponents were succeeding "in some areas" because they were reading Sunzi. He appears to be referring to the various insurgencies, like Vietnam, that were succeeding or had succeeded despite US intervention. His reference to Mao's *Little Red Book* is odd, however, since the few passages that are similar to Sunzi's make up only a tiny portion of the work. He may have confused the *Little Red Book* used during the Cultural Revolution with Mao's military writings.

Clavell says that he first read Sunzi in 1977, after a friend recommended it to him. Given that Clavell had already written several novels set in Asia, *King Rat* (1962), *Tai-Pan* (1966), and *Shōgun* (1975), for which he had done considerable research, his unfamiliarity with Sunzi shows just how limited knowledge of the work was. Sunzi had nowhere near the name recognition in the 1970s that it has now; it would simply be inconceivable for an American (Clavell was originally Australian but became an American citizen) novelist writing about East Asia today to be unaware of Sunzi. He made great use of Sunzi in his subsequent novel *Noble House* (1981), which was set in Hong Kong in 1963. Knowledge of Sunzi became fundamental to his Chinese characters. Unfortunately, at

---

[38] Henry Kissinger, *Years of Upheaval*, Boston: Little, Brown, 1982.

least in America after World War II, Chinese aphorisms cited at moments of crisis had a tendency to appear to be "fortune cookie" wisdom. More concretely, Chinese strategy that argued against a direct assault on one's opponent reinforced the sort of orientalist perspective that contrasted weak, effeminate, but clever Chinese with strong, masculine, direct/thuggish Westerners.

Sunzi's wider recognition extended beyond America in the 1980s, often stimulated by Cold War concerns with the Soviet Union.[39] On November 19–20, 1983, *Le Figaro* published an article that focused on Soviet efforts to break up NATO and Euro-American alliances, arguing that Europe would be conquered without fighting. This was consistent with Sunzi's doctrines, which all Soviet leaders read.[40] Thomas Ries also discussed the connection between Sunzi and Soviet strategy in a 1984 essay, and contrasted Sunzi's approach to warfare to Clausewitz's. Ries viewed Clausewitz as emphasizing the use of violence after war broke out, and Sunzi as emphasizing preparation before a conflict.[41] The assumption or assertion of deep Soviet engagement with Sunzi was apparently widespread, though without much proof being offered to support it. Some writers, it seems, mapped perceived Soviet strategy onto their perception of Sunzi's strategy and then assumed that any similarities had to be the result of Soviet leaders applying Sunzi. Hans Kahler stated, "Lenin turned into a zealous disciple of Sun Tzu," though, assuming it is provable, the main reason to believe this is that Lenin promoted policies that fit the author's conception of Sunzi.[42] S. Steven Powel asserted that the Soviet strategy of "rear attack" (and its psychological effects) was first developed by Sun Tzu about 600 BC, and that the Russians had absorbed Sunzi via the Mongol invasions.[43] As with the lack of real evidence connecting Sunzi to Mao Zedong's military thought, none of these writers acknowledge in their analysis that the Soviet interpretation of Sunzi, if there is one, might be very different from their own.

Captain Louis Le Hegart took up the question of indirect strategy in 1984. Using an earlier definition of indirect strategy, he described it as a way of obtaining one's ends in nonmilitary ways, politically or

---

[39] A French translation of Griffith's translation was published in 1972, so it had been in circulation somewhat earlier.

[40] J. G. Brulon, "L'art de la guerre sans guerre," *Le Figaro*, November 19–20, 1983.

[41] Thomas Ries, "Sun Tzu et la stratégie soviétique," *Revue internationale de défense*, 1984, 4, 391. Ries's discussion is far more extensive than I have included here and certainly warrants more consideration than space allows.

[42] Hans Kahler, "La guerre psychopolitique de l'Union soviétique," *Revue internationale de défense*, 1986, 2, 157.

[43] S. Steven Powel, "Deterrence and the Political Psychological Conflict," *Strategic Review*, Winter 1986, 49–58. The Mongols invaded in the thirteenth century.

economically, or through alternating fighting and negotiating. The key point was that an indirect strategy used unusual or unexpected methods.[44] Le Hegart understood Sunzi's preference for defeating an opponent without fighting as an example of indirect strategy, as well as a proof that such strategy long pre-dated its recent appearance in the modern West. He recognized Liddell Hart's support for indirect strategy, but also that Clauswewitz's strategy of attrition, which he had included along with his strategy of annihilation, was a form of indirect strategy. Attrition achieved its goals without necessarily engaging in armed conflict. Le Hagart's analysis betrays a considerable debt to Hans Delbrück's analysis of Clausewitz, who formulated or revealed the Clausewitzian poles of *Ermattungsstrategie* ("exhausting strategy") versus *Niederwerfungsstrategie* ("throwing-down strategy"), often translated respectively as strategy of attrition versus strategy of annihilation. This also contrasts with Kuo Hua-jo's argument that Sunzi lacked an indirect strategy because it did not include a strategy of attrition.

Corneli himself, whose work has guided much of this discussion, published a work in Italian, "Sun Tzu e la nascita dell'arte della guerra," in 1984. He notes that Griffith's translation of Sunzi was translated into Italian in 1965. Even before that, however, in 1963, General M. Sessich wrote "L'Arte della Guerra di Sun Tzu, il Clausewitz cinese: sua influenza sul pensiero militare di Mao Tse-Tung." At least from General Sessich's perspective in 1963, Sunzi was the Chinese Clausewitz, and he influenced Mao's military thought. Some experts writing on military thought and security studies had been aware of Sunzi in the 1960s, and by the 1980s, as Corneli has argued, that awareness had become much more widespread in America and Western Europe.

The strength and the weakness of this awareness of Sunzi were that it was and is mostly used as a critique of the underlying strategic paradigm of the liberal democracies of the West. The assumption is that the West bases its strategy on Clausewitz, which is too rigid and simplistic. Russia/ the Soviet Union, or any non-Western power, cleverly followed Sunzi because they used intelligence, diplomacy, and guerrilla warfare to defeat direct, Clausewitzian, conventional warfare. Sunzi serves a specific function for critiquing the West, but it seems to mean different things to different people. Of course, Sunzi has always meant different things to different people at different times, but the Western assumption is that it is not necessary actually to determine how, for example, Sunzi was read in the Soviet Union when trying to explain Soviet strategy. The other reason

[44] Louis Le Hégart, "La stratégie et ses sources," *Défense nationale*, February–March, 1984, 32. Cited in Corneli, "Sun Tzu and the Indirect Strategy," 430–431.

for projecting Sunzi onto one's more strategically capable opponent is that the author is advocating for using Sunzi as one's adversary is doing. Yet a careful study of what Sunzi actually said is never included in this advocacy.

The 1980s and Beyond

In 1984, "Ten Important Books: Strategic Thought," by B.D.H. was published in *The Army Historian*.[45] Those ten books were, in order: Griffith's Sunzi translation, Machiavelli's *Art of War*, Jomini's *Art of War*, Clausewitz's *On War*, Mahan's *The Influence of Sea Power on History, 1660–1783*, Douhet's *The Command of the Air*, Liddell Hart's *Strategy*, Mao's *Selected Military Writings*, Beaufre's *An Introduction to Strategy*, and Brodie's *Strategy in the Missile Age*. The discussion of Sunzi begins,

That Sun Tzu wrote his *Art of War* in the fourth century B.C. does not diminish the freshness of his insight into the principles of strategy. Among thinkers of the past perhaps only Clausewitz is comparable, and even that nineteenth-century luminary is more dated than Sun Tzu, although Clausewitz wrote more than two thousand years later.

It goes on to say, "For strategy and military strategy, the thirteen short essays in *The Art of War* are far more useful than the writings of a Thucydides or a Caesar." We see here the now familiar juxtaposition of Sunzi as a classic greater than Clausewitz's historical work, and the elevation of Sunzi above the works of ancient Greece and Rome – certainly an assertion sure to raise the ire of classicists or those insisting upon the pre-eminence of Western culture.

The author does not impute indirect strategy to Sunzi, though s/he does follow Liddell Hart's foreword to Griffith's translation, recounting his encounter with Sunzi in 1927, and its similarity with Liddell Hart's indirect approach (the difference is subtle and carefully nuanced). The author also points out that Sunzi was not discussed in *Makers of Modern Strategy*, but that after the appearance of Griffith's translation, Sunzi "became part of American staff college reading lists." The characterization of Clausewitz is measured, praising *On War*, but lamenting that generals who actually implemented "Clausewitzian" strategy disregarded Clausewitz's qualifications of his extreme theoretical statements.

Liddell Hart in his turn gets credit, with J. F. C. Fuller, as a proponent of tank and air power, and for his indirect approach to strategy. Mao's

---

[45] I was unable to determine the identity of "B.D.H."

ideas are linked directly to Sunzi, and General Beaufre "portrayed world politics as a stark confrontation between a ruthless East, possessing a strategy, and a West without one." Beaufre also "saw strategy as a tune played in two keys: 'direct strategy,' in which force is the essential factor; and 'indirect strategy,' in which force recedes into the background and its place is taken by psychology and planning."[46] Taken as a whole, by 1984 both Griffith's Sunzi translation and Mao Zedong's military writings had become a part of the American military's standard canon of works on strategy. Both were seen as relevant and useful works for strategy, and for some of the threats the US military might face.

Almost twenty years later, on June 9, 2003, Congressman Ike Skelton published his "National Security Book List," containing fifty books that he "recommends as required reading to all officers of the armed forces, to members of Congress, and all others interested in national security issues."[47] Included on that list was Griffith's translation of Sunzi; Robert Coram's biography of John Boyd; Michael Handel's *Masters of War*, which contains the Giles translation of Sunzi, Jomini, and Clausewitz; and the Peter Paret and Michael Howard translation of Clausewitz's *On War*. The rest of the list is made up of military histories, and some military memoirs. Mao's military writings were no longer included, though it contained two Sunzi translations, and two Clausewitz translations. Liddell Hart was gone but John Boyd, the subject of the next chapter, had now entered the list of important military thinkers.

---

[46] B.D.H., "Ten Important Books: Strategic Thought," *Army Historian*, Spring 1984, 3, 11–15.
[47] Ike Skelton, "National Security Book List," *Naval War College Review*, Winter 2004, 57/1, 109–112.

9   Robert Asprey, John Boyd, and Sunzi

Dear Mr. President,
   The attached memorandum applies the lessons of the art of war as developed by Clausewitz and Sun T'zu [*sic*] to the problem of terrorism and "the war against Americans."
   I hope you find it useful and would be delighted to discuss the technical details of applying the classic art of war to planning American strategies against terrorism.

Sincerely,
Newt Gingrich[1]

Sunzi was a household name by the 1980s and continued to establish itself/himself in the popular imagination in the decades that followed. Sunzi was mentioned in Oliver Stone's 1987 movie *Wall Street*. Quite apart from any academic debate as to the universality of Sunzi as a work of strategy, it clearly symbolized the use of strategy for many people. Perhaps the tagline's misquoting and misunderstanding of Sunzi contributed to the movie's defeat at the box office. Newt Gingrich's mention of Clausewitz was used to signal that he was actually well read in strategy, and was serious about national security issues. Putting Sunzi and Clausewitz together was strategic virtue signaling, basically claiming to know strategy from A to Z. Anyone could mention Sunzi; it was the serious student of strategy who would also include Clausewitz.
   Familiarity was widespread in the West, not just in America. In a speech by Dr. Jensen,[2] on November 30, 2015, before the Australian House of Representatives, regarding the Defence Legislation Amendment Bill 2015, he said, concerning procurement of the joint strike fighter,

Sun Tzu, in *The Art of War*, stated that "war is deception" – the idea is to deceive the enemy. Self-deception, almost by definition, aids and abets an enemy. Given

---

[1] Newt Gingrich to Ronald Reagan, June 26, 1985, CIA-RDP87M01152R000400560018-3.
[2] Dennis Geoffrey Jensen (b. 1962), serving at that time in the Australian House of Representatives from the Liberal Party. He held a Ph.D. in materials science.

Defence's capability gap on the issue of energy manoeuvrability of the JSF – and in this, they are either complicit or ignorant, and I am not sure which is worse – how do we believe them in terms of the "secret" capabilities the JSF has? After all, anyone with even a small amount of technical ability in analysis would have been able to see that the JSF would not cut it in terms of energy manoeuvrability.[3]

Dr. Jensen's mention of energy maneuverability was a direct citation (acknowledged) of John Boyd's groundbreaking theory of fighter jet flight and maneuver capabilities. This was an apposite mention in a debate over fighter jet procurement, and shows that he was aware of Boyd's significance as a theoretician of fighter plane design, if, perhaps, not of his subsequent role as a strategic thinker.

John Boyd gained some prominence in the military community as a strategist after he retired from the air force in 1975. Boyd is in one sense the exact opposite of Master Sun. Boyd was a real man who served in the armed forces and was famous and influential for his military strategies, but never himself produced a book explaining his theories. In another sense, however, Boyd is exactly like Master Sun: the majority of what is known of Boyd's military thought has been transmitted by people who attended his lectures, and his slide deck from those lectures. This aspect of a student-produced account of his thought, with the addition of interesting anecdotes, is consistent with the masters literature of Warring States period China.

The vagaries of influence and fashion are fickle, or at least not subject to obvious determinants. A close friend of Griffith's, Robert Asprey, who met Liddell Hart at the same time, was also a marine and wrote on guerrilla warfare, but ultimately fell out with Liddell Hart. Asprey experienced firsthand some of the less pleasant aspects of Liddell Hart's personality, and saw Liddell Hart's struggle for influence. He also saw the decline of that influence in military circles. For Asprey, as for many of those concerned with military education, the perennial question was, how should officers be trained to lead? Given the very limited amount of time that officers are given for training, and the intense struggle over which kinds of intellectual training they should be given, this frequently comes down to which books, on a very short list, they should read. By the 1980s and 1990s, Sunzi, usually Griffith's translation, was on every list in the American military. Liddell Hart began to drop off those lists, and a new book, *Warfighting*, written for the Marine Corps and published in 1989 (heavily influenced by Boyd) started to show up.

---

[3] Commonwealth of Australia, Parliamentary Debates, Defence Legislation Amendment (First Principles) Bill 2015, second reading, SPEECH Monday, November 30, 2015.

The Sunzi remains popular outside the circles of military education, which both aids and hinders the serious consideration of it as a work of strategy. With books ranging from Eric Rogell's *The Art of War for Dating: Master Sun Tzu's Tactics to Win Over Women,*[4] to Catherine Huang and Arthur D. Rosenberg's *Sun Tzu's Art of War for Women: Strategies for Winning without Conflict,*[5] and on to Derek Yuen's *Deciphering Sun Tzu: How to Read* The Art of War,[6] it becomes clear that putting "Sun Tzu" in the title of book raises its value for a variety of audiences. Yet who is to say that the use of Sunzi for dating is not a serious consideration of strategy? Since strategy as a concept and term has come to be applied outside war, there is no particular reason why its use in nonmilitary contexts is any less serious. If the Sunzi is universal, and not tied to a time, place, or activity, then it might well offer useful insights into more effectively achieving goals in many pursuits. An evaluation of the origins of the interpretations proffered by "Sun Tzu" books, usually indirect strategy, winning without fighting, connection to Daoism, and so on, does nothing to enhance or diminish the value of those books to their readers. Criticism by sinologists of mischaracterizations of Chinese culture or history are quite beside the point. To use Sunzi is to be strategic, and invoking Sunzi is an effective tool for getting one's discussions of strategy heard.

Even though the Sunzi became popular, it was still taken seriously by military specialists. Robert Asprey actively promoted Sunzi within military circles, both out of conviction of its value and because of his friendship with Samuel Griffith. Successive waves of reform, large and small, ran through all of the branches of the US military at various times (and were met with similarly strong conservative reactions). The US Army, for example, changed from the mid-1970s "Active Defense" to AirLand Battle in 1982, and then to "Full Spectrum Operations" in the late 1990s. It is impossible meaningfully to quantify Sunzi's influence on any branch of the US military at any given time, but Sunzi and Clausewitz are often drawn upon for apposite quotes. At least in *Warfighting*, the Marine Corps 1989 doctrinal manual (revised in 1997), Liddell Hart is also quoted. The newest strategist to influence the Marine Corps is John Boyd, and while he is only directly mentioned in the footnotes to *Warfighting*, his presence loomed over it.

---

[4] Eric Rogell, *The Art of War for Dating: Master Sun Tzu's Tactics to Win Over Women,* Avon, MA: Adams, 2011.
[5] Catherine Huang and Arthur D. Rosenberg, *Sun Tzu's Art of War for Women: Strategies for Winning without Conflict,* North Clarendon, VT: Tuttle Publishing, 2019.
[6] Derek Yuen, *Deciphering Sun Tzu: How to Read* The Art of War, Oxford: Oxford University Press, 2014.

Robert Asprey

Robert Brown Asprey (1923–2009) had a career very similar to Samuel Griffith's. He was a marine during World War II, and went to college directly after the war. He was at New College, Oxford, on a Fulbright scholarship from 1949 to 1950, when Griffith was also there, at which time he also met Liddell Hart. Asprey served in US Army intelligence in Austria in the 1950s before rejoining the Marine Corps as a captain to participate in the Korean War. After a stint at the University of Vienna from 1955 to 1957, he worked as an editor for the *Marine Corps Gazette*, as well as writing a series of military histories. He is best known for *War in the Shadows: The Guerrilla in History*, published in 1975. Guerrilla warfare was an extremely important area of study for the US military after World War II as the United States became involved in Cold War proxy fights.

The Vietnam War in particular intensified the issue of guerrilla warfare, though there was some question whether the Chinese Army had used guerrilla tactics successfully against the United Nations forces in Korea as well. All this would turn back onto the connection of Sunzi, Mao Zedong, and guerrilla tactics. Liddell Hart's paradigm of Clausewitz/conventional versus Sunzi/unconventional, with unconventional encompassing guerrilla warfare, seemed to carry through at a foundational but unacknowledged level in debates within the US military. Asprey was just as involved in these debates as Griffith, and followed a similar career trajectory. Although Griffith got along with a wide variety of people better than Asprey did, and was usually, but certainly not always, more diplomatic in public, the two men's correspondence (which appeared to always include Belle Griffith, despite their frank communications) is a wonderful window into their time and place. It also puts Griffith's relationship with Liddell Hart into perspective, with Asprey often conveying messages between them. Asprey was far more of a gossip as well, and, after falling out with Liddell Hart, took a certain satisfaction in relaying less flattering anecdotes about him.

Asprey's relationship with Liddell Hart began at or about the same time as Griffith's did. Both Asprey and Griffith were attending New College, Oxford, in 1956, though Asprey appears to have been living in London. Asprey wrote to Liddell Hart on August 6, 1957, on the suggestion of Brigadier Barclay, the editor of the *Army Quarterly*, asking to meet Liddell Hart when he was in London.[7] Liddell Hart wrote back to Asprey on August 8,[8] to try and arrange a meeting. Asprey wrote back on the 20th, saying that he looked forward to seeing Liddell Hart and his wife on

---

[7] Asprey to Liddell Hart, August 6, 1957, LHA.
[8] Liddell Hart to Asprey, August 8, 1957, Boston University Asprey archive; and LHA.

"Thursday."[9] Liddell Hart wrote to Griffith on August 20 inviting Asprey and Griffith to lunch,[10] which took place on August 22.[11] Asprey remained in contact with Liddell Hart, informing him that he would be returning to the United States in November. He wrote to Liddell Hart again in October of 1958 – "Sam gave me hell for not having written to you this summer" – and went on to tell him that he was remaining in America while courting Jennifer Burrows, thus requiring a decent job. In the pursuit of a government job, he was mentioning Liddell Hart's name in Washington.[12] Asprey asked Liddell Hart to write the Foreword to his book in November, and that his agent was trying to sell Liddell Hart's son's book.[13] The other notable people that Asprey's editor at Putnam had suggested were J. Edgar Hoover, Allan Dulles, Wild Bill Donovan, and Walter Bedell Smith. Asprey's relationship with Liddell Hart put him at the top of the list, though it shows how important or famous Liddell Hart was in the late 1950s. He also asked what Liddell Hart's fee was to write the Foreword.

Liddell Hart would reach the height of his fame and influence in the 1960s. John F. Kennedy used the opportunity of reviewing Liddell Hart's 1960 book *Deterrent of Defense* in the *Saturday Review of Literature* of September 3, 1960, to attack the Eisenhower administration's New Look policy and the "Nixon line." Kennedy's review demonstrated the success of Liddell Hart's efforts to rebuild his reputation after World War II: "No expert on military affairs has better earned the right to respectful attention than B. H. Liddell Hart. For two generations, he has brought to the problems of war and peace a rare combination of professional competence and imaginative insight. His predictions and his warnings have often proved correct." Kennedy went on to agree with Liddell Hart's criticisms of Eisenhower's New Look policy, though he dis modify his position to say that "Hart –like many Europeans – underestimates the American task of maintain [*sic*] the security and effectiveness of the American nuclear deterrent." Certainly, by the late 1950s, Liddell Hart

[9] Asprey to Liddell Hart, August 20, 1957, LHA.
[10] Liddell Hart to Griffith, August 20, 1957, LHA.
[11] Liddell Hart to Asprey, August 23, 1957, LHA: "We much enjoyed seeing you here yesterday, and the Griffiths."
[12] Asprey to Liddell Hart, October 25, 1958, Boston University Asprey archive.
[13] Asprey to Liddell Hart, November 16, 1958, Boston University Asprey archive. Adrian Liddell Hart (1922–1991) was Basil Liddell Hart's son by his first wife, Jessie Stone. He had already published two books before 1958, *The Growth of New Germany* (1949), and *Strange Company* (1953). He published a third book, *The Sword and the Pen: Selections from the World's Greatest Military Writings*, in 1975. It isn't clear from Asprey's letter what book Adrian was trying to find a press for.

was extraordinarily influential, and his endorsement of a book, especially by writing a Foreword, highly sought-after.

Liddell Hart quite reasonably told Asprey that he didn't know what the topic of the book was, but that he would be willing to write a Foreword, "If it is on a topic I can effectively introduce, and subject to reading the book." He went on to say that he was "constantly being approached by publishers with requests that I should write a Foreword," as well as being offered "considerable fees or a royalty percentage" for his work. For the most part, he only wrote forewords for friends, and limited the number to preserve their value.[14] The book in question was *A Panther's Feast*, Asprey's biography of Alfred Redl, a homosexual member of the Austro-Hungarian General Staff, who was blackmailed by the Russians. Liddell Hart said that, while he liked the book, it was outside his area of expertise. He could only write a Foreword if the book were sold as historical fiction rather than history.[15] Liddell Hart ultimately concluded that he was not able to write a Foreword for the book, though he did provide an endorsement for the back cover. He apologized both to Asprey and to his editor for not doing the Foreword. Liddell Hart did remain actively supportive of Asprey, however, and, at Asprey's request proposed Asprey for membership in the Institute for Strategic Studies.

Asprey updated Liddell Hart on Sam and Belle Griffith's lives, as well as background gossip. He told Liddell Hart, for example, that Sam Griffith was not invited to speak at the Naval War College because Admiral Ingersol was a big supporter of Chiang Kai-shek, and Madame Chiang Kai-shek had just spoken there.[16] Griffith was still seen, with good reason, as a critic of Chiang and the GMD. Asprey was also on very good terms with Liddell Hart's wife Kathy, and would remain so after Liddell Hart's death. She wrote back to him on one occasion to thank him for flowers he'd sent, but also to follow up with personal questions on his courtship and the Griffiths.[17] Asprey also wrote to Liddell Hart in 1961 to agree with him that Griffith needed to cut the scholarly chapters at the beginning of the Sunzi book.[18]

Asprey and Liddell Hart's correspondence became much friendlier throughout 1961, with Asprey writing to "My dear Basil," rather than his previous "My dear Captain Liddell Hart," while Liddell Hart had long used "My dear Robert." The break in their relationship came in 1962. Asprey was putting together a forum on books that young American

[14] Liddell Hart to Asprey, November 22, 1958, Boston University Asprey archive.
[15] Liddell Hart to Asprey, February 17, 1959, Boston University Asprey archive.
[16] Asprey to Liddell Hart, December 2, 1958, Boston University Asprey archive.
[17] Kathy Liddell Hart to Asprey, January 5, 1959, Boston University Asprey archive.
[18] Asprey to Liddell Hart, June 12, 1961, Boston University Asprey archive.

marine officers should read. He asked various prominent men, including Liddell Hart, to send him a list of ten books that young officers should read.[19] In addition to his list of ten books, Liddell Hart went on to include a supplement advocating for a half-dozen books that he had written.[20] The clash over this forum would bring out many of Liddell Hart's worst characteristics, though Asprey, for his part, was extremely prickly in response. Liddell Hart wanted to be in the forum because it promoted his standing as an important military commentator. That was balanced against the fact that he earned his living by writing. The final component was his careful management, or manipulation, of his place in history, particularly his rewriting of his pre-World War II actions. Unfortunately for him, that rewriting was ignored in the chapter discussing him in *Makers of Modern Strategy*, a work that at least two of the other contributors to the forum put on their lists.

Asprey wrote to the Griffiths on May 25, 1963:

My dear Belle and Albay,[21]

Forum-VII is in and practically done with. The editor liked Forum-VI very much and the Lejeune article got the best poll rating in the Gazette's history. The Crists gave me a letter from Liddell Hart:

"I have just received the April issue and am surprised to see that your Forum is not included – as I had gathered from your earlier request to deliver my contribution by the 1st March that it was going to be for the April issue. Why has it been delayed, and when is it likely to appear?

"As some recompense for the time I spent in meeting your request, I would be grateful for a dozen extra copies of the issue containing it, as I know a number of keen students here who would certainly like to see it . . ."

This was all right, but then came another letter to my proper address:

". . . Thank you also for the small cheque. I appreciate your comment about it – and all the more as the effort to contribute to your Forum put me out of pocket by pounds 190, since I could only squeeze the time by turning down an article request from a popular paper. The cost of friendship can be high! But in this case it was also compensated by the interest of answering the questions you posed . . ."

This is the biggest bunch of shit I've ever heard, and that finishes liddell hart [*sic*] with the Forum and with Asprey. Moreover, he has the gall to carp about Krulak and Craig choosing Makers of Modern Strategy and he himself chose that impossibly superficial Vagts book. No gentleman would ever write to anyone such an insulting paragraph as that above, and while I don't care about dealing with gentlemen I do care about dealing with people who pretend to be and who in fact are conceited scoundrels. I'm just not going to answer his letters, and I'm not

[19] Asprey to Liddell Hart, January 10, 1962, Boston University Asprey archive.
[20] Liddell Hart to Asprey, February 26, 1962, Boston University Asprey archive.
[21] "Albay" or "Albey" was Asprey's nickname for Sam Griffith. I have been unable to determine its origin.

going to send him 12 copies and if starts [sic] screaming I'll jerk his goddam list of books out and tear it up. If he dawdled, at the most it would have taken him a half an hour to write that damn list.[22]

Asprey had, in fact, received a letter from Liddell Hart written on May 21, where Liddell Hart expressed surprise that General Victor "Brute" Krulak (1913–2008) felt that Jomini was "indispensable," or that Krulak and Gordon Craig had both included *Makers of Modern Strategy* since it was "of very uneven quality, some of the chapters being very misleading." Yet Liddell Hart went on in an extremely friendly fashion at the end of the letter.[23] The break in the relationship was driven by Asprey rather than Liddell Hart, and Asprey afterward seemed to enjoy passing along or collecting unflattering stories about Liddell Hart. Liddell Hart's congenial tone, and Asprey's strong reaction to the issue of the article, suggest that he had built up some resentment over time, perhaps after Liddell Hart had refused to write the Foreword to his book. Asprey related a story to General Brocas Burrows about Liddell Hart peddling his memoirs in New York. The publisher offered 2,000 dollars and Liddell Hart, who had expected a minimum offer of 15,000, got pale and indignant.[24]

Asprey also kept a clipping of the June 19, 1969, *Times Literary Supplement* review of the book *Churchill: Four Faces and the Man*, which offered different perspectives on Churchill by four different authors, one of whom was Liddell Hart:

Sir Basil Liddell Hart on "The Military Strategist" indulges in a good deal of special pleading along with a good deal of justificatory autobiography. He begins his summing up with a conventional tribute to "a wonderful man", but his conclusion is that Churchill, though he had every advantage including the advice of Sir Basil himself [underlined in the original] was a failure both as a strategist and a statesman.

Despite all of his difficulties with Liddell Hart, he remained in touch with Kathy Liddell Hart after her husband's death, even visiting her in England. And the fact remains that Liddell Hart, whatever his foibles, had truly supported Asprey and his career. Liddell Hart's influence was at its greatest in the 1960s and carried through into the 1970s. His fame in military circles only gradually declined in the 1980s as the people who knew him, had read him, or heard him speak got older.

---

[22] Asprey to Belle and Sam Griffith, May 25, 1962, Asprey collection, Boston University.
[23] Liddell Hart to Asprey, May 21, 1962, Asprey collection, Boston University.
[24] Asprey to General Brocas Burrows, October 8, 1963, Asprey collection, Boston University.

Asprey began a correspondence with David Hackworth (1930–2005) in the late 1980s. Hackworth was recognized during the Vietnam War for employing guerrilla tactics against the Vietcong, having served with distinction in the wars in both Korea and Vietnam. Hackworth was one of the most decorated, if not the most decorated, soldiers in the US military when he retired as a colonel. He became deeply disillusioned with the US military's handling of the Vietnam War and gave a television interview in 1971 where he said the United States should withdraw from Vietnam, after saying the war could not be won. After retiring Hackworth moved to Australia, where he became a successful businessman for a while before returning to the United States in the 1980s. Once back in the United States, he began a new career writing and offering commentary on military subjects. His background as a decorated combat veteran in two wars, with particular knowledge of guerrilla warfare, made him an important analyst and speaker. He also worked as a war correspondent in several conflicts. His autobiography, *About Face*, was published in 1989.[25]

The Hackworth–Asprey connection appears to have started sometime after Hackworth returned to the United States. Asprey wrote back to Hackworth in December 1989,

You suggest an interesting point on the essential loneliness of generals. As a military correspondent I got to know scores of them and they really are lonely. I was told the most incredible top secret stuff and at one point almost became a king-maker in the Marine Corps – just like Basil Liddell Hart who was one in the late 'thirties. I knew Basil well and disapproved of most of what he wrote. We finally had a falling out. Have you read Mearshimer's [*sic*] new biography of him? If not, please do.[26]

Hackworth wrote to Asprey on February 15, 1990,

My favorite book which I have read a dozen times and it is my travelling companion is: General Griffith's THE ART OF WAR. He thanks you for your "valuable critical suggestions." That wonderful little book covers what generalship is all about. Suspect not many of today's Army or USMC generals follow its wisdom.[27]

Asprey was quite pleased with Hackworth's praise of Griffith's book, "Glad you like THE ART OF WAR. Sammy was my chief of staff and eventually one of my best friends."[28]

There were ongoing debates within the military regarding the lessons to be learned from the Vietnam War. Asprey and Hackworth were

---

[25] David Hackworth and Julie Sherman, *About Face: The Odyssey of an American Warrior*, New York: Touchstone, 1989.

[26] Asprey to Hackworth, December 9, 1989, Asprey collection, Boston University.

[27] Hackworth to Asprey, February 15, 1990, Asprey collection, Boston University.

[28] Asprey to Hackworth, June 14, 1990, Asprey collection, Boston University.

apparently in agreement about the US military's failure to learn, or indeed resistance to learning, the lessons of the war. A particular object of their contempt was Harry Summers: "Am reading Harry Summers screed at the moment and certainly agree with your comments – in spades. This kind of crap is absolutely typical of the NWC[29] –one experience with those guys was enough for me."[30] Harry G. Summers, Jr. (1932–1999) was an army colonel who had also served in the Korean and Vietnam Wars. In 1982, he published *On Strategy: A Critical Analysis of the Vietnam War*, in which he adopted a Clausewitzian or Neo-Clausewitzian approach that argued that the US Army had won many tactical victories in Vietnam, but failed on the strategic level because politicians and the top military commanders failed to develop strategic objectives commensurate with their resources. This was a more sophisticated version of the popular concept that the army had won every battle by conventional means, and was failed on the home front.

For men like Asprey and Hackworth, Summers's analysis was merely the army leadership's preferred interpretation, since it absolved them of any responsibility, or any need to adapt to guerrilla warfare. The Clausewitzian perspective, and it was self-consciously understood as such, allowed Summers to ignore the enormous number of skirmishes that the US failed to win, and the negative effect that conventional operations often had on the local population. Where the guerrilla understood that every military action was part of a political struggle, the Clausewitzian approach of Summers separated out only the actions that the army saw as its responsibility, and, by that standard, declared them successful. This was symptomatic of the US Army, whose leadership has always been inclined toward, as David Fitzgerald titled his book, "learning to forget."[31] Fitzgerald argues that, with remarkable consistency, the US Army has repeatedly and intentionally forgotten the lessons of insurgency and fighting guerrillas, and then been forced to relearn those lessons the next time it encounters that kind of fighting.

Hackworth was unquestionably on the side of Sunzi and learning guerrilla warfare: "I will speak at Quantico on 7 April 1994," he wrote to Asprey, "and I'm going to hold up your book to the young officers of the Amphibious Warfare School as the bible, along with Sun Tzu."[32] Asprey and Griffith connected together, perhaps inadvertently, guerrilla warfare and Sunzi. Asprey certainly connected Mao and Sunzi in his

---

[29] The Naval War College.
[30] Asprey to Hackworth, July 22, 1992, Asprey collection, Boston University.
[31] David Fitzgerald, *Learning to Forget: US Army Counterinsurgency Doctrine and Practice from Vietnam to Iraq*, Stanford: Stanford University Press, 2013.
[32] Hackworth to Asprey, March 29, 1994, Asprey collection, Boston University.

writing, and Hackworth's advocacy further amplified this. Interestingly, as far as I was able to tell in Asprey's papers, neither Asprey nor Hackworth mention John Boyd in their discussions of warfare and the Marine Corps. Outside a narrow group of supporters, Boyd's fame took some time to spread.

John Boyd

Colonel John Boyd (1927–1997) embarked upon a career as a strategist after retiring from the air force in 1975. His place as a strategist, and his relative valuation in that role, are strongly dependent upon who is asked. In 2001, Grant T. Hammond wrote of John Boyd,

Many officers in the military, people in business and the academy, are rediscovering his message. They are joining a movement to teach others about the moral dimension of human conduct, the need for creative adaptation, the evils of business as usual, the rigors of successful competition, and the Boydian trinity of people first, ideas second, things third. His legacy endures through Internet exchanges, Web sites, courses at public and private schools throughout the world, and articles and books that continue to spread the word. Internationally, there have been articles in South Korean newspapers, Internet discussions of Boyd in Chinese, and graduate business courses in Denmark.[33]

By 2018, however, General Paul K. Van Riper wrote,

I believe the world's greatest military theorists are Carl von Clausewitz, Sun Tzu, and John Boyd. The first two left an extraordinary legacy with their written words; Boyd, however, did not, which is unfortunate and no doubt the reason his lessons are fading into the distance for active duty military officers today.[34]

General Van Riper was writing in support of studying Boyd, and Ian Brown's book on Boyd's teachings. Yet even in 2001 Grant Hammond had to assert that people were "rediscovering" Boyd. Given that Boyd had been active from the late 1970s to the late 1990s, it is remarkable that by the early twenty-first century he had to be rediscovered. It is particularly surprising that a marine general had to lament the fading importance of Boyd. Boyd had been a major influence on the composition of *Warfighting*, the marine doctrinal manual produced in 1989. *Warfighting* was the product of a major reform effort in the Marine Corps, and represented the formal adoption of the infelicitously named "maneuver warfare" doctrine. Boyd's

---

[33] Grant T. Hammond, *The Mind of War: John Boyd and American Security*, Washington, DC: Smithsonian Books, 2001, 193–194.
[34] Lieutenant General Paul K. Van Riper, USMC (Ret), Foreword to Ian T. Brown, *A New Conception of War: John Boyd, The US Marines, and Maneuver Warfare*, Quantico: Marine Corps University Press, 2018, xi.

influence outside the Marine Corps was limited, and even the aspects of strategic thought that he did contribute were highly circumscribed by the fact that he did not write a manual himself. Without a specific book to his name, only specialists knew to attribute his concepts to him. Liddell Hart's name and explicit influence also faded very quickly after he died, and he had been far more famous as a strategist than Boyd.

Boyd's supporters often compared him to Sunzi. In Richard Coram's 2002 biography of Colonel John Boyd, Coram asserted that Boyd was undoubtedly the most influential strategist since Sunzi.[35] This was at a minimum hyperbole, and much more likely a gross overstatement, but it is important in demonstrating that, in 2002, at least for some people, Sunzi was the preeminent strategist by which to compare all others. Boyd himself severely criticized Clausewitz and strongly praised Sunzi, as a long line of twentieth-century Western strategists had already done before him. Nevertheless, even that most Boydian of texts, *Warfighting*, quoted Clausewitz more than anyone else. Very little of what Boyd had to say was new, and most of it seemed to repeat things that Liddell Hart had said. This is not to say that Boyd plagiarized Liddell Hart, but rather that he arrived at similar conclusions.

Boyd had collected around himself a group of self-identified "acolytes" to promote his influence and reputation. The success of the first Gulf War was attributed by several influential people, including Dick Cheney, to Boyd. The Marine Corps embraced Boyd even as his own service, the air force, disavowed him. Yet it remains to be seen whether Boyd's thoughts will persist. Without a text to his name, he is almost impossible to quote, though, as Grant Hammond argues, "A synthesis of Clausewitz, Sun Tzu, Liddell Hart, Napoleon, Patton, and, most especially, John Boyd tailored to the Marine Corps, 'Warfighting' is the essay Boyd should have written instead of only giving briefings." Hammond goes on to argue that much of the language in *Warfighting* is taken verbatim from his presentations.[36]

The fact remains, however, that Boyd did not write *Warfighting* and the manual itself is a synthesis of the writings of other strategists. *Warfighting* is, in fact, a superbly crafted work of strategy that deserves to be read and reread. But without its endnotes, Boyd disappears by name from the text. Clausewitz predominates, followed by Sunzi (in Griffith's translation). Boyd is mentioned in two footnotes:

Tempo is often associated with a mental process known variously as the "Decision Cycle," "OODA Loop," or "Boyd Cycle," after retired Air Force Colonel John Boyd who pioneered the concept in his lecture, "The Patterns of Conflict." Boyd

---

[35] Richard Coram, *Boyd: The Fighter Pilot Who Changed the Art of War*, New York: Back Bay Books, 2002, 445.
[36] Hammond, *The Mind of War*, 195.

identified a four-step mental process: observation, orientation, decision, and action. Boyd theorized that each party to a conflict first observes the situation. On the basis of the observation, he orients; that is, he makes an estimate of the situation. On the basis of the orientation, he makes a decision. And, finally, he implements the decision – he acts. Because his action has created a new situation, the process begins anew. Boyd argued that the party that consistently completes the cycle faster gains an advantage that increases with each cycle. His enemy's reactions become increasingly slower by comparison and therefore less effective until, finally, he is overcome by events.[37]

The second mention of Boyd also refers to a lecture of his: "Boyd introduces the idea of implicit communications as a command tool in his lecture, 'An Organic Design for Command and Control.'"[38] The first endnote makes a strangely tentative connection of tempo to Boyd, explaining his concept without stating that they are one and the same as tempo. The OODA loop is probably Boyd's most distinctive concept and, while its strategic logic is questionable, it can be firmly attributed to him. Unfortunately for his reputation, it is usually encountered as simply the "OODA loop" without attribution. Having discussed the trajectory of the concept of "indirect strategy" in this book, I wonder whether the OODA loop will also be attributed to Sunzi later in the twenty-first century. Just as likely, only specialists in strategic thought will know who John Boyd was and what he contributed to military thought.

Even the endnotes to *Warfighting* make Clausewitz, Sunzi, and Liddell Hart important figures. Contrast the mentions of Boyd with the mentions of Clausewitz and Sunzi. "For the definitive treatment of the nature and theory of war, see the unfinished classic, *On War*, by Clausewitz. All Marine officers should consider this book essential reading."[39] Liddell Hart is actually the second person quoted in the manual, right after Clausewitz. The first endnote to a Sunzi quote reads,

Sun Tzu, *The Art of War*, trans. S. B. Griffith (New York: Oxford University Press, 1982) p. 85. Like *On War*, *The Art of War* should be on every Marine officer's list of essential reading. Short and simple to read, *The Art of War* is every bit as valuable today as when it was written about 400 B.C.[40]

Even if *Warfighting* is as close to a Boydian statement of strategy as we are likely to get, its strong emphasis on Clausewitz throughout conflicts with his avowed dislike of the Prussian.

John Boyd was by most accounts an inspiring teacher. His education in military history and strategy was eclectic and unsystematic, which

---

[37] United States Marine Corps, *Warfighting*, Washington, DC: United States Marine Corps, 1989 (hereafter *Warfighting*), 106 fn. 20.
[38] *Warfighting*, 109 fn. 5.   [39] *Warfighting*, 101 fn. 4.   [40] *Warfighting*, 103 fn. 2.

allowed him to move comfortably across disciplines and information. His goal was to engage an audience of officers in an interactive discussion to foster their judgment and strategic thinking. As a teacher of students in class, however, his goal was not strictly to parse which ideas came from which thinkers and carve out a space wherein he could define his unique contributions to the field.[41] Boyd also faced the eternal educational problem that once he set down his ideas in writing the tendency of people interested in learning from him would be to follow rigidly the written text. A written text is often a barrier to thinking for oneself as it becomes a road map rather than a guide to navigation. And, of course, Boyd himself was in a continual state of rethinking the issues under discussion.

Whether Boyd knew it or not, or whether he cared, by not writing his own book he left the understanding, dissemination, and interpretation of his ideas to others. Even if he had written a book, later readers would interpret it as they would, but he would have at least controlled their starting point. He could have tried to provide a sufficient basis for a clear understanding of what he meant. Ian Brown frames this in a very telling manner:

Boyd had a complex interpretation of conflict, and his nuances were not always appreciated by his proponents, let alone his critics. The friction was not just because Boyd and his critics disagreed but because his ideas were often interpreted by friends who missed his deeper points or simplified them too much, especially as they concerned attrition and the OODA loop.[42]

It may well be true that almost everyone, beside Ian Brown, has misunderstood the finer points of Boyd's thinking, but he seems to imply that a more accurate understanding of Boyd's ideas would do away with opposition to those ideas.

Brown returns to this theme, Boyd's qualities as a teacher and the difficulties of really understanding the OODA loop: "Listening to the audio of 'Patterns of Conflict,' it is clear that Boyd's audiences were engaged and enthusiastically absorbed in his material. But not all of that material was effectively transmitted beyond the classroom." He goes on to point out,

The OODA loop was another friction point between maneuverists and their critics. The loop remains the most well known of Boyd's ideas, yet even Boyd's acolytes tended to gloss over its nuances as they strove to share it with a larger

---

[41] Boyd's decision not to write a book may also suggest that he saw himself as a teacher, not a writer. He was also well aware that the individual components of what he was teaching, barring perhaps the OODA loop, were not original.
[42] Brown, *A New Conception of War*, 109.

community of warfighters. From its perceived origin to its application, the OODA loop was often misrepresented.[43]

Here he at least concedes that Boyd's acolytes themselves understood the finer aspects of the OODA loop, even if they erred in their transmission to a broader audience.

Brown does not, however, accept that there might be reasonable grounds for disagreeing or even criticizing Boyd,

As maneuver warfare discussions proliferated, the concept drew its fair share of criticism, and it still does to some degree today. Such critiques came from (1) a failure to understand Boyd's ideas holistically –sometimes due to intellectual laziness on the part of the critic, but other times because the critic did not have access to Boyd's ideas directly or accessed them through the imperfect interpretation of maneuver proponents; (2) a natural resistance to radical change; and (3) it must be said, by personality conflicts, often generated by the well-meaning but acerbic admonitions of William Lind.[44]

This level of advocacy simply denies any reasonable grounds for a well-informed person to object to maneuver warfare or to Boyd. By definition, to object is to be lazy, ill-informed, reflexively conservative, or overcome with personal animosity. It is perhaps a sign of how fiercely fought the battles to change Marine Corps doctrine were in the 1980s that they are still being fought decades later.

Many people were debating military reforms, and many had been reaching toward the concepts that would become maneuver warfare independent of Boyd, like then lieutenant Stephen Miller in a 1975 article, "Camouflage and Deception," in the *Marine Corps Gazette*:

The extent to which the elements of the debate and ultimate solution to come were present in Miller's article is extraordinary. He captured the problem – winning while outnumbered and outgunned – and forecast the kernels that Boyd supplied to undergird maneuver warfare doctrine: time as a weapon; using decision making to deceive, confuse, and slow an enemy's response; launching unexpected strength against critical weaknesses to make an enemy unravel. These parallels are even more remarkable considering that Miller, by his own admission, was not yet familiar with Boyd, Boyd's ideas, or any of the other individuals who later played key roles in the maneuver warfare movement.[45]

Warfighting itself grew out of the more general struggle for reform, but it was commissioned by then marine commandant Alfred M. Gray Jr., and written by John Schmitt. Gray "used maneuver techniques long before Boyd synthesized his OODA loop. Already a dedicated student

---

[43] Brown, *A New Conception of War*, 116.   [44] Brown, *A New Conception of War*, 121.

[45] Brown, *A New Conception of War*, 79. I would like to thank Mr. Miller for kindly taking the time to answer some of my questions concerning his background.

of history, two decades of service and combat experience in the Far East brought him to embrace the outlook on war defined by Sun Tzu."[46] Gray gave Schmitt wide latitude to write the manual, and Brown was disappointed that Gray's attitudes toward military principles cannot be proven to have been the result of contact with Boyd. Gray had long studied on his own.[47] Schmitt was chosen because he already supported maneuver warfare, but he directly consulted with Boyd by phone, and had a copy of his lecture slides. Because of this influence, in Brown's description, "Boyd's name was suddenly ranked among the august company of Clausewitz and Sun Tzu."[48] As we have seen in our discussion of *Warfighting* above, this was something of an overstatement.

From a textual perspective, John Schmitt should rank highly as a strategist and strategic thinker. Even with Boyd's direct influence by phone, it was ultimately Schmitt who wrote *Warfighting* and Gray who made it official Marine Corps doctrine. It is extremely telling that Schmitt is not held up on par with Boyd, and has in some sense been unfairly relegated to the roll of clerk, for either Gray's or Boyd's ideas. This characterization has been explicitly denied by people, like Gray, who were part of the formulation of *Warfighting*, but it does not fit into the myth narrative promoting the position of Boyd as a late twentieth-century equivalent to Sunzi. It is Boyd who has been transformed from an inspirational teacher and incisive strategic thinker into a transcendental strategist.

Boyd and Sunzi

There are several reasons for bringing Boyd into a consideration of the use of Sunzi in the West. Robert Coram passed over the entire Western tradition of military thinkers to put Boyd on a par with Sunzi, without actually arguing why that was the case. Sunzi has become *the* paradigmatic strategist, *sans pareil et sans reproche*, whom Boyd could not be suggested to have either matched or exceeded. The best he could do was be second, and certainly ahead of every other Western strategist or military writer, including Clausewitz and Liddell Hart. Yet whatever Boyd's future status as a strategist, there is no particular reason in the early twenty-first century to place his influence above that of his predecessors.

This leads to the second reason to consider Boyd in this context. Boyd's strategy is very similar to that of Master Sun in that the written accounts

---

[46] Brown, *A New Conception of War*, 159.   [47] Brown, *A New Conception of War*, 169.
[48] Brown, *A New Conception of War*, 171.

of both are collections of notes, aphorisms, and attributions but were not composed by their putative authors. In Sunzi's case, this was because he did not exist. Boyd most certainly existed, but left virtually the same legacy of his thought. Moreover, Boyd's legitimacy is based upon several anecdotes that are very hard to corroborate. These stories were similar to Sima Qian's account of Sunzi forming a military unit using palace women, or attributing great military victories to him. They make a point about the subject as a means to prove that their thought was effective and therefore correct. Boyd's reputation as a fighter pilot, for example, is an important part of his biography, but he never shot down an enemy plane, and his greatest feats were as an instructor in simulated combat. The reality of battlefield accomplishment was always just out of reach.

A third reason to consider Boyd returns us once again to the Marine Corps. The Marine Corps's embrace of Boyd is one of the main props to his status as an important strategist. Most obviously, they accepted and maintain his personal papers, demonstrating that they value him as a subject of study.[49] The air force did not archive his papers, as would be more usual for an air force officer. The Marine Corps went further, including him in their pantheon of important figures at Marine Corps Research Center at Quantico, the only non-marine to hold such an honor. As with any individual, an institution demonstrates its values by the heroes it chooses. There were, in fact, sound reasons for the air force to have honored Boyd, but its choice not to do so was not just an expression of individual animosity; it was also an expression of institutional values.[50] The marines honored Boyd because he argued for things they valued at that time.

Finally, although Boyd's criticism of Clausewitz and praise for Sunzi may well have been his honest opinion of both, it also reflects a late twentieth-century reading of both strategists. Because Coram praised Boyd he associated him with Sunzi. It is hard to find a strategist praised as the greatest strategist since Clausewitz, or a new Clausewitz. Nor was Boyd called a new Liddell Hart. Clausewitz came with considerable

---

[49] I should thank, once again, Jim Ginther, the senior archivist for the Archives Branch of the Marine Corps History Division, for making available Boyd's papers to me, and for much useful information that I would never have been aware of otherwise.

[50] Setting aside clashes of personality and different subjective evaluations of events, the air force had three institutional reasons to reject Boyd. First, he was an inveterate rebel, always ready, willing, and able to work around the air force's system of command. Second, he frequently undermined the established goals of the air force as set by his superiors in order to promote what he believed to be better goals. Third, he claimed individual credit for developments more usually credited to the air force or a group as a whole. While Boyd and his partisans, for example, credit the creation of the F-16 to him, many other people were also involved. The truth of that claim, and the value of the F-16 as opposed to what might otherwise have been built, is hard to evaluate.

Western baggage, whether deserved or not, and was a nearby figure whose cultural similarities made him easy to place in context. Sunzi was distant, foreign, and exotic, rendering him a classic, timeless strategist with whom anything could be done. Only a sinologist might object, something which troubled no one.

Had the Marine Corps not adopted Boyd he might well have disappeared from the historical record. The accomplishments attributed to him were hidden from the general public and most of the United States government and military. Boyd operated not just within the military world, but more particularly within the bureaucracy of the Pentagon. He did not command troops in battle or demonstrate his fighting prowess in war.[51] Whatever his contributions to the war plans for Desert Storm, he was not responsible for the decision to fight, for the decision of how to fight, or for the consequences of the campaign. He would not have been blamed if it had failed or if the victory were not so lopsided.

While the efforts to apotheosize John Boyd by his acolytes and supporters seem genuine and well meaning, the evidence for Boyd's importance is more equivocal. From an outside perspective, Boyd has been constructed into exactly the same sort of mythical strategist as Sunzi. It is hard to argue for Boyd's enduring significance because he produced so little in the way of a written statement of his ideas. Yet as a mythical persona (as contrasted with the historical John Boyd), his lack of written text is actually an advantage. Boyd can now become the idealized figure that those promoting an interpretation of his ideas want, rather than the author of a specific text that can be attacked, criticized, or discounted. Whereas Sunzi, Clausewitz, or Liddell Hart can be placed on or removed from reading lists for officers, Boyd is immune to those measures of status and influence.

---

[51] Although he flew combat missions in Korea, he never shot down an enemy plane. He did command troops during the Vietnam War, but not in any significant combat role or engagement.

Conclusion

There are no Sunzi police to enforce an orthodox interpretation of *The Art of War* decided upon by an official Sunzi authority. But there was also no single author called Master Sun who wrote *The Art of War* with a unified, coherent meaning that could or can be uncovered or determined by careful study. Many hands wrote, compiled, and edited the work that would be attributed to the fictional Master Sun, and as a result it is complex, generally coherent, and displays several underlying lines of argument. *The Art of War* was interpreted differently by its many commentators starting in the third century CE and continuing to the present. Those interpretations were the product of their respective authors, and the times and places in which they wrote.

I have argued in this book that the modern, Western reading, or perhaps Anglo-American reading, of Sunzi put forth in 1963 has far more to do with B. H. Liddell Hart's thinking than with Master Sun's. Whether or not Liddell Hart took indirect strategy from the Giles translation of Sunzi, he was responsible for popularizing it in the West. Even without a single author, the compilation on *bingfa* that was attributed to Master Sun was a product of the military, political, and social context in which it was put together some time in the fourth or third centuries BCE in China. It reflected the interstate warfare of its time, rather than that of the imperial era beginning in 221 BCE. All this is simply to say that while a great deal is open to interpretation, *The Art of War* cannot mean anything an interpreter wants. The work has meaning, and an interpreter may well produce a reading inconsistent with that meaning, or one that overemphasizes a part of the text that does not represent the whole. While I believe the reduction of the text to the indirect strategy is a misreading of Sunzi, I am well aware that I have no power or authority to compel compliance with my views, and that the vast majority of readers who believe that Sunzi presents an indirect strategy will ignore my arguments.

The Western reading of Sunzi is not consistent with the Chinese reading of Sunzi. Yet, if we are all at liberty to interpret texts as we will, then there is surely no harm in believing that the twentieth-century interpretation of Sunzi by an American and an Englishman is perfectly acceptable. For purposes of entertainment, this is true. But this Western interpretation is a significant cause for concern when we move out of popular culture, books of business strategy, and dating advice into issues of national security, scholarship, and cultural understanding. Leaving aside the extent to which Sunzi in fact influences current Chinese strategy, it is clear that one cannot use a Western reading of Sunzi to understand Chinese militazry policy today. At a minimum, one should, for example, use the current Chinese People's Liberation Army interpretation of Sunzi to understand how Sunzi might influence current PLA strategy. And one should also recognize that if Sunzi influences the Chinese government's strategy (also a big "if"), then one should use the Chinese government's interpretation of Sunzi, which may well be different from that of the PLA.

There is now some respectable scholarship on current Chinese military strategy and operations, and while it is of high quality it is still not extensive. The overwhelming focus on Sunzi as the key to understanding Chinese strategy, and the substitution of reading a translation of Sunzi for actual knowledge of Chinese doctrine and Chinese military history, have stunted what should otherwise be a well-studied field. Western military services do not appear to be particularly interested in carefully studying Chinese strategy or military history as a whole because they can simply accept the Anglo-American interpretation of Sunzi as a total explanation for Chinese strategy. To be fair, very few Western military services study any real strategic works or real military history, beyond a very carefully selected set of examples that supports their current doctrine. Still, it might be wise to examine the Chinese military's own carefully selected examples from their own and others' histories that support their current doctrine. This would only make sense if one understood what those examples were and what their selection signified. When an organization chooses its models, it is critical also to understand what was not chosen. Real understanding requires more than reading one book, let alone one idiosyncratic interpretation of that book.

When Samuel Griffith's Sunzi translation appeared in 1963 it followed obvious signs of the rise of modern China presented by a militarily experienced and academically credible author. It would have seemed likely that a dedicated subfield of Chinese military studies would have developed in that environment. Ten years later, the Kierman and Fairbank volume *Chinese Ways in War* attempted to do just that, to begin the field of Chinese military history in the West. Despite the prestige of John King Fairbank and Harvard University Press, almost nothing happened. Military history was (and sometimes still is) anathema to academic departments, and the study of China was far too complicated and demanding for the military. Chinese studies in the United States and Europe was a small, peripheral field more generally, leaving a very small pool of scholars to draw from. The argument that Sunzi represented all one needed to know about Chinese war because war wasn't important in Chinese history anyway only served to further undermine an almost nonexistent field. A tautological loop then supported the unimportance of war in Chinese history. It wasn't important so it wasn't written about, thus there was no reason to write about it because it wasn't important.

All of this fed into larger, and more pernicious, generalizations about China, and the non-West in general. The most basic generalization was that there was a fundamental split between Western and Chinese ways of doing things, and Western and Chinese culture. The problem was not so much that there weren't differences, but rather how extensive those differences were and what one did about them. In the American education system, which has seldom been very encouraging of foreign-language study, even of European languages, Chinese or Asian languages were usually regarded as impossible to learn. At the same time, the awareness of the depth and complexity of Chinese history made it a subject beyond anyone in the West's ability to understand. Since real study and engagement were impossible, the shortcut of relying solely upon a very specific interpretation of Sunzi that fit preconceived Western notions of China made perfect sense. Clarity was more compelling than complete ignorance. Sunzi's indirect strategy at least provided an explanation for an otherwise unknowable subject.

While business strategy and dating or relationship advice are important in their own way, the need for accuracy is more important in the military sphere. There is also the question of how conceptions of Chinese warfare and strategy affected conceptions of Chinese culture. Military power is often used as a proxy for the overall value of a culture. Military strength equals culture value, so winning at war shows not just that a culture is good at war, but that it is a good culture overall. For example, Prussian/ German culture was highly regarded in the Anglo-American world between 1870 and 1914, and indeed well into the Nazi period, because of its perceived martial prowess. By contrast, losing a war shows a failed culture. From the mid-nineteenth to the late twentieth centuries, China was a military failure, suggesting that its entire culture was a failure for having led up to this circumstance. Twenty-first-century China has been at pains to demonstrate that its military power has grown along with its economy. Among the many reasons the current government is so concerned to develop military power is precisely to demonstrate the value of its culture.

The military weakness of the Qing dynasty in the nineteenth century was projected back onto all of Chinese history, creating the ahistorical modern concept, repeated almost as much inside China as outside it, that China was never militarily capable. Normative antiwar ideals of core thinkers were transmogrified into an explanation that China was militarily weak because of its antiwar culture. That dislike of fighting, at least the direct clash of arms, produced a strategy that sought to win without fighting: the indirect strategy. This thesis could only exist, and persist even today, because there is no military history of China available in the West, and very little academic military history in China. It is not an accident that thousands of years of battles, campaigns, and wars continue to be actively overlooked. Many people wanted to find in China a nonmilitary culture, and they did so by refusing to study its military history and reducing its military thought to a strategy of avoiding fighting.

The construction of Chinese culture as nonmilitary has long been an important touchstone in descriptions of Chinese culture. This nonmilitary nature is assumed, and then used to explain or justify all sorts of other generalizations. A classic formulation was Joseph Needham's explanation that the Chinese did not develop guns to the extent the Europeans did, despite inventing gunpowder, because of lack of interest in war and because of Daoist ideas that disinclined them to use such inventions for war. This effectively answered one of the great questions of history, why the Chinese were able to invent gunpowder but not take over the world or fend off the West. It also made the Chinese into a technologically capable, if perhaps too idealistic, even naive, culture. They chose not to make weapons because those were bad things to do. But their wonderful ideals doomed them in the face of outside aggression.

As You Like It

Misreading the Sunzi and misusing it to guide one's decisions or draw one's own conclusions is, to judge by the frequency with which Sunzi or Sun Tzu is mentioned in the titles of books and articles far outside the military or China fields, big business. It tells us nothing, however, about China, Chinese military thought, Chinese military history, or Chinese culture. To the extent that indirect strategy is, in fact, Liddell Hart's strategy, it might have some value in the field of strategic thought as a whole. Of course, a necessary first step in actually thinking critically about indirect strategy as a strategy would be agreeing upon a clear definition of what it is and, perhaps just as importantly, what it is not. Given the lack of clarity for terms like "guerrilla warfare" or "mobile warfare," it is not surprising that no such understanding of indirect strategy has been generally agreed upon.

"Sun Tzu" and indirect strategy have also been invoked in works on strategy and the military in order to promote the author's own thoughts on strategy or war. In sharp contrast, Clausewitz or any of the dozens of other Western thinkers on strategy or war are only put in the titles of books on history. Sunzi is seen as classic and timeless, and Clausewitz as merely historical. To the extent that Clausewitz has a "popular" reputation outside the academy, it is as the straw man created by Liddell Hart, responsible for the grinding bloodshed of World War I. Liddell Hart's views have been remarkably persistent among the popular readership for history, not just his views of World War I, and blitzkrieg, but also with respect to William Tecumseh Sherman, and Chinggis Khan, neither of whom he knew much about.

This should not be surprising, since Liddell Hart was an intelligent and fluent writer who published many books for the popular audience. His heroes and villains, and clear distinctions between good and bad practice, made military history understandable. Before his indirect approach to strategy there was no "direct" approach, explicitly understood as such. Or was there? Some Western advocates for Clausewitz and Western culture more broadly have reacted against Sunzi because of the inherent criticism of the West such advocacy implies. If China was always and fundamentally committed to the indirect approach, then the West must be the opposite of that, and always and fundamentally committed to the direct approach.[1] And, since the West dominates the world in the twenty-first century, then the direct approach is obviously superior. These stark positions ignore innumerable battles, generals, and strategic thinkers from all cultures who do not reflect such reductionist views of history. Yet the obvious historical inaccuracy of this indirect-versus-direct paradigm does not matter for those exploiting it because history has always been beside the point.

Sunzi has been used in the West as part of struggles within the West over power and ideas. Father Amiot translated the Sunzi for a French audience interested in learning about China, but also to contribute to struggles for power and influence in France. Accuracy was hoped for, and Amiot did a fair job for his time and place, but his translations were driven by contemporary French concerns. The audience for a translation is those who speak the language the original text was translated into. Samuel Griffith translated Sunzi for a Western audience that faced a new Communist government in China after a cataclysmic world war. The

---

[1] The current paradigmatic example of this view being Hanson, *The Western Way of War*.

Chinese Communist model of guerrilla warfare seemed to be a looming threat to Western, and American, power. Why was the greatest conventional power in the world struggling to suppress insurgents and guerrillas? Why was direct military force so costly and ineffective? Sunzi arrived to provide a Chinese explanation that fit neatly into the framework that the great strategist Liddell Hart had built. Liddell Hart had built that framework to promote his own views and reputation, but he was kind or wise enough to support Griffith in his translation of Sunzi. And it is truly important to remember that, for all of his foibles, Liddell Hart generously supported many people in establishing themselves as military historians. The field owes him an eternal debt, even if we find much to disagree with in his *oeuvre*.

If Liddell Hart's name has been forgotten outside the ranks of military historians, Sunzi now symbolizes strategy itself. The real irony is that Liddell Hart's ideas remain tremendously influential, if unacknowledged, and the actual content of the Sunzi is rarely discussed, overridden by pre-existing assertions of indirect strategy, Daoist influence, or connection to Mao Zedong. Some Chinese scholars have posited a connection to Daoism for over a thousand years, but indirect strategy and Mao are strongly connected to Griffith's translation. The many very good Sunzi translations into English that followed those of Giles and Griffith, and extremely limited number of translations of Chinese strategic texts other than the Sunzi, suggest that there is a large audience for Sunzi but not for Chinese strategy more generally, or even strategy itself.

Perhaps, then, in the final analysis, there is something about Sunzi the myth and Sunzi the text that has allowed *The Art of War* to establish itself as the pre-eminent work on strategy in China for 2,000 years, and now the pre-eminent work on strategy beyond China as well. A book on strategy in war, and only in war, has been transformed into a handbook on strategy applicable to every aspect of life. Liddell Hart certainly thought that strategy could be applied beyond warfare to business and other pursuits. That, of course, required a very different conception of "strategy," just as the introduction of Sunzi to France in 1772 contributed to a new understanding of "strategy." In that sense, Sunzi has in fact always been part of the modern Western conception of strategy.

Bibliography

Adcock, F.E. *The Greek and Macedonian Art of War*, Berkeley and Los Angeles: University of California Press, 1957.

Alexander, Joseph H. *Edson's Raiders: The 1st Marine Raider Battalion in World War II*, Annapolis: Naval Institute Press, 2001

Anonymous *The Book of War: The Military Classic of the Far East, United Services Magazine*, 1908–1909, 38.

Anonymous review of Thomas R. Phillips (ed.), Roots of Strategy,*Military Engineer*, July–August 1940, 32/184, 312.

Aurousseau, Léonard Review of *Sun Tzŭ on the Art of War*. 孫子兵法, *the Oldest Military Treatise in the world* by Lionel Giles, *Bulletin de l'École française d'Extrême-Orient*, October–December 1910, 10/4, 709–710.

Ball, J. Dyer Review of "*Sun Tzu on the Art of War* by Lionel Giles," *Journal of the Royal Asiatic Society of Great Britain and Ireland*, July 1910, 961–966.

Ban, Peter Y. "Brigadier General Samuel B. Griffith II, USMC: Marine Translator and Interpreter of Chinese Military Thought," MA thesis, United States Marine Corps Command and Staff College, 2012

B.D.H. "Ten Important Books: Strategic Thought," *Army Historian*, Spring 1984, 3, 11–15.

Boltz, William G. "Lao tzu Tao te Ching 老子道德經," in Michael Loewe (ed.), *Early Chinese Texts: A Bibliographic Guide*, Berkeley: The Society for the Study of Early China, 1993, 269–271.

Bond, Brian *Liddell Hart: A Study of His Military Thought*, New Brunswick: Rutgers, 1976.

Bonnet, Gabriel *Les guerres insurrectionelles et révolutionnaires*, Paris: Payot, 1958.

Boorman, Scott A. and Howard L. Boorman "Mao Tse-tung and the *Art of War*," *Journal of Asian Studies*, November 1964, 24/1, 129–131.

Brady, Anne-Marie *Making the Foreign Serve China*, London: Rowman and Littlefield Publishers, 2003.

Brown, Ian T. *A New Conception of War: John Boyd, the US Marines, and Maneuver Warfare*, Quantico: Marine Corps University Press, 2018.

Brulon, J. G. "L'art de la guerre sans guerre," *Le Figaro*, November 19–20, 1983.

Calthrop, Everard Ferguson *The Book of War*, London: John Murray, 1908.

Carlson, Evans *Twin Stars of China*, New York: Dodd, Mead and Company, 1940

Castel, Albert "Liddell Hart's "Sherman": Propaganda as History," *Journal of Military History*, April 2003, 67/2, 405–426.

Childs, David J. *A Peripheral Weapon? The Production and Employment of British Tanks in the First World War*, Westport, CT: Greenwood Press, 1999.

Cipolla, Carlo *Guns, Sails, and Empires: Technological Innovation and the Early Phases of European Expansion, 1400–1700*, New York: Pantheon Books, 1965.

Clausewitz, Carl von (trans. Michael Howard and Peter Paret) *On War*, Princeton: Princeton University Press, 1976.

Clavell, James "Foreword," in Lionel Giles (trans.), *The Art of War by Sun Tzu*, New York: Dell Publishing, 1983.

Coram, Richard *Boyd: The Fighter Pilot Who Changed the Art of War*, New York: Back Bay Books, 2002.

Corneli, Alessandro "Sun Tzu and the Indirect Strategy," *Rivista di Studi Politici Internazionali*, July–September 1987, 54/3, 215.

Danchev, Alex *Alchemist of War: The Life of Basil Liddell Hart*, London: Phoenix Gant, 1998.

David, Alexandre "'L'interprète des plus grands maîtres': Paul Gédéon Joly de Maizeroy l'inventeur de la stratégie," *Strategique*, 2010, 1, 63–85.

David, Alexandre *Joly de Maizeroy: L'inventeur de la stratégie*, Paris: L'École de guerre, 2018.

De Crespigny, Rafe *Imperial Warlord: A Biography of Cao Cao 155–220 AD*, Leiden: Brill, 2010.

Denecke,Wiebke *The Dynamics of Masters Literature: Early Chinese Thought from Confucius to Han Feizi*, Cambridge, MA: Harvard University Press, 2011.

Dobson, Sebastian "Lieutenant-Colonel Everard Ferguson Calthrop (1876–1915)," in Hugh Cortazzi (ed.), *Britain and Japan: Biographical Portraits*, Volume 8, Leiden: Brill, 2013, 86–87.

Earle, Edward Mead (ed.) *Makers of Modern Strategy*, Princeton: Princeton University Press, 1944.

Finch, Michael P. M. "Edward Mead Earle and the Unfinished *Makers of Modern Strategy*," *Journal of Military History*, July 2016, 80, 781–814.

Finlay, John *Henri Bertin and the Representation of China in Eighteenth-Century France*, London: Routledge, 2020.

Fitzgerald, David *Learning to Forget: US Army Counterinsurgency Doctrine and Practice from Vietnam to Iraq*, Stanford: Stanford University Press, 2013.

Galvany, Albert "Philosophy, Biography, and Anecdote: On the Portrait of Sun Wu," *Philosophy East and West*, October 2011, 61/4, 630–646.

Garsia, Clive Review of Thomas R. Phillips (ed.), Roots of Strategy,*International Affairs Review Supplement*, September 1943, 19/13, 676–677.

Gat, Azar *A History of Military Thought: From the Enlightenment to the Cold War*, Oxford: Oxford University Press, 2002.

George, Alexander L. *The Chinese Communist Army in Action: The Korean War and Its Aftermath*, New York: Columbia University Press, 1967.

Giles, Lionel (trans.), *The Art of War by Sun Tzu*, New York: Dell Publishing, 1983.

Giles, Lionel (trans.), *The Art of War: Bilingual Chinese and English Text*, Burlington, VT: Tuttle, 2014.

Graff, David *Medieval Chinese Warfare, 300–900*, London and New York: Routledge, 2001.

Graff, David "Sun Tzu," in Daniel Coetzee and Lee W. Eysturlid (eds.), *Philosophers of War*, Volume 1, Santa Barbara, Denver, and Oxford: Praeger, 2013, 175.

Griffith, Samuel B. "Some Chinese Thoughts on War," *Marine Corps Gazette*, April 1961, 40–42.

Griffith, Samuel B. "Sun Tzu, First of the Military Philosophers," D.Phil. thesis, University of Oxford, 1961.

Griffith, Samuel B. *The Art of War*, Oxford: Oxford University Press, 1963.

Griffith, Samuel B. *The Battle For Guadalcanal*, New York: Bantam Books, 1963.

Groft, Marlin and Larry Alexander *Bloody Ridge and Beyond*, New York: Berkeley Cailber, 2014.

Guderian, Heinz (trans. Constantine Fitzgibbon) *Panzer Leader*, London: Joseph, 1952.

Hackworth, David and Julie Sherman, *About Face: The Odyssey of an American Warrior*, New York: Touchstone, 1989.

Hammond, Grant T. *The Mind of War: John Boyd and American Security*, Washington, DC: Smithsonian Books, 2001.

Hanson, Victor Davis *The Western Way of War*, Oxford: Oxford University Press, 1989.

Hanson, Victor Davis *Wars of the Ancient Greeks*, New York: Smithsonian Books (HarperCollins), 2004.

Heuser, Beatrice *The Evolution of Strategy*, Cambridge: Cambridge University Press, 2010.

Hoffman, Jon T. *Once a Legend: "Red Mike" Edson of the Marine Raiders*, Novato, CA: Presidio Press, 1994.

Howard, Michael *"Temperamenta Belli:* Can War be Controlled?", in Michael Howard (ed.) *Restraints on War*, Oxford: Oxford University Press, 1979, 1–15.

Huang, Catherine and Arthur D. Rosenberg, *Sun Tzu's Art of War for Women: Strategies for Winning without Conflict*, North Clarendon, VT: Tuttle Publishing, 2019.

Kagan, Donald and Gregory Viggiano (eds.) *Men of Bronze*, Princeton: Princeton University Press, 2013.

Kahler, Hans *"La guerre psychopolitique de l'Union soviétique,"* Revue international de défense, 1986, 2., 157–160.

Kierman, Frank A. "Phases and Modes of Combat in Early China," in Frank A. Kierman and John K. Fairbank (eds.), *Chinese Ways in Warfare*, Cambridge, MA: Harvard University Press, 1974, 27–66.

Kierman, Frank A. and John K. Fairbank (eds.) *Chinese Ways in Warfare*, Cambridge, MA: Harvard University Press, 1974.

Kissinger, Henry *Years of Upheaval*, Boston: Little, Brown, 1982.

Lau, D. C. "Some Notes on the 'Sun tzu' 孫子," *Bulletin of the School of Oriental and African Studies, University of London*, 1965, 28/2, 319–335.

Lau, D. C. and Roger Ames, (trans.) *Sun Bin: The Art of Warfare. A Translation of the Classic Chinese Work of Philosophy and Strategy*, Albany: State University of New York Press, 2003

Le Hégart, Louis "La stratégie et ses sources," *Défense nationale*, February–March 1984, 25–42.

Le Hégart, Louis "La stratégie: Théorie d'une pratique?" *Défense nationale*, March 1984, 51–68.

Lew, Christopher *The Third Chinese Revolutionary Civil War, 1945–49: An Analysis of Communist Strategy and Leadership*, London and New York: Routledge, 2009.

Lewis, Mark Edward Lewis *Sanctioned Violence in Early China*, New York: SUNY Press, 1989.

Li Ling 李零 "Lideer Hete, 'Huidao Sunzi,'" *Sunzi Xuekan* 孫子學刊, 1992/4, 12–13.

Li Ling 李零 *Bing yi zhali: Wo du Sunzi*兵以诈立 : 我读孙子, Beijing: Zhonghua Shuju, 2006.

Li Ling 李零 *Sunzi Yizhu* 孫子譯注, Beijing: Zhonghua Shuju, 2012 (2nd ed.)

Liang, Chin-tung *General Stilwell in China, 1942–1944: The Full Story*, New York: St. John's University Press, 1972.

Liddell Hart, B. H. *The German Generals Talk*, New York: Morrow, 1948.

Liddell Hart, B.H. *Strategy*, New York: Frederick A. Praeger, 1954.

Liddell Hart, B.H. *The Liddell Hart Memoirs* (2 vols.), New York: G. P. Putnam's Sons, 1965.

Liu Xu 劉煦 and Zhang Zhaoyuan 張昭遠 *Jiu Tangshu* 舊唐書, Beijing: Zhonghua shuju, 1975.

Lorge, Peter (ed.) *Debating War in Chinese History*, Leiden: Brill, 2013.

Lorge, Peter "Discovering War in Chinese History," *Extrême-Orient Extrême-Occident*, 2014, 38, 21–46.

Lorge, Peter "Early Chinese Works on Martial Arts," in Paul Bowman (ed.), *The Martial Arts Studies Reader*, London: Rowman and Littlefield, 2018, 13–25.

Loewe, Michael A. N. "*Sun Tzu: The Art of War* by Samuel Griffith," *Journal of the Royal Asiatic Society of Great Britain and Ireland*, October 1963, 3/4, 252.

Luvaas, Jay "Liddell Hart and the Mearsheimer Critique: A Pupil's Retrospective," *Parameters*, March 1990, 9–19.

Macksey, Kenneth *Guderian: Creator of the Blitzkrieg*, New York: Stein and Day, 1976.

Machiavelli, Niccolò, *The Art of War* (trans. Christopher Lynch), Chicago: The University of Chicago Press, 2003.

Mair, Victor (trans.) *The Art of War: Sun Zi's Military Method*, New York: Columbia University Press, 2007.

Mearsheimer, John J. *Liddell Hart and the Weight of History*, Ithaca: Cornell University Press, 1988.

Millis, Walter *Military History*, Washington, DC: Service Center for Teachers of History, 1961.

Minford, John (trans.) *Sun-tzu The Art of War*, New York: Penguin Books, 2002.

Minford, John "Foreword," in Lionel Giles, *Sunzi: The Art of War*, Vermont: Tuttle, 2008, vii–xxv.

Mitter, Rana *Forgotten Ally: China's World War II, 1937–1945: The Full Story*, Boston: Houghton Mifflin Harcourt, 2013.

Montgomery, Bernard *A History of Warfare*, London: Collins, 1968.

Needham, Joseph *Science and Civilization in China*, Volume 5, Part 7, Cambridge: Cambridge University Press, 1986.

Neumann, Sigmund and Mark von Hagen, "Engels and Marx on Revolution, War, and the Army in Society," in Peter Paret (ed.), *Makers of Modern Strategy*, Princeton: Princeton University Press, 1986, 262–280.

Nixon, Richard *The Real War*, New York: Warner Books, 1980.

O'Neill, Robert "Liddell Hart Unveiled," *Twentieth-Century British History*, 1990, 1/1, 101–113.

Paret, Peter (ed.) *Makers of Modern Strategy*, Princeton: Princeton University Press, 1986.

Paret, Peter Review of Werner Hahlweg (ed.), *Schriften-Aufsätze-Studien-Briefe (Volume II, Parts 1 and 2)* by Carl von Clausewitz, Göttingen: Vandenhoeck and Ruprecht, 1990, *Journal of Military History*, October 1, 1991, 55/4, 536–537.

Parr, Adam "John Clarke's *Military Institutions of Vegetius* and Joseph Amiot's *Art Militaire des Chinois*: Translating Classical Military Theory in the Aftermath of the Seven Years' War," Ph.D. diss., University College London, 2016.

Parr, Adam *The Mandate of Heaven: Strategy, Revolution, and the First European Translation of* Sunzi's Art of War, Leiden: Brill, 2019.

Perdue, Peter *China Marches West*, Cambridge, MA: Belknap Press, 2005.

Petersen, Jens Østergård "What's in a Name?", *Asia Major*, 1992, 5/1, 1–31.

Peterson, Charles A. "The Huai-hsi Campaign, 815–817," in Frank A. Kierman and John K. Fairbank (eds.), *Chinese Ways in Warfare*, Cambridge, MA: Harvard University Press, 1974, 123–149.

Phillips, Thomas (ed.) *Roots of Strategy*, London: John Land and the Bodley Head, 1943.

Pichichero, Christy *The Military Enlightenment: War and Culture in the French Empire from Louis XIV to Napoleon*, Ithaca: Cornell University Press, 2018.

Pokora, Timoteus "*Sun Tzu: The Art of War* by Samuel Griffith," *Revue bibliographique de sinologie*, 1963, 9, 372.

Powel, S. Steven "Deterrence and the Political Psychological Conflict," *Strategic Review*, Winter 1986, 49–58.

Rand, Christopher "Li Ch'üan and Chinese Military Thought," *Harvard Journal of Asiatic Studies*, June 1979, 39/1, 107–137.

Reardon, Carol *With a Sword in One Hand and Jomini in the Other: The Problem of Military Thought in the Civil War North*, Chapel Hill: University of North Carolina Press, 2012.

Reid, Brian Holden *J. F. C. Fuller: Military Thinker*, New York: St. Martin's Press, 1987.

Ries, Thomas "Sun Tzu et la stratégie soviétique," *Revue internationale de défense*, 1984, 4, 391.

Rogell, Eric *The Art of War for Dating: Master Sun Tzu's Tactics to Win Over Women*, Avon, MA: Adams, 2011.

Rooney, David *Stilwell the Patriot*, London: Greenhill Books, 2005.

Said, Edward *Orientalism*, New York: Vintage Books, 1978.

Sawyer, Ralph D. and Mei-chün Sawyer *The Seven Military Classics of Ancient China*, Boulder: Westview Press, 1993.

Sawyer, Ralph D. and Mei-chün Sawyer *Sun Pin: Military Methods*, Boulder: Westview Press, 1995.

Schram, Stuart (ed.) *Mao's Road to Power: Revolutionary Writings, 1912–49*, Volume 1, London and New York: Routledge, 1992.

Scobell, Andrew *China's Use of Military Force: Beyond the Great Wall and the Long March*, Cambridge and New York: Cambridge University Press, 2003.

Sidebottom, Harry *Ancient Warfare: A Very Short Introduction*, Oxford: Oxford University Press, 2004.

Skelton, Ike "National Security Book List," *Naval War College Review*, Winter 2004, 57/1, 109–112.

Smedley, Agnes *The Great Road: The Life and Times of Chu Teh*, New York: Monthly Review Press, 1956.

Smith, George W. *Carlson's Raid: The Daring Marine Assault on Makin*, New York: Berkeley Publishing Group, 2001.

Snow, Edgar *Red Star over China* (revised and enlarged ed.), New York: Grove Press, 1961.

Song Qi 宋祁 and Ouyang Xiu 歐陽修 *Xin Tangshu* 新唐書, Beijing: Zhonghua shuju, 1975.

Spence, Jonathan *Emperor of China*, New York: Alfred A. Knopf, 1974.

Tang, Zi-Chang *Principles of Conflict: Recompilation and New English Translation with Annotation on Sun Zi's* Art of War, San Rafael, CA: T. C. Press, 1969.

Tanner, Harold *The Battle for Manchuria and the Fate of China: Siping, 1946*, Bloomington: Indiana University Press, 2013.

Tanner, Harold *Where Chiang Kai-shek Lost China: The Liao–Shen Campaign, 1948*, Bloomington: Indiana University Press, 2015.

Tanner, Harold "The Shangdang Campaign," paper presented at the 2020 Chinese Military History Society.

Taylor, Jay *The Generalissimo: Chiang Kai-shek and the Struggle for Modern China*, Cambridge, MA: Belknap Press, 2009.

Toqto'a 脫脫 *Songshi* 宋史, Beijing: Zhonghua shuju, 1995.

Tuchman, Barbara *Stilwell and the American Experience in China, 1911–45*, New York: The Macmillan Company, 1971.

United States Marine Corps, *Warfighting*, Washington, DC: United States Marine Corps, 1989.

Van de Ven, Hans *War and Nationalism in China: 1925–1945*, Routledge, 2003.

Wallacker, Benjamin E. "*Sun Tzu: The Art of War* by Samuel Griffith," *Journal of the American Oriental Society*, April–June 1963, 83/2, 268–271.

Wallacker, Benjamin E. "Two Concepts in Early Chinese Military Thought," *Language*, April–June 1966, 42/2, 295–299.

Wei Zheng 魏徵 *Suishu* 隋書, Beijing: Zhonghua shuju, 1973.

Wilkinson, Endymion *Chinese History: A Manual*, Cambridge, MA: Harvard University Press, 1998.

Williams-Ellis, Clough and Amabel Williams-Ellis *The Tank Corps*, New York: George H. Doran Company, 1919.

Woolbert, Robert Gale capsule review of *Thunder out of China*, *Foreign Affairs*, April 1947, 531.

Wukovits, John *American Commando*, New York: NAL Caliber, 2009.

Xiong Huayuan 熊華源 "Mao Zedong jiujing heshi dude *Sunzi bingfa* 毛澤東究竟何時讀的《孫子兵法》," *Dangde wenxian* 黨的文獻, 2006/3, online.

Ye Shi 葉適 *Xixue Jiyan Xumu* 習學記言序目, Beijing: Zhonghua shuju, 1977.

Yuen, Derek *Deciphering Sun Tzu: How to Read* The Art of War, Oxford: Oxford University Press, 2014.

Zhang Tingyu 張廷玉 *Mingshi* 明史, Beijing: Zhonghua shuju, 1995.

Index

Page numbers in **bold** refer to footnotes.

Adcock, F. E., 12
Amiot, Joseph (1718–1793)
  biographical details, 46
  Chinese antimilitarism promoted by, 61
  identification of Sunzi as on the military
    profession (*art des guerriers*), 9
  translation of the *Sima fa* 司馬法
    (Methods of the Minister of War), 47
Amiot, Joseph (1718–1793) – *Art militaire
    des chinois*
  and Amiot's interest in the Chinese clas-
    sical tradition, 47
  and Enlightenment military thought in
    France, 45, 48, 219
  Giles's criticism of, 56
  Maizeroy's transformation of the word
    "strategy" influenced by, 2, 49–50,
    51
  minimal impact of, 173, 182
ancient Greek civilization and warfare
  and the construction of Western super-
    iority, 12, 13–15
  exposition of a person's moral stature as
    the focus of biography during, 21
  military strategists identified by
    Griffith, 156
  and the Romans, 156
  use of deception and maneuvering by, 14
  the West's fundamental culture defined
    by, 170
Asprey, Robert
  career of, 200
  correspondence with Hackworth,
    205–207
  and Griffith, 137, 199, 200
  and Liddell Hart, 79, 198, 200–201,
    203, 204
  the Sunzi promoted within military circles
    by, 199

*War in the Shadows: The Guerrilla in
  History*, 200
Aurousseau, Léonard Eugène, 58

B.D.H.
  ten books on strategic thought identified,
    195–196
Ball, J. Dyer (1847–1919)
  biographical details, **58**
  review of Giles's translation of Sunzi,
    58–59
Battle of Midway (June 4–7, 1942), 99, 118,
  127, 136
Battle of the Coral Sea (May 4–8, 1942),
  99, 127
Beaufre, General, 195, 196
Bertin, Henri Léonard Jean Baptiste
  (1720–1792), 44, 46–47, 50
blitzkrieg (mobile, mechanized warfare)
  de Gaulle's contributions to Liddell
    Hart's theorizing of, 79, 83
  Fuller's influence on the origins of, 64,
    74, 79, 81, 83
  German generals admired for their man-
    euver warfare, 108
  Liddell Hart on lightning warfare and its
    limits, 76
  Liddell Hart's claim to have theorized
    blitzkrieg, 65, 79–82, 84, 186
  Martel's contributions to Liddell Hart's
    theorizing of, 64, 74, 79, 81, 83, 86
  and Sunzi's emphasis on deception,
    intelligence, and mobility, 39–40
  Sunzi on attacking the mind of the enemy
    compared with Liddell Hart's strategy
    of mobile warfare, 154
  and war games tactics demonstrated by
    Stilwell, 99
Bond, Brian, 79, 80

Lightning Source UK Ltd.
Milton Keynes UK
UKHW022011191122
412508UK00022B/405

9 781108 822466